The search for an excellent business book is over!

"A hilariously, elegantly crafted book . . . gracefully dissects the common failings of business and government." —*The New York Times Book Review*

"A joyous pleasure from a remarkably gifted talent . . . Indeed, Norman Augustine comes as close to being the Mark Twain of the business world as anyone in the field."
—W. Gregor MacFarlan, Vice President, Harbridge House Inc.

"Insightful, delightful, and fascinating . . . Certain to be of interest and value to managers in all walks of life." —Donald Rumsford, former Secretary of Defense

"A fascinating book written with a truly delightful sense of humor." —Sanford N. McDonnell, Chairman and CEO, McDonnell Douglas Corporation

"In the diverting tradition of C. Northcote Parkinson, Laurence J. Peter, and Robert Townsend: a nice bit of comic relief from deadly serious guides that mistake management for leadership."
—*Kirkus Reviews*

PENGUIN BOOKS

AUGUSTINE'S LAWS

Norman R. Augustine is President and Chief Operating Officer of Martin Marietta Corporation, one of the nation's hundred largest firms. He has held numerous high-level posts in government and private industry, including Undersecretary of the Army and Vice President at LTV Corporation, and President of the American Institute of Aeronautics and Astronautics. He lives in Washington, D.C.

Aviation Week & Space Technology

Augustine's
LAWS

Norman R. Augustine

PENGUIN BOOKS

PENGUIN BOOKS

Viking Penguin Inc., 40 West 23rd Street,
New York, New York 10010, U.S.A.
Penguin Books Ltd., Harmondsworth,
Middlesex, England
Penguin Books Australia Ltd., Ringwood,
Victoria, Australia
Penguin Books Canada Limited, 2801 John Street,
Markham, Ontario, Canada L3R 1B4
Penguin Books (N.Z.) Ltd, 182–190 Wairau Road,
Auckland 10, New Zealand

First published in the United States of America by the
American Institute of Aeronautics and Astronautics, Inc. 1983
This revised and expanded edition first published by
Viking Penguin Inc. 1986
Published in Penguin Books 1987
Copyright © Norman R. Augustine, 1983, 1986
All rights reserved

LIBRARY OF CONGRESS CATALOGING IN PUBLICATION DATA
Augustine, Norman R.
Augustine's laws.
1. Industrial project management—Anecdotes, facetiae,
satire, etc. 2. Management—Anecdotes, facetiae, satire,
etc. I. Title.
T56.8.A92 1987 658.4 86-15122
ISBN 0 14 00.9446 6
Printed in the United States of America by
Offset Paperback Mfrs., Dallas, Pennsylvania

*To those many individuals
in the private sector and especially those
in government who through sheer ability and
dedication have achieved so very much, too often in
spite of aspects of the system intended to support them*

Columbia Business School

"You can see a lot by observing."
    —Yogi Berra

Preface

Insight into the problems of business can be found in unexpected places. For example, A. A. Milne could well have been writing about the vicissitudes of management in the opening paragraph of *Winnie-the-Pooh*. "Here is Edward Bear," he wrote, "coming downstairs now, bump, bump, bump, on the back of his head, behind Christopher Robin. It is, as far as he knows, the only way of coming downstairs, but sometimes he feels that there really is another way . . . if only he could stop bumping for a moment and think of it!"

Like bears, businesspersons all too seldom take the time to stand back from the trials of their day-to-day pursuits to seek to learn from their experiences. An excellent example is the problem reported by the newspaper *Midlands of England,* where long queues of would-be passengers wishing to use the Bagnall-to-Greenfields bus service were being passed by drivers in half-empty buses. A bus company official reportedly countered the public's objections to this annoying practice by pointing out that "It is impossible for the drivers to keep their timetables if they must stop for passengers." Impeccable logic. But, somehow, something seems to have been missed.

This book on management seeks to take respite from the pressures of everyday business life for a moment of introspection to see if in fact there might not be, as Edward Bear suggests, a better way. One authority, Thomas Edison, *assures* us that "There *is* a better way," and counsels, "Find it!"

Indeed, there is a better way, as innumerable highly successful businesses have demonstrated. Still, there remains that large set of much maligned activities which, were they ever to be documented into a movie, might best be viewed with the film run backward in order to conclude with a happy ending.

It is largely from this latter category of business undertakings that "Augustine's Laws" have been formulated. The laws are dedicated to the proposition that, with a better understanding of the history of past pursuits, one need only *selectively* repeat history in the future. In Bismarck's words, "Fools you are . . . to say you learn by your experience. . . . I prefer to profit by others' mistakes and avoid the price of my own." This is in keeping with Augustine's Fundamental Law of Aeronautics: "Never fly on an airplane with a tail number less than ten."

Perhaps the principal dilemma posed in these pages is not for managers but rather for librarians: Should the book be categorized as comedy or as tragedy? Possibly it is best simply described as science *friction*. There is ample room for book critics to assert that in reality (or unreality, as the case may be) it should have begun "Once upon a time . . ." But the subject with which it deals, namely management, is very real and very serious and permeates our entire existence—for we are continually called upon to manage not only our business lives but also our personal lives.

This book did not start out to be a book. Rather, it was a collection of vignettes prepared for various speeches and articles on management which, at the author's young daughter's urging, took its present form upon the occasion of the author's encounter with appendicitis while away from home on a business trip . . . and the need to fill time while recovering. Thus, a trade was established: one appendix for one book.

In its original form the book was specifically written for the manager of large aerospace engineering projects (the author's field) and was as such published by the New York-based American Institute of Aeronautics and Astronautics—as was the second version. To virtually everyone's amazement, nearly 10,000 copies promptly sold—nearly all by mail order. The readership, however, seemed to extend far beyond the aerospace specialist for whom the book was intended and it found itself read and quoted by senators, secretaries of state, medical doctors, lawyers, and all vintages of people interested in a range of business undertakings literally spanning from women's clothing to rollaway beds. The book also found its way into the curricula of a number of universities and as a subject of discussion in congressional hearings as well as being quoted in the general media in publications ranging from *Time* and *The Wall Street Journal* to the *Atlantic Monthly*, *Fortune* and the *National Geographic*. It was the subject of a special segment on the *CBS Evening News* and portions of it have been translated into Japanese and German for overseas readers.

The present version of the book grew out of the observation by many of its earlier readers that the management problems associated with designing spacecraft to fly to Mars seem to have much in common with those encountered by small and large businesses of all ilks. Thus, at the suggestion of Gerald Howard of Viking Penguin, a new version of *Augustine's Laws* was born for use by what Howard called, to the author's chagrin, "regular people"—presumably meaning the *general* business community. The book nonetheless continues to draw relatively heavily upon the author's own experiences in managing aerospace projects as well as his years in government. That this should be the case is mainly because of the author's desire to violate the custom of most Washington speakers and writers and talk about something of which he has some degree of knowledge.

There have been many superb books published in recent years dealing with successful business undertakings. This book, however, takes a contrapuntal viewpoint and adopts the perspective of learning from a business gone awry. It is much as is the practice at medical conventions—where it is generally considered that a great deal can be learned by *not* focusing on healthy people.

The author, in his own business experience (which began at the very top—in the distribution field—spreading tar on roofs while in college), has had the good fortune of being associated with a series of truly superb organizations and groups of people, including those in the organization he has most recently been privileged to lead and which, so great is its dedication to serving its customers that in nineteen years of flying spacecraft and large launch vehicles—forty in the last three years alone—it has had but one mission fail. But at the same time the author has had abundant opportunity to observe the nature of large and small organizations under duress—seemingly possessing an innate sense of timing that resulted in his joining the Board of Directors of one small company just as it was bought by a larger firm; or his leaving Douglas Aircraft just prior to its being acquired by McDonnell Aircraft; accepting a position in the Pentagon just as a war broke out; arriving at the giant LTV Corporation the same week that its founder, Jimmy Ling, was relieved of control; joining the federal government as a presidential appointee just in time to see the nation's president and vice-president forced to resign; and assuming the presidency of Martin Marietta's largest operating element just as the Bendix Corporation initiated its widely publicized (and unsuccessful) takeover assault on Martin Marietta. Scar tissue is probably a valuable asset in business, albeit not always pleasantly acquired.

Writing this book was undertaken with some degree of trepidation in view of the astute advice offered by a friend, Gene Zuckert, former Secretary of the Air Force and now partner in Zuckert, Scoutt, Rasenberger & Johnson, to wit: "Why is it that so many veteran [government] administrators develop their incisive perception and reform proposals when they are no longer in a position to act to improve the situation?" An appropriate question indeed.

Although treated in a sometimes tongue-in-cheek manner, the problems addressed in *Augustine's Laws* are nonetheless unmistakably real and deserving of attention. At times slightly irreverent toward business in general and "the system" in particular, the author hopes through this treatise on organizational misbehavior to contribute toward improving upon that process, which has, in spite of its many pratfalls, demonstrated truly enormous inherent strength and accomplishment, largely because of the dedication and native ability of the individuals who *make* it work. The author is proud to have counted these people as his colleagues, both inside government and out, and holds an abiding respect for their dedication, their integrity, and their accomplishments. Needless to say, he is an unwavering believer in the free enterprise system.

The author would like to express his appreciation to Paul Blumhardt and James Morrison for their assistance in collecting several segments of statistical data contained herein, to Pamela Seats for reviewing parts of the material, to Rhoda Glaser for her help in typing certain sections previously published by the Defense Systems Management College, to Joel Makower of Tilden Press, Inc., for the research support he provided, and especially to Glenda McFarlin for the overall processing of the manuscript.

The present volume of fifty-two laws—one for each week of the year—actually constitutes the third edition (with the second version representing a 20 percent increase in length at a cost increase of one-third . . . stimulating Augustine's First Law of Publishing which, happily, has been violated by the present version). The original, less complete collection of these laws was referred to as "The Compleat Augustine's Laws." But such is the transitory nature of immutable laws.

Washington Star

Once out of control, problems can be difficult to correct . . . or "the seventh month of a pregnancy is a poor time to address family planning."

Contents

Daedalus (dĕd'a-lŭs), craftsman and inventor,
fashioned two sets of wings from feathers and wax
and together with his son Icarus soared high into the sky
until Icarus,
so near to the sun that his wings melted,
crashed and drowned in the ocean.
—Greek mythology

Jane's Publishing Company, Limited

"Even the exuberant should have a contingency plan."

PART I

UNBOUNDED
ENTHUSIASM

1

The Beginning of
the End

"Free Gondwanaland!"
—Graffito at Duke University

*With the excitement of business school now barely
behind them, it had been disappointing to realize
at so early an age that nothing but the future lay
ahead. Yet they possessed the exuberance of youth
and the ambition to conquer the business world
and then move on to something difficult. Both
had been trained to take over immediately as
chairman of one of America's leading corporations or, if things didn't work out, to start as
president. In fact, they had both graduated with
honors, largely on the basis of the thesis they co-
authored entitled* Top Management for the Beginner. *But as luck would have it, not one of the
Fortune 500 had an opening for a chairman or
even a president. Having no experience which
would qualify them for any other jobs, the only
remaining alternative was to form their own small*

3

firm. *Even the exuberant should have a contingency plan. But in the words of C. D. Jackson, "Great ideas need landing gear as well as wings." Thus on a wing and a prayer began the fledgling Daedalus Model Airplane Company, the confluence of an enduring interest they had shared in model airplanes and their unfortunate inability to find a position helping someone else make a lot of money. Necessity truly is the mother of invention. Out of little acorns mighty oaks grow— and hadn't every successful firm in America once been small? Or could it be that one just hears more of General Electric, General Motors, and General MacArthur than, for some reason, General Candle, General Carriage, and General Custer. Little indeed did the burgeoning entrepreneurs realize at this point that from here on up it would all be downhill. That is one of the problems that new companies and new humans share, being born at a young age.*

The concept of "profit-or-loss" stands right up there alongside baseball and apple pie as a fundamental element of the American way of life. This heritage can be traced all the way back to the year 1606, when shares of stock were sold for $62 in the Jamestown venture to establish the first permanent settlement in America.

Captain John Smith, writing about the struggling Virginia colony just a few years later, pointed to the power of the free enterprise system and the incentives it embraces in the following words: "When our people were fed out of the common store and laboured jointly together, glad was he who could slip from his labour, or slumber over his taske, he cared not how; nay, the most honest among them would hardly take so much true paines in a week, as now for themselves they will do in a day."

Ironically, however, perhaps no finer example of free enterprise in America exists than that observed, appropriately, in the nation's capital just a few years ago when a group of students formed a commercial "protesting firm." The idea was sort of a "Rent-a-Picket," whereby one wishing to stage a demonstration on the White House sidewalk could do so for a mere few dollars an hour—with signs provided free. Discounts were available for larger demonstrations. There was a natural appeal to those embracing important causes but not to such an extent as to be worth personally parading up and down a cold sidewalk.

Thus is the underpinning of American business—on a stage richly populated with adventurers and pioneers in their very own right. But enthusiasm, energy, and euphoria, it will be seen, are not always enough to steer one safely through the hazardous rapids of modern enterprise. A Booz–Allen & Hamilton report describes one such disastrous case with the words "Managerial intellect wilted in competition with managerial adrenaline."

Tom Watson, Jr., chairman of IBM, wrote some years ago that "of the top 25 industrial corporations in the United States in 1900, only two remain in that select company today. One retains its original identity; the other is a merger of seven corporations on that original list. Two of those 25 failed. Three others merged and dropped behind. The remaining 12 have continued in business, but each has fallen substantially in its standing."

The grim reaper of businesses is, unfortunately, alive and well today. Fifteen years ago *Forbes* magazine selected the ten then most "profitable" U.S. companies, giving special consideration to overall solidity in terms of equity, growth and five-year performance. By 1985, three of them no longer even existed as independent companies. Four others had returns on equity that barely rivaled bank certificates. In fact, one of the above mentioned three had a return on equity below that achievable by hiding one's money under the mattress: It was involved, following a takeover, in bankruptcy proceedings.

Of seventy-five computer companies founded in the late 1960s, according to a study conducted at Columbia University, only ten still survive. According to Thomas Willmott of International Data Corporation, defending a niche "is like being in the Alamo." And in the words of Calvin Coolidge, "When large numbers of men are unable to find work, unemployment results."

In a *Business Week* cover story entitled "Oops!" Thomas Peters' and Robert Waterman's incisive book *In Search of Excellence* has been subjected to a dose of 20-20 hindsight. The verdict, according to *Business Week:* ". . . at least 14 of the 43 companies highlighted by Peters and . . . Waterman in their book just two years ago have lost their luster."

All eleven new professional basketball leagues founded in the last seven years have gone belly-up—but number twelve is now being formed.

Somehow these odds take most people by surprise, just as it seems amazing when Vic Braden, the tennis pro, reminds his incredulous students that half the people who play tennis *lose*.

Why, when one can start with a blank sheet of paper, hand-pick one's own products, markets, facilities, and even employees, should it be so extraordinarily difficult to get one's footing in business? To many it looks easy— but the simplicity should be viewed in the same light as the ease of a first step onto a stationary escalator: It's not as easy as it looks.

The founder of Osborne Computer is reported in *Inc.* magazine—together with the editorial comment about his firm that "This . . . was no two-bit start-up"—as stating, "I didn't have a degree in electronics and never had run a manufacturing operation." Nonetheless, "I *knew* we would succeed," he said, confidently, in 1983, shortly before his company went bankrupt. Unabashedly quoted about his *new* company a short time later, he observed, "I've come to the conclusion that gold is lying around and somebody should pick it up."

According to *Computer & Software News,* not surprisingly "the stock market is getting tired of computer chains who double sales only to double losses." Raymond Rose of Oliver Rose Securities notes, unarguably, that "The P/E ratio doesn't mean anything when there is no E."

Yet, America's 600 business schools alone churn out 63,000 budding entrepreneurs each year—second only to the number receiving master's degrees in education. One institution offers an MBA program on New York commuter trains. Some say they might more usefully offer the course on the subway leading to the bankruptcy court. Interestingly, as reported in *Forbes,* the blue chip General Electric Company hires fewer than fifty MBA recipients among the 2000 college graduates it recruits annually. Robert Mills, a manager of university relations and professional recruitment for GE, states flatly, "There's no value to the MBA degree."

If one cannot learn the path to business success, or even survival, from the nation's erudite institutions of higher learning, perhaps then the great truths are to be discovered at the other end of the academic spectrum—from the school of hard knocks. Frank Perdue, the sixty-four-year-old champion of the American chicken, sums it all up with no textbooks, no commuter trains, and no campaigns for alumni donations, in just three sentences: "Eighty percent of all newly advertised products fail. The manufacturer decides the consumer is a fool. *That's* why the product fails." Period.

A study reported in *The Economist* concerning the introduction of new products into the commercial marketplace found, to the chagrin of the executive office, that 58 percent of all innovations ultimately fail. Except, that is, for those originated by top management—these fail at a rate of 74 percent.

The director of research for Sodyeco, a manufacturer of fabric dyes, has stated that his firm synthesized 13,000 dyes to get just twenty-eight on the market. Among those that *did* make it was a long-sought fade-proof dye for blue jeans. This promising new discovery, the product of years of intensive research, arrived on the market just in time to be greeted by the exploding fad in prefaded jeans. It will be recalled that even Thomas Edison had several hundred failures before he eventually found a substance suitable for use as a filament in the electric light bulb. In fact, of the 1069 patents obtained by Edison, only thirteen fundamentally new products encompassing them are said to have made it to the marketplace.

According to the book *In One Day* by Tom Parker, 300 inventors seek a patent from the U.S. Patent Office each day. About 180 are successful in obtaining the desired protection—but for most that is unnecessary since fewer than three of them ever make any money from their invention anyway. What the other 297 need is protection from themselves.

But it's not enough for a business merely to be successful. It must be *more* successful than the financial community *expects* it to be. On December 27, 1984, Toys 'Я' Us, Inc., announced that its sales over the Christmas season had grown a spectacular 17 percent. There was only one problem. The brokerage firms had been telling everyone the growth would be 30 percent. The day following the announcement, Toys 'Я' Us stock dropped seven points—from 47 to 40—and continued downward in the weeks that followed.

It is a risky business—that's what starting a new business is. Just how risky is summarized in Figure 1. Founding a firm ranks right up there with going over Niagara Falls in a barrel, and sometimes seems to make about as much sense. In terms of survival probability, it makes parachuting, sports car racing, and astronauting look pretty tame. A more descriptive term for "venture capitalists" would perhaps be "adventure capitalists." When the author once asked Jimmy Doolittle what was the greatest hazard encountered in the early days of aviation, the highly respected aviation pioneer immediately replied, "Starvation." His observation seems to have applicability to most infant fields of business endeavor.

The Law of Eternal Optimism, Augustine's Law Number I, is derivable from the above evidence:

Dangerous Business

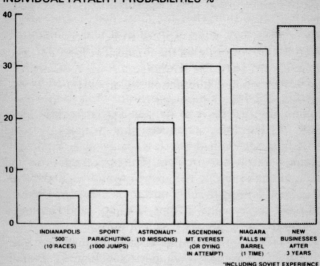

INDIANAPOLIS 500 (10 RACES) / SPORT PARACHUTING (1000 JUMPS) / ASTRONAUT* (10 MISSIONS) / ASCENDING MT. EVEREST (OR DYING IN ATTEMPT) / NIAGARA FALLS IN BARREL (1 TIME) / NEW BUSINESSES AFTER 3 YEARS

*INCLUDING SOVIET EXPERIENCE

Figure 1. There are many risky undertakings in this world, but few have a failure probability as intimidating as starting a new business. (Note that the data for astronauts includes both the United States and Soviet Union.)

LAW NUMBER I

The best way to make a silk purse from a sow's ear is to begin with a silk sow. The same is true of money.

For every firm that drowns in a pool of red ink there are hundreds that are merely doused. During one recent year, a bad year, the kind of year euphemistically described in shareholders' annual reports as "a year of retrenchment," 528,870 of the nation's 1,468,725 active corporations recorded a net loss. This *truly* is the bottom line.

Even operations which appear to be successful may sometimes be suffering on the financial ledger. For example, according to *The Washington Post*, W. Clement Stone of Combined International Corporation "never succeeded in wringing a profit from . . . *Success* magazine." On the other side of the ledger, Fred Smith, founder of Federal Express, elected to disregard the "C" he received on his college term paper wherein he laid out the concept of overnight small-package delivery—and went on to found what is today a $4-billion-and-climbing industry.

The ability to balance risks and potential gains is the very essence of decision-making in business—and, for that matter, in private life as well. A truly classic example of this fact was recorded on film in an unrehearsed session of the James R. Neuman Corporation's program for executives called "PACE." On this particular occasion the lecturer singled out an individual from the audience and asked if he would be willing to walk across a narrow steel beam hypothetically resting on the floor in exchange for $20 if he succeeded. Answering affirmatively, the question was then changed to one of the same beam suspended between two forty-story buildings with the result that the student-executive promptly indicated he would not undertake the walk under such circumstances and certainly not for $20. Having seemingly made his point, the lecturer inadvisedly continued, posing still another question: "Supposing I were standing on one of the same two buildings holding one of your children over the edge and told you I would drop your kid if you didn't walk across the beam. *Now* what would you do?" Pondering momentarily, the executive made a shambles of the decorum of the class when he inquired, "Which kid do you have?"

Some of history's most significant new ventures have been the result not solely of enormous risk-taking but rather of pure dumb luck—combined with an astute individual's powers of observation and imagination. Penicillin was of course discovered when Sir Alexander Fleming happened to observe that bacteria did not grow in a portion of a culture that had been *accidentally* contaminated by mold. Synthetic fibers were the result of a Du Pont researcher's observation while washing a reaction vessel used in unrelated polymer research. A catalyst critical to the formulation of artificial rubber was found when a mercury thermometer being unjudiciously used as a stirring rod accidentally broke. The search for artificial sweeteners was unexpectedly propelled forward when a researcher working in another field noticed a sweet taste to a cigarette that had been resting on a laboratory bench. Ivory Soap—"It Floats"—was discovered when a worker accidentally released high-pressure air into a soap-making vat. William Roentgen discovered X rays while investigating cathode rays. And America was "discovered" when Columbus failed in his search for the Indies.

In a superb series of advertisements, Harry Gray, on behalf of his firm, United Technologies Corporation, eloquently summarized the reason that there is, fortunately, an unending line of adventurists willing, even eager, to challenge the odds. "R. H. Macy," one ad explains, "failed seven times before his store in New York caught on. English novelist John Creasey got 753 rejection slips before he published 564 books. Babe

Ruth struck out 1,330 times, but also hit 714 home runs." The same series of ads tells of a fellow who ". . . dropped out of grade school. Ran a country store. Went broke. Took 15 years to pay off his bills. Took a wife. Unhappy marriage. Ran for House. Lost twice. Ran for Senate. Lost twice. Delivered a speech that became a classic. Audience indifferent. Attacked daily by the press and despised by half the country.

"He signed his name A. Lincoln."

2

Wait Till Last Year

"Why rob banks? That's where the money is."
—W. Sutton

The first cut at a five-year plan looked fantastic—too good to be true. Only the one-year plan seemed a bit shaky . . . but our budding giants of Corporate America were in this enterprise for the long-haul, so there was little future in dwelling upon the short term. Thus enveloped in euphoria, neither noted that the market projection which had been made would require every man, woman, and child in America to build one model airplane each day for the rest of their lives. But then, the Daedalus Model Airplane Company was obtaining the best planning advice money could buy . . . from people with the very same training as those who had generated the sales projections for the Concorde supersonic aircraft, the Edsel automobile, and the home video game market. It would perhaps be poetic justice if all planners were paid in Susan B. Anthony dollars. The data base relating to the model airplane market was sparse, to say the least, but everyone knows that the nation's capital is filled with renowned economists who have made their reputations extrapolating from a single data point. Furthermore, when beginning a new undertaking one must focus on the big picture. The incumbent government itself was forecasting, in the face of the intensely fought upcoming election, a huge growth in the economy as a whole. And these projections most assuredly were not the mere passing figment of some forecaster's inexperience—the same projections had now been made each year for four consecutive years. They had stature. Only the starting point for the soon-to-be realized recovery seemed to be in doubt—slipping to the right at a rate of about one year per year.

As the old vaudeville line goes, "They told me to cheer up, things could be worse; so I cheered up and, sure enough . . . things got worse." Consider, for example, the number of combatant ships in the U.S. Navy. For a number of years projections have been made recognizing that budgetary austerity would force a near-term decline in the number of ships in the fleet. These projections, however, always predicted that the longer term would see a strong recovery. As shown in Figure 2, this projection has proven to be fully half-correct: The number of ships has indeed declined in the near term just as projected, but in the *real-world* longer term, sure enough, things got still worse.

Planners all too often become so enamored with the

Reality Sinks In

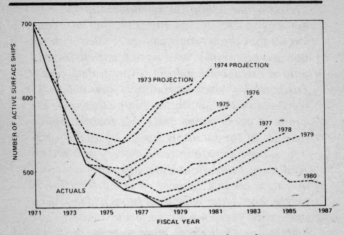

Figure 2. For many years, official projections have shown an eventual large increase in the size of the fleet. For many years this has not been happening . . . at least not until the late 1980s.

elegance of the planning process that they forget what is the ultimate measure of a plan. After all, even Custer had a plan.

In the words of Quintus Ennius some twenty-two centuries ago, perhaps concerned over the future of the Roman fleet, "No one regards what is before his feet; we all gaze at the stars." In fact, it seems to have been characteristic for centuries for planners to stumble over their feet as they gazed into the distance. When dealing with sales projections and the availability of funds, planners have traditionally been too optimistic when they view the longer term. The one major exception to this appears to be in the area of technology projections wherein planners have tended to be overly optimistic in the near term but not optimistic *enough* in the longer term. It has been said that a good planner is a person comfortable living with the outcomes of wrong predictions.

The problem with continual "get-well-fast" forecasts is that they eventually become self-reinforcing and are *actually believed*, not only by those who do the forecasting itself, but also by corporate marketing managers in a sort of inverse "crying wolf" phenomenon. Francis Bacon properly observed that "Man prefers to believe that which he prefers to be true."

President Thomas Jefferson explained this tendency of forecasters to view the world through rose-colored glasses in these words: "I like the dreams of the future better than the history of the past." "President" Thomas Dewey would probably also agree with this.

In such an environment, large numbers of new products are often initiated, betting that funds will become available to complete them in the good times which almost assuredly lie ahead. The difficulty is that the good times that lie ahead always seem to do exactly that: lie ahead. A tortuous cycle thus occurs wherein many projects are begun; inadequate funds are subsequently available to conduct them as planned; in order to avoid the obvious waste of canceling efforts in which substantial investments have been sunk, all projects are stretched in schedule; these stretchouts increase costs; the increased costs exacerbate funding shortfalls; further stretchouts are then required; and so on *ad destructum*.

The Air Force's F-15 air superiority fighter aircraft is an example of a project which experienced exactly such a course when unprojected budgetary limitations precluded the planned production rate from being achieved. A substantial number of airplanes that were to have been built during a peak production period had to be pushed downstream and patched onto the end of the production line some three years later in order to make funds available to cover the unforeseen needs of other programs. The result was that, although the total number of F-15 aircraft to be purchased remained constant at 729, the total cost of these same aircraft increased by nearly $2 billion due to the stretchout. Although the stakes are sometimes higher when manufacturing airplanes than, say, skate boards, the same principle applies. These additional funds could have been used to purchase an extra wing of seventy-two aircraft had in fact fewer other programs been started and the original, more efficient production plan completed.

Unfortunately, or perhaps fortunately, this problem is not peculiar to the planning for any particular commodity or even of any particular nation: witness the Soviet five-year economic plans. As in the United States, everything is always projected to recover—in the Soviet case within five years. What may, in fact, be needed is a *one-year* plan, for then forecasters almost certainly would project complete recovery in just one year and everyone wouldn't have to wait so long to find out they were in trouble.

When looking at forecasts such as those shown in Figure 2, there seems to be a convoluted belief that what goes down must come up; or, as the old adage states, the grass is always greener on the other side of the mountain. Erma Bombeck has made the more appropriate observation that the grass is always greener over the septic tank.

The British/French supersonic transport, the Concorde, is an example of a fine technological product which nonetheless has been an economic-planning disaster. Originally forecast in November 1962 to cost £160 million in development, the bill eventually ran out to £1065 million in June of 1973 when the development was complete. The initial estimate of the size of the marketplace called for 400 aircraft. In actuality, sixteen aircraft were built and nine sold—all to the captive airlines of the two governments participating in the development.

James Cook, writing in *Forbes* about the nuclear power industry, observes that at 7 percent annual growth the needed capacity doubles every ten years. On the other hand, from the "rule of 72," which says that the number of years required to double one's "investment" approximately equals 72 divided by the interest rate, at 1 percent, the doubling time is about seventy years. By the time the industry belatedly realized that something very, very fundamental was afoot in their marketplace, the Tennessee Valley Authority had canceled eight out of seventeen nuclear projects, Public Service Electric and Gas five out of eight, Duke Power six of thirteen, and Detroit Edison three of four . . . so far. In the words of Silas Marner, "Nothing is so good as it seems beforehand."

As but one example from the commercial world of consumer products, there is now the case of Coca-Cola, the phoenix of the soft drink business. In this renowned case planners, aided and abetted by their bubbling colleagues in marketing, giddily decided to replace Old Coke with New Coke; but New Coke rose from the remains of Old Coke so that *both* New Coke and New Old Coke had to be kept on the market. Clearly, the rumors of Old Coke's demise were much exaggerated.

The problem is not limited solely to "big picture"

long-range planning but is endemic to in-the-trenches short-range planning as well. Oliver Wight, president of the firm by the same name, has noted that "The average American foreman spends 60 to 80 percent of his time on activities other than those he's being paid for. Because the schedules are bad, he is expediting . . . looking for material." Then there is the case in Beckley, West Virginia, reported by the United Press International: "State highway officials say they did not realize until too late they were building a two-lane bridge for a three-lane section of the West Virginia turnpike. Explains John Gallagher, a spokesman for the Department of Highways, 'It sounds a lot worse than it is.' "

Too many projects are predestined for disaster by planning so faulty as to leave no real opportunity for subsequent managers to work their way into a success. President Lyndon Johnson is said to have often related the story of a man who had applied for a job as a flagman at a railroad crossing and was told he would be given the job if he could pass a test consisting of but a single question. Agreeing, the applicant was told to imagine he was a flagman at a crossing having but a single track when he suddenly observed the Continental Express approaching from the east at 95 mph and, looking in the other direction, saw the Century Limited bearing down from the west at 100 mph. Having further been told that the two trains were at the time 100 yards apart, the job-seeker was then asked what he would do under such a circumstance. Without hesitation, the would-be flagman responded that he would go and get his brother-in-law. Puzzled, the railroad's examiner inquired what good that would do, to which the job-seeker promptly replied, "He ain't never seen a train wreck!"

Sad to say, much of the planning conducted by American business has, as the old saying goes, made astrology look respectable.

All of which leads to Augustine's pragmatic Law of Surrealistic Planning:

LAW NUMBER II

If today were half as good as tomorrow is supposed to be, it would probably be twice as good as yesterday was.

Houston Oiler coach of three weeks, Chuck Studley, commenting at midseason on his team's fifteen consecutive losses, noted, "We're certainly in a position to go either way."

But at least most planners are consistent. Consistently wrong. Like the legendary admiral who actually projected a shrinking fleet . . . and now, in recognition of his unwelcome prescience, is probably the Supreme Allied Commander of Lake Mojave.

3

Easy Doesn't It

"He has exceeded my expectations and done even better."
—Yogi Berra, about Don Mattingly

It was growing a bit tedious to hear over and over from their friends (who merely sold their time and abilities to work for others) about how nice it must be to be one's own boss. Although it certainly was true that one could select where one wanted to work and when one wanted to work, it was also turning out to be true that there was nobody to whom one could complain when the payroll was late. Nonetheless, Daedalus Model Airplane Company was now legally established, being duly licensed by the city, county, state, FAA, DOT, DOC, CAB, SBA, ICC, IRS, and most every other permutation of twenty-six letters taken three at a time. Now all that was needed was to sit back, relax, and wait for financial success to come pouring forth. The business strategy of Daedalus Model Airplane Company was ac-

tually a simple one—to sell a quality product at a lesser price than its competitors. This tried-and-true approach turns out to be a sure way to capture a large market share. The difficult part arises if one also seeks to sell at a lesser cost than one's competitors. It happens that there is an important difference between price and cost . . . sometimes referred to as "profit." Mathematicians refer to it as a small difference between two large numbers—the most tenuous type of calculation of all. As one newly-made millionaire acquaintance of the founders of Daedalus (a colleague who had the misfortune of having his business school experience prematurely terminated by action of the faculty) explained of his own burgeoning business, "It costs me a dollar each to make my product, and I can sell all I care to make for four dollars apiece. You just wouldn't believe the profit there is in that three percent."

According to Robert Half International, an executive recruiting firm, top executives work an average of fifty-seven hours a week and middle managers fifty hours a week. The general work force averages on the order of forty hours a week. The accountants have a word for this executive practice: "FILO"—"First In, Last Out." Thus we see what is considered "success" by the kind of people who populate the upper strata of corporate organization charts. No wonder we are in trouble.

It has been determined that the average American worker in 1929 devoted 2342 hours a year to his job. In comparison, today's worker devotes 1582 hours (in contrast to his Japanese counterpart at 2140 hours).

While one can certainly and legitimately debate relative quality of lifestyle, such statistics probably do not bode well for U.S. productivity in the international competitive marketplace. In fact, at the above relaxation rate no one will be working at all in just another 120 years.

While one must be cautious not to confuse cause and effect, there is in fact a great deal of evidence that success in most endeavors is more likely to go to the individual with the self-discipline and will to squeeze from himself or herself "that last tiny bit" of personal performance. All other things being equal, as they often are in contests among well-balanced organizations or closely-matched individuals, the one capable of reaching down deepest for that final ounce of accomplishment will often be the one to emerge victorious. Studies show that competitions for new contracts are usually decided by very narrow margins. The same is true in sports, politics, and most other fields of human endeavor. And as Yogi Berra has explained, "Ninety percent of this game is half mental."

In the finals of the 1984 Olympics the difference separating the gold medal winner in the 100-meter dash from the performer who finished dead last, after years and years of individual preparation, was a mere sliver of time—0.36 seconds to be exact. Between the second-place, silver medal winner and the last-place finisher, a minuscule 0.16 seconds elapsed. Susan Butcher, in 1982, missed winning the grueling sixteen-day Alaskan dogsled race over 1131 miles in winds up to 60 mph and temperatures of fifty degrees below zero—by a mere three minutes and forty-three seconds. Such is the margin between fame and oblivion in corporate affairs as well.

Company number 501 of the Fortune 500 falls short

of company number 500 by a minuscule one-tenth of one percent of sales. Yet no one will read about number 501. Many a football team has spent the off-season agonizing over a single missed tackle, dropped pass, penalty, field goal attempt that hit a goal post, or fumble that made the difference in what otherwise might have been a truly outstanding season.

For a century or more, runners throughout the world had been trying to break the four-minute-mile mark, a barrier which had proven impenetrable until now-widely-remembered Roger Bannister shattered it in 1954. In the three decades that followed, there were no less than twenty-seven instances when individuals, mostly nameless today, set new records below the three-minute-fifty-second mark. Two athletes have now each run over 100 four-minute races themselves. Runners even hold the dubious distinction of having run a four-minute mile and finished last in their race. The world presumably abounds with athletes, businesspersons, and individuals of all persuasions who look back upon a narrow margin to lament "if only. . . ."

Figure 3 suggests just how narrow the margin of victory can be in the world of sports. The difference between being first in one's chosen field and being an also-ran is almost always microscopic when the also-rans are also seeking to be world-class performers in their own right. This is seen to be particularly true in such endeavors as golf, race-car driving, and track and field.

There is no finer example to be found of the potential payoff resulting from the will to win, the discipline to reach for the last bit of personal commitment, than the field of politics. "President" Samuel Tilden would be a household word today had he not lacked one single undisputed vote to carry the electoral college—having

The Margin of Achievement

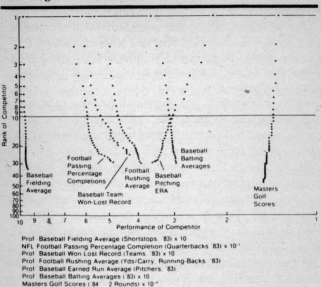

Figure 3. The margin between victory and defeat is often very, very small—whether one is dealing with the world of sports, business, politics, or a host of other undertakings.

already compiled a popular majority. A special Electoral Commission finally determined by a vote of 8–7, after one member switched his vote at the last minute, that history would instead remember Rutherford Hayes as president. Winfield Hancock lost by 3510 swing votes out of 8,891,088 votes cast between himself and James Garfield (although the electoral vote was much more decisive). Grover Cleveland escaped with his political life by defeating James Blaine by less than one percent of the popular vote (0.32 percent, to be exact) only to be defeated himself, just four years later, when he fell short of the needed electoral votes even though carrying the popular vote by a correspondingly narrow margin.

One of the most popular presidents of this century, John Kennedy, defeated Richard Nixon by a tiny 0.09 percent swing out of the 68 million votes they shared. And Nixon overcame Hubert Humphrey by a similarly narrow margin—0.4 percent. More recently, in 1976, in an election in which over 81 million votes were cast, Jimmy Carter would not have been president had 1.3 percent of the votes in a single state (Pennsylvania) and 3687 votes in Hawaii been cast differently.

Such "if only's" are of course by no means confined to *presidential* politics. In Senate races they are also abundant, as shown in the table at the bottom of the page, and in House races they positively abound.

Interestingly, in a sample of tight races in the Senate, Democrats seemed to be more likely than Republicans to win the close ones by odds of about two to one.

Some "If Only's" from Politics

U.S. Senate Races

Margin (Votes)	Total Vote	Margin, %	State	Year	Winning Party
2	221,850	–	New Hampshire	1974	Republican*
21	16,116	0.13	Nevada	1914	Democrat
25	134,624	0.02	Nevada	1964	Democrat
31	73,848	0.04	Delaware	1922	Democrat
46	15,795	0.29	Nevada	1912	Democrat
94	228,048	0.04	N. Dakota	1974	Republican
282	116,937	0.24	Utah	1922	Democrat
300	254,319	0.12	S. Dakota	1962	Democrat
313	158,586	0.20	Nevada	1974	Republican
339	118,294	0.29	Mississippi	1941	Democrat
378	894,434	0.04	Iowa	1924	Republican
486	95,964	0.51	Idaho	1918	Democrat
901	1,556,258	0.06	Missouri	1944	Republican
1489	2,512,773	0.06	Ohio	1954	Republican
4653	5,318,626	0.09	New York	1980	Republican

*John Durkin (D) Defeated Louis Wyman in Runoff

Taking just one example from the other side of the Capitol building, in a 1984 Indiana race for a seat in the U.S. House of Representatives, Frank McCloskey, a Democrat, was reported by the media as having defeated Richard McIntyre. Another count caused state officials to declare McIntyre the victor by just thirty-four votes from among the 233,613 cast between the two—about 0.01 percent. After one lawsuit, three recounts, and six months, the House had still refused to seat either candidate. Ultimately, Congress's General Accounting Office concluded that McCloskey had won—by four votes. In such cases a candidate could hardly help but wonder, if he had shaken just one more hand or kissed one more baby . . .

The margin of victory thus is narrow indeed—and to achieve it demands the utmost of dedication and concentration from both individuals and organizations. With this in mind, Bill Peterson, former coach of the Houston Oilers, exhorted *his* team, "Just concentrate on *one* word—'Super Bowl.'"

Put in terms of this premise, Augustine's Law of the Last Ounce can be promulgated:

LAW NUMBER III

There are no lazy veteran lion hunters.

4

Madison Avenue Crosses Wall Street

"You can do anything with a bayonet except sit on it."
—Napoleon

The business genius of the two founders of the Daedalus Model Airplane Company had combined to produce an eminently marketable product. The problem was that no one had ever heard of it. Customers were literally staying away in droves. In this case the solution was straightforward: advertise. Truly, if one puts one's light under a basket either no one will see it or the basket will catch on fire. Both bad. In the words of a renowned Big Ten football coach of the "grind 'em out" school of offense, "If you throw the ball there are only three things that can happen and two of them are bad." The Daedalus Model Airplane Company was learning a similar lesson about the odds in most business decisions and thus set forth to find an established PR firm which would launch the huge advertising cam-

paign that was so desperately needed. The first advice given by the firm was to open an exhibit booth at the Paris Air Show, an event with a culinary and social pace so demanding it is known among veteran partakers of the libations as the "Paris Death March." Business is tough indeed . . . sometimes even demanding that one devote one's own body to the corporate good.

It takes only a few moments and a little arithmetic to arrive at the conclusion that by the time the average American youth has graduated from high school he or she will have been conditioned, cajoled, pushed, and pulled by an average of 400,000 television commercials. The average number of commercials per week has, according to *Television/Radio Age,* increased from 1,839 in 1965 to 4,997 in 1983. Soon it will be necessary to interrupt the commercials to bring you a program.

William Wrigley of Wrigley Chewing Gum fame was once asked by a fellow-passenger on a commuter train why his firm continued to advertise when it already had almost totally captured the chewing gum market. Wrigley's answer was to observe that the train on which they were riding at the time was moving along very well, hence, "Why don't we just take off the engine?"

Although it can presumably be debated whether advertising is the engine or more nearly the caboose, there can be little debate that advertising is a part of the great American way of life. But, as with so much else in the business world, there are curious traps in logic that await the unwary. The first of these concerns the question of which companies and products need to advertise the most? The answer might include such fluid products as the now-defunct Billy Beer (Remember it? "Billy" as in "Carter"—the Hula Hoop of the brewing business) or perhaps Lone Star, or Fox Head, Dixie, Pearl, LA, Brew 102, Henry Weinhard's, or Moosehead. Old Frothingslosh would be a prime candidate for a few minutes of prime-time Super Bowl exposure. On the other end of the name-recognition spectrum, who hasn't heard of Bud, Miller Lite, and Coors? The illogic of the marketing world is shown in Figure 4, wherein it can be seen that when it comes to advertising, Bud and Miller don't need to and Old Frothingslosh and Billy can't afford to—a situation which is drawn to a head in Augustine's Law of the Hired Gun, which states:

The Price of Fame

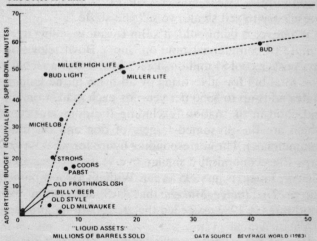

Figure 4. Products that are well known are generally produced by firms possessing ample funds with which to advertise them. Unknown products, on the other hand, are likely to stay that way because their producers have insufficient funds to tell anyone about their products.

LAW NUMBER IV

If you can afford to advertise, you don't need to.

Truth *is* stranger than fiction when it comes to the wonderful world of business—for the next observation about this convoluted state of affairs is that much advertising doesn't really try to sell the thing you are *trying* to sell! Charles Revson, founder of the enormously successful cosmetic manufacturing firm Revlon, explains, "In our factory we make lipstick. In our advertising, we sell hope." A salesman for a nationwide chain of medium-priced steak-houses confides, "Our advertising doesn't try to sell steak, we sell the sizzle."

Whatever *is* being sold, it's Big Business selling it. A minute of commercial time on Super Bowl television now costs a cool $1 million. That's $16,666.67 a *second*. The total bill for advertising by all firms in the United States adds up to $350 per year for each man, woman, and child in the nation (excluding the dogs and cats, which are the presumed targets of dog and cat food commercials). The corresponding figure for what is perhaps the economically similar overseas consumerized society, Japan, is just $95 a year. William Meyers points out in *The Image Makers* that U.S. advertising expenditures in 1983 exceeded the gross national product of Saudi Arabia.

Part of the trick to understanding advertising is of course to be able to think illogically. For example, when selling luxury items (perfumes, furs, fashionwear), the old standby is that if an item isn't moving, change its name and *raise* the price. Yes, raise; not lower. Sinclair Lewis, the author, has correspondingly noted that "people will buy anything that is one to a customer." Similarly, when Ted Turner of cable TV fame was starting his ascent, he took over a struggling station that could afford little more in the way of programming than re-runs of old black-and-white movies. His marketing gimmick? Extol to potential advertisers that only on his channel would their full-color advertisements *really* stand out in contrast with the rest of the pictorially dull material being presented. The argument apparently worked: The station picked up business and the rest is history. When sporting goods factories turn out tennis balls that are too dead to pass the "bounce test" (a tournament requirement that all balls dropped from 100 inches must bounce to a certain height), do those factories discard the balls and write off a loss? Of course not. They put the reject-balls in a special can, *raise* the price, and ship them to the Mountain states for sale as "high-altitude" balls. Ivar Bombach, vice-president of AeroVironment Inc., faced with charges that single-engine aircraft are less safe than multi-engine flying machines, accurately reports in *Inc.* magazine, "The basic points about the twin (engine) are that there is twice as much chance of an engine failure . . ." (No-engine airplanes should *really* be safe.) When Bob Uecker couldn't make it as a baseball player he went on television and got rich telling people he couldn't play baseball! And then there are the commonplace ads for "genuine imitation leather," "real diamond-like" jewelry, genuine simulated marble, solid walnut veneer, and so on.

There are of course the independent testing houses which profess to help the consumer extricate himself from this maze. In his book *All Out of Step,* Gerard Lambert (Lambert Pharmaceutical, etc.) tells of the amusement that abounded in the executive washroom at Gillette when one such consumer laboratory recommended Tuxedo razor blades over Gillette's own blades. Tuxedo, it seems, was the name under which Gillette sold its factory rejects—or "seconds," as they are more delicately called in the trade.

Not only are there research organizations striving to help the consumer, there is also an abundance of market research organizations ready and willing to aid the supplier. Truly profound findings are sometimes unearthed. According to *The Wall Street Journal,* as but one example, "An aspirin manufacturer wanted to time its ads to run when a cold spell was about to begin. But research revealed that people buy more aspirin whenever they run out, regardless of the weather." Seems reasonable. Marilyn Machlowitz, head of a New York-based management consulting firm, has written that ". . . one of New York's leading cultural institutions was about to undertake a costly study to find out which of its many exhibits was the most popular with visitors. Just before the consulting contract was signed, a committee member suddenly suggested asking the janitor where he had to mop the most."

Another imaginative avenue for market research into customer preferences is to be found in the Institute for Highway Safety's yearly report of the top ten automobiles in terms of demand. Demand, that is, by car thieves. It seems that the prestigious list includes eight European models, one Japanese model, and, alas, but a single U.S. finisher—the number-ten-placed Cadillac Brougham. Particularly disappointing was the performance of the Corvette, long a favorite, which fell completely off the 1984 list. This lack of consumer loyalty is a particularly distressing aspect of the business world.

There is also the long-enduring, probably apocryphal, story of the two market researchers who were independently dispatched some years ago to one of the world's less-developed countries by one of the world's larger shoe manufacturers. When their initial telegram-reports arrived at the corporate headquarters, one message read, "No market here. Nobody wears shoes"; whereas the other promised, "Great market here. Nobody has any." Most surveys similarly show that almost no one says they read advertisements. Other surveys, however, show that most people know what was *in* the advertisements (that they did not read). Such is the way of market research.

No discussion of the marketing process would be complete without a few words on packaging—the art of shrinking the candy bar while holding the wrapper fixed in a manner such that no one even notices when there is no candy included whatsoever. According to the prevailing illogic, what is inside the package may be less important than how it is wrapped. There is more than a little evidence of the correctness of this unfortunate thesis. As recorded in *Forbes,* Paul Fussel reports,

> Molloy posed as a middle-class man who had left his wallet home and had somehow to get back to the suburbs. At the rush hour, he tried to borrow 75 cents for his bus fare, the first hour wearing a suit but no tie, the second hour properly dressed, tie and all. "In the first hour," he reports, "I made

$7.23, but in the second, with my tie on, I made
$26, and one man even gave me extra money for
a newspaper."

Then there is the entire spectrum of promotional gim-
micks that have become so popular, such as the one
wherein Trans World Airlines offered some incredibly
lucrative discount coupons to individuals who purchased a camera from their partner in the undertaking,
Polaroid Corp. The problem, according to Stewart Long,
TWA senior vice-president for marketing and sales, was
that "Buyers will find a loophole if there is a loophole
there, and we left some big ones." In this case Long
was not wrong. The buyers found the loopholes all
right . . . with a vengeance—including the lack of a
"one per customer" rule and the absence of a restriction
on international travel. Maritz Travel Co. promptly
purchased 10,000 cameras to obtain access to the discounts. Frequent Flyer Ltd., according to *Business Week*,
found a Polaroid dealer who would sell at a discount
and bought enough cameras to get more than 7000 flight
coupons (Polaroid allegedly canceled the dealership's
privileges). Brokers quickly sprang up and a secondary
market developed. TWA's international traffic nearly
doubled—with the company apparently seeking to make
up the loss on each passenger by achieving higher volume. Competing airlines Pan American World Airways
Inc. and Northwest Airlines Inc., seeing their market
disappearing into clear sky, were also dragged into the
tar pit—having to agree to accept TWA's Polaroid coupons on their own flights. The glut of Polaroid cameras
which accompanied this high-flying promotion was finally eased somewhat when Polaroid gave 2000 cameras
to its own employees—cameras which its corporate travel

department had accumulated when it became a leader in the parade to jump on the lucrative giveaway bandwagon!

Not all advertising campaigns are as "successful" as TWA's, which is perhaps fortunate for the already beleaguered airline industry and others in similar straits. The 1985 Super Bowl experience is an example of how fickle the public can be—even when $1 million-per-minute TV commercials are being dangled before it. Asked after the Super Bowl which commercial first came to mind, by far the favorite answer according to an SRI Research Center survey, turned out to be "none"—the lasting recollection of fully 65 percent of the viewers. This was in spite of eleven different advertisers pushing everything from cars to hamburgers, and one particularly spectacular spot for the Apple Macintosh Office Line. But the news gets still worse. According to *Advertising Age,* "Nearly seven out of every ten people . . . who said they had seen an Apple commercial said they didn't know what product was being advertised." Still worse, referring to the ad-extravaganza, nearly half the people who *did* remember the Apple commercial indicated they "disliked it a lot." Oh yes, by the time the commercial appeared, the lopsided game had driven droves of people away from their TV sets. (Perhaps this can be used to promote advertising the following years—by pointing out that by the time the ad which so many people disliked was aired, no one was watching.) Other than that, Mrs. Lincoln . . .

By and large, however, advertising does seem to work. Lewis Kornfeld, vice-chairman of Tandy Corp., cites in his book a 1927 study by Robert Vaile on advertising during the economic depression of 1920–24. Using that data, which relates to 230 firms, one can ascertain that when times grew tough and corporations were hard-pressed to find cash, those firms which nonetheless increased their advertising expenditures generated 14–20 percent more relative sales (and a modest but still positive net profit) than those who decreased their advertising.

The key to the whole thing is probably to be found in the title to Kornfeld's book, namely: *To Catch a Mouse, Make a Noise Like a Cheese.*

5

Striving to Be Average

Cave canem.*
—Latin proverb

In spite of all the difficulties encountered, the *Daedalus Model Airplane Company* was looking as if it conceivably might possibly be starting to eventually begin to prosper. For example, no longer could its two founders handle all the operations by themselves. It had become necessary to hire a few additional employees, most notably a lawyer, an accountant, an advertising expert, a plant guard, a public relations expert, a personnel manager, and seven secretaries. It was concluded that this would greatly increase productivity. As the founders set out on their hiring campaign they quickly confirmed the suspicion which is held by a vast majority of average individuals, namely, that very few individuals come

*"Beware of the dog."

up to the average. Our new executives also discovered the non sequiturs of the hiring business: (1) anyone who needs a job is not someone you would want to give a job; (2) envelopes addressed to the president of the firm marked "personal" are either from strangers seeking jobs or from stock brokers seeking accounts; (3) calls intercepted by one's secretary from "personal friends" are invariably from unknown job applicants; and (4) about the last place anyone would ever find a job is by applying to the personnel department. As Terry Bradshaw once remarked with regard to the requirements of the speaking circuit he was pursuing after he had retired from professional football, "When you're unemployed you have to work all the time." Armed with all these bits of illogic, the Daedalus Model Airplane Company began to grow. And grow.

Robert Frost was among the first to note that the world is full of willing people—"some willing to work, and the rest willing to let them."

The contribution made by any given group of people working in a common endeavor tends to be highly concentrated in the achievements of a few members of that group. The degree of this concentration is observed to obey a fundamental law, as indicated by the data in Figure 5. It is seen from the figure that the great predominance of output is produced by a disproportionately small segment of the participants—with the same result seeming to apply nearly within a pencil-width whether one is addressing authors, pilots, engineers, policemen, or football players. Unfortunately, it also

Concentrating on Productivity

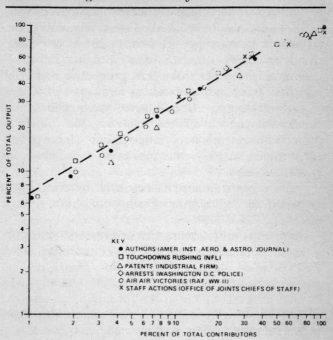

Figure 5. In virtually any undertaking it is found that a very small fraction of the participants produces a very large fraction of the accomplishments. It must, in fairness, be pointed out that a very small fraction of the participants also produces a very large fraction of the problems.

seems to apply to arrests by the Washington, D.C., police force and to beer consumption.

As one digs deeper into the barrel, so to speak, if the manpower assigned to a given task is increased, the *average output* is merely driven *downward*. This is the essence of Figure 5. Ultimately, large numbers of participants are added with hardly any increase in productive output at all (unless, of course, changes in work methods are also introduced). Conversely, substantial reductions in manning—eliminating the least productive contributors—can be effected with little impact on overall output. In fact, the least productive half of all participants seems to generate no more than 20 percent of the total output. Bob Whalen, vice-president and general manager of Global Analytics, Inc., refers to projects drawing upon this latter half as "Statue of Liberty Projects . . . 'Give me your tired, your poor, your huddled masses. . . .' "

Groucho Marx summed it all up in the following words: "I would not join a group which would have me as a member."

It might be more accurate to describe the above observation as merely a generalization or corollary of V. Pareto's work published in 1897, in which it is demonstrated that the proportion of people with any given income falls off rapidly as the income increases—the so-called Pareto Principle, a principle found to have wide applicability. The world is made up of those who make things happen; those who watch things happen; and those who ask what happened.

The results presented in Figure 5 are in fact probably *understated*, since the data base considers only participants who made at least some contribution, such as obtaining one patent or writing one article, when in reality there are many who obtain no patents and write no articles. Worse yet, there are those who produce negative output, such as the researcher who writes incorrect treatises or the worker who makes so many mistakes that a great deal of the time of other potentially productive workers is consumed in rectifying the problems the former has created. This can be very frustrating to those assigned the clean-up duty—which highlights the importance of properly motivating and rewarding the high performers so they will not leave their present employer and move along to other challenges. Such was the case in the story told about a homeowner who, incensed over a $40 charge by a plumber for a mere ten minutes' work, protested, "Why, that's more money than I make and I am a surgeon," to which the plumber is said to have replied, "Yes, and it's more than I used to make when *I* was a surgeon, too."

Only about one-third of all workers typically achieve a level of contribution equal to the average of those who contribute. In a moment of frustration a second-string National Football League quarterback summed up the problem in the following terms: "It's hard to soar like an eagle if you are surrounded by turkeys!"

The task of the personnel department, and in fact the primary job of every manager, thus becomes one of finding and motivating "eagles." But in most companies there are few departments more criticized for their handling of people than the personnel department. That this should be the case is ironic—but not necessarily altogether bad. Consider the case of the convicted Soviet spy Charles Boyce, Jr. In the book *The Falcon and the Snowman,* a chronicle of his adventures, it is noted that when he grew tired of his work at TRW in California he was encouraged by his Soviet managers to take a position at Martin Marietta Aerospace in Colorado. The book concludes this aborted episode by noting that the company's employment department lost his application. Members of that employment group are even today asking the age-old question, "Where did we go right?"

Ironically, most people think of *themselves* as being eagles, well *above* average and well above the standards set by their colleagues. This is of course exactly as it should be—no organization with a low opinion of itself is likely to be very successful. But the statistical dichotomy is nonetheless real. As pointed out in a General Electric survey some years ago, the average person surveyed placed themselves in the 77th percentile; that is, their view was that their performance exceeded that of 76 percent of their associates. In fact, only 2 percent of the respondents placed themselves as below average. (When the same group was rated by their supervisor, 85 percent were rated *lower* than they had rated themselves.) "You never met a money manager," says Bruce Hauptman, head of a firm that evaluates money managers, "that isn't in somebody's top quartile."

All of which leads to Augustine's productivity law, more rigorously known as the Law of Averages, which relates to the allocation of manpower. It can be stated as follows:

LAW NUMBER V

One-tenth of the participants produce over one-third of the output. Increasing the number of participants merely reduces the average output.

Astonishingly, the top 1 percent produce nearly twenty times the per capita output of the bottom half in many measurable undertakings. Building a work force comprised entirely of the top 1 percent is not easy, either mathematically or socially. Nonetheless, it is the essence of success for organizations large and small. How is this accomplished? The recruiting motto of Ross Perot's enormously successful company EDS advises, "Eagles don't flock—you have to find them one at a time."

6

A Hungry Dog
Hunts Best

"You canna expect to be baith grand and comfortable."
—James Matthew Barrie, 1891

*Daedalus was a success—at least if the measure
of success is how much money a company's owners owe. In their more contemplative moments
they were reminded of the words of professional
golfer George Archer: "If it wasn't for golf, I'd
probably be a caddie today." Truly, Daedalus's
growth had been remarkable, with the payroll
now exceeding thirty people and the founders
generally answering the question "How many
people work for you?" by explaining, "Nearly
half." But it was at this very point that organizers
from the local union set out to enlist Daedalus's
employees. Concerned that any collective bar-
gaining agreement might inordinately raise costs,
the company was advised by numerous larger
and more experienced corporations to fight fire
with fire: namely, blunt the union's efforts by*

46

*offering all the employees substantially higher
pay than any of their unionized counterparts were
receiving. That would surely keep the union at
bay—and make all the employees happy and
motivated at the same time. To offset this, prices
were increased for the employee food cart service, already affectionately referred to by the
workers as the Roach Coach.*

A motivated, capable work force has already been seen
to be the *sine qua non* of successful companies. But it
is very difficult to purchase motivation, especially over
the long haul, just as it is difficult to buy loyalty, dedication, integrity, or a host of other intangible but essential work force attributes.

A report published by the *St. Petersburg Times* enum-
erating the payroll of each of the twenty-eight teams in
the National Football League affords a rare opportunity
to correlate the performance of a complex organization
with its degree of profligacy when it comes to its payroll.
As the players might perhaps admit, many a team's
willingness to try to buy performance seems to be limited only when "debt do us part."

If one measures, to a first order, the output of a
football team by its won-lost record, the chart in Figure
6 can be produced. The chart shows the output (winning
percentage) versus input (team payroll) for each club
in the National Football League for a recent season. If
there were a strong relationship between pay and performance, one would expect that all the data points in
the chart would gather tightly along the dotted line
shown trending upward and to the right. In contrast, if
there were no relationship at all between pay and performance, one would expect to see a loose "shotgun"

The Good Life

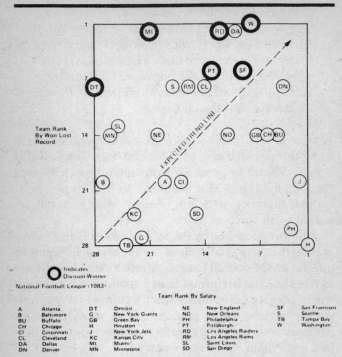

Figure 6. Although it can be shown mathematically to be an exercise in futility to risk losing outstanding employees because of salary deficiencies, the idea of "buying" performance seems to be equally specious.

pattern. One certainly could not confuse the results in the figure with the former.

To suggest that these findings might be somewhat disappointing to executives who would hope to buy output from a work force is a bit of an understatement.

For example, the following observations can be made for the year examined:

- The highest paid team in the NFL finished dead last.
- The lowest paid team won its division.
- The upper salary quartile produced no division winners.
- Two of the eight poorest paid teams won their division.
- Only one team in the upper salary quartile won over half of its games.
- The three highest paid teams finished last, second to last, and eighth to last.

One might argue that salary should be viewed as an investment in the future and therefore the proper metric is how well each team performed the *next* year. Here, too, the record is not very comforting since the top five teams in pay averaged a nineteenth place finish *both* seasons.

So much for the power of the dollar—alone.

Turning to individual performers, data for the same season show that only four of the dozen highest-paid quarterbacks led their teams to a record of better than .500. Five of them led their colleagues to a solid position among the nine worst teams in the twenty-eight-team league.

If nothing else, the remark attributed to Will Rogers that "We have the best politicians money can buy" certainly doesn't seem to apply to football players.

In a recent interview in *Inc.* magazine, Tom Peters, coauthor of *In Search of Excellence*, arrives at a similar conclusion: "I grew up in Baltimore. The Baltimore

Orioles, who for years ranked 23 out of 26 on salary, have put together teams that executed exceptionally well! Over the past 27 years (in terms of victories) Baltimore is well over 100 games ahead of the number two team in all of major league baseball."

This is not to suggest that pay is altogether unimportant; it merely implies that there are other much more forceful ingredients to success than what one puts in pay envelopes. This is, of course, not a new discovery by any stretch of the imagination. Perhaps the best known experiment in this regard is the one conducted years ago at the Hawthorne Works of the Western Electric Company. In that case, personnel researchers were seeking to determine the impact on the output of production workers who were performing detailed piecework when the ambient-light level was increased. Indeed, as the lighting was intensified so also did the work pace, with the result that new production records were set almost daily. But to the consternation of the researchers, if not the stockholders, as the light level was subsequently *decreased,* production continued to *increase*! Ultimately, new high levels of performance were being achieved in lighting conditions said to be little better than a full moonlit night. The reason, of course, was that the employees had been told beforehand that the company needed their help in performing an important experiment, with the result that the motivational effect of the employee's realization that they had an important function to perform far outweighed anything having to do with visual acuity.

There are, it would seem, matters that affect productivity which are far more important than mere financial incentives or management pressure. It is, for example, interesting that the home-team advantage in sports, in terms of won/lost percentages, is greatest in games such as basketball and hockey where the crowd is close to the players and can best cheer them on to greater performance.

Clearly, one cannot afford to lose able employees because of shortfalls in pay relative to one's competitors. The costs of recruiting, relocating, and absorbing a new worker into the work force makes this a specious saving in nearly all instances. On the other hand, if a firm is too generous with its payroll, it may—all other things being equal (which they seldom are)—find it difficult to produce products which can be priced competitively in the marketplace.

As far as can be determined, the principal incentive of the salary system in the National Basketball Association is to encourage one to be tall. The four highest paid centers, according to the *Detroit Free Press,* receive an average of $1.538 million for six months (about $25,000 per inch) whereas the corresponding forwards receive only $1.326 million and guards a mere $1.323 million. There are eleven players in the league making over $1 million per season. As at least one fan pointed out in conjunction with a potential baseball strike, it is tough to get too worked up over the plight of a union whose members average $329,408 a year! The median salary of the people who teach these budding millionaires, their coaches, naturally is only a little over half what the players earn. The *Business Week* survey of executive remuneration for American firms lists eighteen individuals in the multimillion dollar league. Symbolically, four of the five highest paid executives in the United States during 1984 were employed by a toy retailer. Similarly, a survey of the remuneration of labor union presidents revealed fifteen individuals receiving between $100,000 and $200,000 each year—not including bonuses—and one collecting $491,000. But these salaries barely get one to first base when compared with the thirty-six baseball players picking off between $1 million and $2.1 million of guaranteed annual salary. For the record, the President of the United States receives an annual salary of $200,000. But then, as Babe Ruth said in response to criticism that he was making more money than President Hoover, "Why not? I had a better year than he did."

Apparently a lot of people have had better years than the President of the United States, including one actor on a TV series who earned fifteen times the President's salary, a movie star who garnered for a single film twenty-five times the President's earnings, or the singer who pulled down for a single record album ninety times the President's yearly income. It can be a real downer to give up the movies and become President.

But far more importantly, the evidence does confirm, as every country boy already knows, "A Hungry Dog Hunts Best." In fact, one can even promulgate the Law of Good Times:

LAW NUMBER VI

A hungry dog hunts best.
A hungrier dog hunts even better.

"This was no time to be asking fundamental questions—certainly not in the formative stages of a project."

PART II

BOUNDED
ENTHUSIASM

7

What Goes Up . . . Stays Up

"They couldn't hit an elephant from this dist__"
—Last Words of General John Sedgwick,
Battle of Spotsylvania, 1864

*Not including its chairman and president, Dae-
dalus now counted among its fifty employees
twenty-five vice-presidents and twenty-four individuals with the rank of supervisor. You just
can't hire people into new and risky businesses
without offering incentives. As the owners quickly
discovered, titles are cheap. To most of Daedalus's management, which by now had become
accustomed to the good life, "roughing it" had
come to mean a slow bell-hop. Daedalus was
falling into the pattern of newly growing businesses with surprising ease. But why then were
they having to struggle so mightily to control
costs when, as everyone knows, as a business
grows, overhead cost, as a fraction of total cost,
goes down? It was concluded that to tackle so
contentious a topic an independent and detached*

*group of examiners would be needed. Thus, the
Headquarters Staff established itself. Early in
the overhead cost investigation which followed,
this staff actually found two of its own members
who, when asked what they did, both pronounced out of utter frustration, "Nothing . . . absolutely nothing." To demonstrate the
corporate staff's remarkable diligence and
toughness the overhead committee recommended that one of the two be discharged. It
also appeared that it might be necessary to lay-
off four robots. It was at about this time that a
cartoon surreptitiously appeared on the bulletin
board near the new executive athletic center displaying two well-fed executives contemplating a
chart which depicted a plummeting sales trend.
The caption had one of the bosses exclaiming
excitedly, "What do you mean, 'cut the fat'? We
are the fat!"*

There are probably few areas of management more
challenging or fundamentally cantankerous than seeking to control overhead costs. This is perhaps in part
because there are few areas in management wherein
managers themselves can be claimed to be so literally
a part of the problem—or, as it is sometimes called in
moments of descriptive candor, "The Burden." A still
better description was that used frequently by Bill Carl-
son of TRW: "The real problem is not overhead," he
said, "what is really stifling is the underfoot."

It is, of course, a widely accepted tenet of business
economics that in hard times overhead rates tend to
creep upward. This is logically explained by the need

to spread fixed costs over a smaller business base, exacerbated by less efficient production rates and the need for increased research and marketing to help reverse the downward sales trend. Managers therefore happily anticipate the day of an increasing sales base when the opposite will be true and overhead rates will properly and almost automatically reduce themselves.

Figure 7 addresses this concept based on industry-wide overhead rates collected for one segment of the nation's business establishment by the Department of Commerce. The figure clearly confirms that in times of

Sales Base and Overhead

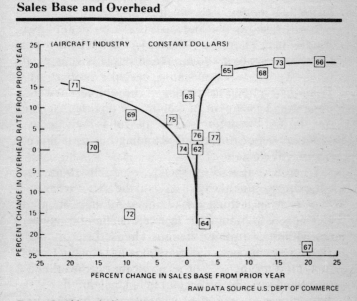

Figure 7. Although data relating overhead costs to business volume are varied, there is little evidence to support the conventional wisdom that increased business base begets reduced overhead.

decreasing base, overheads do indeed increase. But, alas, it additionally confirms, as is widely suspected by most modern-day practicing Don Quixotes of management who have jousted with overhead costs, that in prosperous times overhead rates *also* tend to increase. Through some sneak-circuit of nature, overheads, software, entropy, and laws all seem to share a common property—they increase. But more of this in later chapters.

It has been widely observed in this vein that, for example, adding floor space to house more people causes employment to decline. The additional cost of the space leaves less money with which to pay a staff.

Figure 8 shows that the most visible element of overheads—fringe benefits—themselves abide by the same trend as described above. When business goes down, fringes go up. When business goes up, fringes go up—even when stated as a fraction of the total cost of wages. Thus the Department of Commerce reports that some one-third of the nation's entire payroll is in the form of "fringes"—that innocuous-sounding but certainly not peripheral element of cost.

When it comes to overheads, especially fringe benefits, entertainment expenses, and the like, it seems that there is no such thing as bad times: All times are good, although, as seen from the figure, some may be "gooder" than others. To quote the most dreaded words among the professional sales and marketeering community, "He took me for lunch." For most businesses, overhead is their single largest project—but seldom does it get the management attention of whatever may be their next largest project.

Several years ago, a newly elected chairman of LTV,

The Impact of Good Times and Bad Times on Fringe Benefits

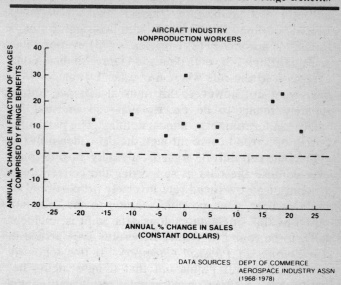

Figure 8. The persistent growth in fringe benefits is an increasingly important element of overhead costs and has proved to be quite resilient to changes in business conditions.

a large corporate conglomerate, was making his initial visit to a steel mill which had just come under his jurisdiction. Having observed several times during the course of the tour one worker slowly running a small hand-file over a huge steel billet, the executive finally overcame his reluctance to exhibit his lack of familiarity with the steel business and inquired of the worker, "What are you making?" The answer shot back, straightforwardly, "Six dollars and eighty cents an hour. Why?"

Addressing the loss of U.S. jobs to foreign competition, due in part to high overheads and in part to plain old-fashioned inefficiency, James Baker of General Electric outlined the future choices in straightforward terms: (1) automate, (2) emigrate, or (3) evaporate.

Tantalizingly, the data points in Figure 7 indicate one exception to the rule wherein overhead went *down* as base went up; however, this unusual instance unfortunately seems to be exactly that—an unusual instance—a forerunner to almost nothing. The particular fairing of a trend curve through the data shown in the chart could certainly be argued, but, sadly, no one could ever confuse the data as supporting the conventional wisdom of an overhead rate inversely proportional to business base. One possible solution to the dilemma posed by this single anomalous data point is, incidentally, to be found in Wilder Bancroft's 1931 article in *The Journal of Physical Chemistry*. In this scholarly treatise, Bancroft points out that disagreements between theoretical and experimental results can generally be resolved if one multiplies the experimental findings by a factor equal to the ratio of the theoretical expectation to the experimental measurement. However, seeking, at least for the moment, some other approach, it is instructive to examine the expanding universe theory as it applies to the dynamics of overheads. The astronomical theory of Black Holes also has a degree of relevance.

Hardly a manager is alive today who has not experienced surprise and puzzlement at finding both base and overhead rates rising, contrary to all expectations and diligent efforts, during a period of good times. Perhaps such periods are simply aptly named. It is much as if the established laws of economics have been repealed, hurtling us toward the zenith of a policy that may have been espoused prophetically during the Carter administration and known as "Zero Base Budgeting." But to the eternal frustration of managers who seek to put major overhead reductions into effect, the principal impact of their actions is usually no more than to set into motion once again what has historically come to be known at firms throughout America as "The Great Timecard Hunt," wherein all employees immediately shift first priority to seeking each day the timecard which authorizes them to remain on the payroll.

This same phenomenon is, incidentally, familiar to any design engineer who understands the widely taught principle that the costs of nearly all major systems— say trains, automobiles, ships, or aircraft—correlate closely and directly with their weight. This same individual will nonetheless simultaneously accept without question the fact that if one attempts to take weight out of such a machine, its cost will dramatically *increase*! As usual, there are explanations: "The use of exotic lightweight materials *always* increases cost"; or, in the case of overhead, "Increases in workload *always* increase costs due to the need for additional hiring, training, and facilities . . . not to mention the impact of operating with less experienced employees." Somehow, reductions in one account merely seem to produce bulges in other accounts, a phenomenon known in overhead management circles as the "Mattress Effect." In the words of Yogi Berra, when asked what he would do if he found a million dollars that someone had lost, "If the guy was real poor, I'd give it back to him."

Any pragmatic manager having had the facts of life explained by his subordinates will thus dutifully realize that Augustine's Law of Insatiable Comfort must, regrettably, be recognized:

LAW NUMBER VII

Decreased business base increases overhead.
So does increased business base.

In the words of John Newbauer of the American
Institute of Aeronautics and Astronautics, "When lux-
uries become necessities, *that's* decadence!"

8

Certain Uncertainty

> "It seems to me that no soothsayer should be able to look at another soothsayer without laughing."
>
> —Cicero to Roman Senate

As new products were brought on line, everyone was beginning to understand how one well-known professional football coach, after being granted an unlimited budget by the club's owner, was accused even before the season had begun of overspending it. In Daedalus's case, it was proving to be utterly impossible to control costs since every time a new product was almost ready for the marketplace the engineers would all start redesigning it to make it better. It was also becoming painfully evident that estimating the cost of technologically state-of-the-art projects was an inexact science. The experts, in spite of their mountains of numbers, seemingly used an approach descended from the technique widely used to weigh hogs in Texas. It is alleged that in this process, after catching the hog and tying it to one end of a teeter-totter arrangement, everyone searches for a stone which, when placed on the other end of the apparatus, exactly balances the weight of the hog. When such a stone is eventually found, everyone gathers around and tries to guess the weight of the stone. Such is the science of cost estimating. But then, economics has always been known as the dismal science.

Two types of uncertainty plague most efforts to introduce major new products: known-unknowns and unknown-unknowns. The known-unknowns, such as the composition of the moon's surface at the exact location of the first Apollo landing, can be accommodated and an approach planned which minimizes their consequences. The second category, the unknown-unknowns, cannot be specifically identified in advance, but their existence in the aggregate can be predicted with every bit as much confidence as insurance companies place in actuarial statistics. An example of the latter category of unknown is the lightning that struck Apollo XII shortly after its launch on the way to the moon. Somehow, in every major business pursuit, "lightning" strikes *somewhere*. It cannot be predicted *where* it will strike, only that it *will* strike. But, unfortunately, the budgeting system used in planning most projects has not permitted the recognition of such contingencies and thus the provision of "lightning rods." This is in part due to the vulnerability of so-called management "reserves" to budget cutting, and partly due to optimistic bids engendered in cost-reimbursable competitive contract award environments such as building custom homes, purchasing auto repairs, or developing military aircraft.

To illustrate the perversity of nature insofar as it seeks to disrupt the best planned new-product and development projects, a picture may be worth a thousand words. In Figure 9, an aerial photo is shown of the site of a large NASA wind tunnel. The effects of an explosion can clearly be seen in the upper right-hand corner of the photograph. The tunnel has obviously been destroyed and only a pile of pipe remains, all in the vicinity of where the tunnel had once resided. All, that is, except for one large section of pipe. For some reason this particular section chose to fly over the entire building complex—and land on the only automobile within sight, at the lower left corner of the photograph.

In the words of Robert Burns, "The best laid schemes 'o mice and men gang aft a-gley." Those involved in the process of estimating costs would also be well advised to heed the words of John Gay, "Lest man suspect your tale untrue, keep probability in view."

The need to recognize uncertainty when making cost estimates is not an altogether new problem. On March 27, 1794, for example, the Congress authorized building six large frigates to form the backbone of the U.S. Navy. The War Department first began to lay the keels seventeen months later, shortly after which cost overruns and schedule slippages caused the program to be cut back to three ships.

The problem is not endemic to any one side of the Potomac or to any one industry. There is the Washington Metro and—the overrun one never hears much about—the computer system installed by the government's own watchdog against cost overruns, the General Accounting Office. In 1972 the U.S. Senate proposed constructing a new office building—hardly an overwhelming challenge of technological prowess or

Figure 9. Highlighting an unfortunate coincidence in terminology, the large blown-down wind tunnel shown in the upper right-hand corner of the figure was destroyed when it was inadvertently overpressurized.

uncertainty—at a cost of $48 million. The cost of a stripped-down version of the building soon became $137.7 million. Senator John Chafee notes that this is a mere ten times the cost of the Louisiana Purchase. Some sage soul has pointed out that a conservative is a liberal who has been mugged.

Abundant evidence indicates that it is not human nature to learn from well-documented history, but rather to repeat it. The Great Mahaiwe Bank of Great Barrington, Massachusetts, recently discovered this when a check written in payment for a book titled *How to Balance Your Budget* had to be returned due to insufficient funds.

Poor cost estimating is on occasion difficult to dismiss merely with the vagaries of probability. Rather, it suggests some ulterior association with certain of the growth companies of industry that, to everyone's detriment, espouse the motto, "Bid 'em low; watch 'em grow."

Although many more sophisticated ways of predicting program costs are available were one in fact to use them, the cost-estimating correction factor presented in Figure 10 would, in the aggregate, have eliminated overruns on major programs conducted by the Department of Defense during the recent decade had it been available and applied. But taking prudent steps such as that could destroy one's bad reputation.

It should be noted that when the data in Figure 10

Predicting Cost (R&D Plus Procurement)

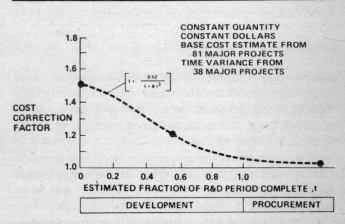

Figure 10. Historical evidence can be used to determine the correction factor, which if used, at least in the past, would have dramatically improved upon the otherwise generally poor cost-estimating track record accrued by the professionals in the field.

are in fact applied, the decision-maker will undoubtedly have been misinformed as to what fraction of the program is actually complete. This distortion has been compensated for in Figure 10 using Law Number XXIII (see page 204). By establishing adequate contingency reserves, realistic estimates of needed resources can thus be established. Caution is, of course, in order with respect to the delegation of authority for the management of the necessary reserves lest Parkinson's Law exert itself and costs rise to match the accessible funds. This is, however, an altogether solvable problem—a "done deal," as they say in the Southwest.

An adviser to a recent President of the United States is said to have expressed the view that there should be two requirements met before anyone becomes an economics reporter. First, the individual ought to have taken a basic economics course; second, he ought to have passed it. It is suspected that too many cost analysts have as their principal credential that they once won an award for "Most Enthusiastic in Arithmetic." Simply stated, the prevailing cost-estimating practices are resulting in a record whereby the average estimator has predicted eleven of the last two underruns.

At least our cost control record offers a lot of potential for improvement.

In order to better the record of cost estimators of the past few decades, it is thus necessary to recognize unknown-unknowns, to work twice as hard, and to be twice as smart. Fortunately, this is not difficult.

All of which leads to Augustine's Law of Inestimable Consequences:

LAW NUMBER VIII

The most unsuccessful four years in the education of a cost estimator is fifth-grade arithmetic.

9

FYI

"We sure liberated the hell out of this place."
—An American soldier, World War II

There was good news and there was bad news. At the end of its first year of operations the Daedalus Model Airplane Company had an income. That was the good news. The bad news was that it owed income tax. The really bad news was that nobody seemed to have the faintest idea how much. Somehow, the progenitors of the tax laws had created them in such a fashion that one needs the services of a lawyer, two accountants, and three semanticists to interpret them. Thus, a tax department was added to the headquarters staff to lead the company safely through the thickets of IRA's, FICA's, RRTA's, and the likes. This nomenclatural search for a means to impress the uninitiated is said to reach its ultimate form on the stone inscriptions above the columns of large public buildings—inscriptions offering

> *the names of the buildings for the edification of tourists—in* Latin. *Similarly, it may be that few really know what "E Pluribus Unum" really means . . . but who can deny that it is impressive?*

Communications, two-way communications, are as essential in business as is having a product to sell. Yet many companies create near-insurmountable barriers to effective communication by loading their corporate vocabularies with OBEs, TDYs, ASAPs, COBs, TGIFs, PDQs, and worse. The most important attribute a listener can have is ESP.

Most major business activities—particularly in the new product development area—depend on widespread public understanding for their funding, their acceptance, or both. Yet, in spite of the many examples of contributions to mankind made possible, for example, through modern technology, the general public still harbors a considerable skepticism of the net benefit wrought by past technological advances. As a result, budgetary and environmental limitations abound and support for basic research has eroded in many quarters of the United States. The problem is exacerbated by the very language which engineers and managers use to communicate their achievements, a language which appears to be formulated to assure that no information might be transmitted, either to the public or, frequently, among themselves.

According to Talleyrand, writing some 200 years ago, language was given to man to conceal thought. This would certainly appear to be the case in the twentieth century. There are, for example, engineers working in the information systems [sic] field who can speak entire paragraphs without using a single word. These are the same people to whom a mouse is a "peripheral."

A former senior official in the Department of Defense, Gerald Dineen, met this problem head-on, pointing out, "We go to the Congress and tell them that our WWMCCS has got to have a BMEWS upgrade, our Fuzzy Sevens have to be replaced by PAVE PAWS, we want to keep our PARCS and DEW in operation, we have to harden the NEACP, and we have to improve our MEECN with more TACAMO and begin planning to replace AFSATCOM with Triple-S . . . and then we wonder why no one understands."

The extent of the problem faced by the uninitiated can begin to be appreciated by considering the following excerpt from an Air Force document on the implementation of a new acquisition policy, itself known as A-109:

- "The HQ USAF/RD sends the draft MENS through SAF/ALR to OUSDRE for OSAF, OSD, DIA, and OJCS staff-level comment."
- "The HQ USAF/RD OPR develops the for-coordination draft MENS and presents the MENS comments and proposed solution approach to the HQ USAF RRG for corporate review in lieu of the underlying SON."

To the unwashed, this passage might convey a message something like:

- "The blank blank/blank sends the draft blank through blank/blank to blank for blank, blank blank, and blank staff-level comment."
- "The blank blank/blank blank develops for-

> coordination draft blank and presents the blank
> comments and proposed solution approach to
> the blank blank blank for corporate review in
> lieu of the underlying blank(s)."

Clearly, having drawn such a blank when dealing with
the process of replacing ROCs (Required Operational
Capabilities) with MENs (Mission Element Needs),
GORs (General Operational Requirements), and SONs
(System Operational Needs), one can understand why
there are those who have been able to conclude only
that somehow SON of MEN must have been GOR'd
by a ROC.

Turning to football, there is the statement "when NY
blocked the LA PAT following the TD on the bomb
from the QB to the WR during the O/T, OJ, speaking
on CBS, said there'd be no SB XX for LA if they didn't
get a FG or TD PDQ." From the world of finance we
have, "When the low IRR and ROI reduced the firm's
ROE and PBT shown on their P&L, the P/E dropped
and their NYSE growth lagged GE, GM, AT&T and
IBM—and even the IRS was P.O.'d." Or, from the
engineering world, there is the following excerpt from
Signal magazine:

> *JINTACCS and USMTF:* A second major influ-
> ence on the JINTACCS program will be the U.S.
> Message Text Formatting Program (USMTF), es-
> tablished by JCS Publication 6, "The Joint Re-
> porting Structure." The merging of JINTACCS
> and USMTF efforts is an essential step in reducing
> the U.S. Commanders' burden of dual reporting
> between tactical and strategic elements as well as
> U.S. and NATO separate reporting systems. JIN-

TACCS message formatting rules agree with the U.S. rules documented in JCS Publication 6, and the NATO rules documented in STANAG 5500. These rules use key words with unique meanings. In order to maintain this uniqueness, JINTACCS is cooperating with the JCS and Defense Communications Agency (DCA) to develop the U.S. Message Text Formatting Software System (USMTFSS). This software capability will enable the JCS to establish a U.S. data base that encompasses JINTACCS, JRS, NATO and service/agency key words. The USMTF/JINTACCS relationships will be defined as the USMTF Software System begins maturing.

One wonders if this might not all be related to the Boeing Utility Retrieval Program—or BURP, as it is better known. Of course, the liberal use of abbreviations, acronyms, and other means of obfuscation does have the advantage of making sometimes pedestrian material appear rather erudite in that it becomes more difficult to comprehend. Who, for example, would pay a medical doctor twenty dollars in exchange for his scribbling on a piece of paper "Take two aspirin"? Hence, the practice of writing prescriptions in Latin or, at the very least, using indecipherable handwriting. A practitioner who, rather than admonishing "Take two aspirin," can prescribe "Take two tablets of acetylsalicylic acid," and in addition do so with poor penmanship, could very likely qualify as a specialist and thereby command at least forty dollars for the same services rendered.

As might be expected, the potential of uncommunicative communication has not gone unnoticed by the federal government or most other large organizations. That most intimidating of all documents, the Federal Income Tax Form 1040, is for example generously sprinkled with IRAs, HRs, IRSs, FICAs, RRTAs, R&RPs, EIs, EICs, ZIPs and —ignominiously—something called "WINs."

Furthermore, the IRS's own computers don't speak acronymese—as, for example, some holders of ALCOA stock discovered when the always diligent computers unearthed the fact that these shareholders had not reported their Aluminum Company of America dividends. They promptly received Form CP2000s from their friendly computers.

A recent newspaper report trumpeted the headline "MAZE, MOXA merge"—and then went on to clarify for all, "MAZE acquired about 57 percent of the stock of MOXA, which were merged into MAZE Energy, Inc.; a new subsidiary of MAZE." *That* surely cleared up any confusion that might have prevailed about what previously perhaps sounded like merely another amazin', mixed-up merger.

A few years ago when in the midst of the national antiballistic missile debate the name of the then-troubled Zeus missile was changed to SPARTAN, it was only a matter of hours until some knowing wag had posted a sign on a Pentagon bulletin board proclaiming: "SPARTAN: Special Political Advantages Realized Through Advanced Names." A few years later, the oft-analyzed but never deployed Advanced Manned Strategic Aircraft, AMSA, became known among its much-suffering advocates as "America's Most Studied Aircraft."

Similarly, at a security gate at Cape Kennedy on the approach to one of the launch pads is a sign which, among a number of cautions about matches, explosives, flammable liquids, falling objects, high voltages, etc., conspicuously warns visitors that "POVs are prohibited." Now, this is a cause for consternation among those who may wish to enter but are not exactly certain whether or not they have a "POV" in their possession. It therefore can be with no inconsiderable relief that one learns that a POV is merely governmentese for a "Personally Owned Vehicle," i.e., a bureaucratically shortened form of the word *car*. To the government, cutting red tape often means slicing it into long strips lengthwise.

There are those individuals, both outside the federal government and inside, who are endowed with that special talent to take fairly lucid concepts and, through suitable embellishment, make them very nearly incomprehensible. The original statement of the acquisition policy which David Packard, then Deputy Secretary of Defense and a founder of the Hewlett-Packard Corporation, was to promulgate for the Department of Defense was written by himself and had an acronym content of only 0.2 percent of the words contained therein. However, by the time this statement was translated by Pentagon acronymologists so that it could, presumably, be more readily understood, into the regulation which underpins much of the Defense Department's present acquisition policy, acronyms comprised fully *ten times* the above fraction of all the words in the document. It seems doubtful that Secretary Packard himself would recognize his carefully thought-out policy in its "improved" form.

It is suggested that a measurement of the percent of words that take the form of acronyms in a particular work can be used to determine the implicit worth of that work. Clearly, the greater the number of acronyms the greater the intellectual value of the material since, obviously, the last thing anyone engaged in communicating would wish to do would be to deny a portion of the audience the message being conveyed by using unfamiliar terminology. Thus, in view of their widespread use, acronyms can only be concluded to be valuable contributors to the worth of written or spoken material.

Figure 11 examines this premise and presents for a number of documents their acronym-use factor, called the Acronym Activity Index (AAI), measured in the fundamental unit known as a "GLOP" (itself an acronym for "Groups of Letters for Obfuscating Points"). The success achieved in the bountiful usage of acronyms in various documents is evident from the enviable rat-

Clear Obfuscation

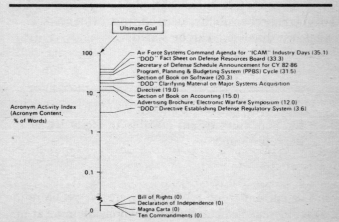

Figure 11. The excessive use of trade jargon, abbreviations, and acronyms is a major impediment to the communication of ideas.

ings shown. These ratings are particularly creditable when contrasted with those of the more acronymically impoverished examples from other writings which are also included in the figure at the bottom of the scale.

In the government procurement arena, where purchases are made of everything the government uses, acronymology has risen to a very high plateau. In fact, one government document provides a list of 10,000 official abbreviations to be used in specifications for items to be purchased. Appropriately, the document is referred to as "DOD STD-12."

Complex concepts are of course often characterized by their difficulty of being understood; therefore, persons unfamiliar with Greek or Latin should give intellectual depth to their ideas by utilizing acronyms to a degree more or less proportionate with the lack of sophistication of the ideas being presented. Such is the advantage of being obscure clearly.

Augustine's Law Number IX, the Comprehensive Law of Incomprehensibility, derived from evidence such as that just discussed, can be stated:

LAW NUMBER IX

Acronyms and abbreviations should be used to the maximum extent possible to make trivial ideas profound.

—Q.E.D.

The current trend toward ever-greater proliferation of acronyms, particularly in the national defense arena, does, however, introduce a specter of danger: the potential advent of an *Acronym Gap*.

The Defense Marketing Survey has stated that it has compiled a list of over one million acronyms which are in common usage in defense matters alone. These acronyms consist principally of "words" made up of five or fewer letters. Since the number of possible five-letter (or less) acronyms that can be formed with the English alphabet is no more than about 14 million, it can be seen that nearly 10 percent of all possible reasonable acronyms have already been used up. With the accelerating use of such nomenclature, the day when the creation of new products and ideas will no longer be possible thus may not be too distant. This, of course, portends ill since the Soviet Union enjoys a position of inherent acronymical superiority over the United States due to its clever possession of an alphabet containing not twenty-six but thirty-two letters. Some form of accommodation with China and its enormous language population of 14,000 characters would appear to be prudent. The dire consequences for commercial firms in the United States which seek to compete with Japan will be equally evident. Placed in this context, today's worldwide economic and military situations can thus be readily explained.

A possible solution to the acronymical gap would, of course, be to adopt even longer and less pronounceable letter groupings, an arena in which the U.S. Navy has been in the forefront for many years. One wonders, however, the impact on an organization's or individual's self-esteem to be known as the NAVHLTHRSCHEN, the NAVIDISTCOMDTS, COMNAVOCEANCOM, or the NAVMEDRSCHU. On the other hand, this identity might not appear all that unattractive to individuals assigned to such real organizations in being today as ARF, ARG, NEMISIS, DRAG, AGED, MORASS, or AFWL (pronounced "awful")—but might represent a considerable come-down to the Chief of Naval Air Training, CNATRA, better known simply as "Sinatra."

Many acronyms do not mean that which an inexperienced observer might suspect—ANTS, GNATS, DOG, FROG, COD, APE, RAT, BAT, RAM, and CLAM have, in military jargon, nothing whatsoever to do with Noah's ark; they are simply references to various items of hardware. The author himself experienced the type of problem which can arise from such double meanings on the very first day of a tour of service with the federal government. While faithfully carrying out an assigned appointment schedule on Capitol Hill in preparation for a forthcoming confirmation hearing, the author considered it rather inappropriate that typed after the name of several senators on the daily calendar was the notation "OLD SOB." It was only some time later that it was learned that "OLD SOB" can, in Washington, also mean "old Senate Office Building."

This strange practice is best explained by the words of Mark Twain: "They spell it Vinci and pronounce it Vinchy; foreigners always spell better than they pronounce." Michael Lewis, twenty-one, traveling in early 1985 from Los Angeles to Oakland, learned to his chagrin that some people talk pretty funny right here at home. Speaking to the media shortly after his arrival in Auckland, New Zealand, he remarked of the people in Los Angeles, "They didn't say Auckland. They said Oakland. They talk different."

Writing in *The Washington Post,* Rick Atkinson and Fred Hiatt succinctly summarized a long series of reorganizations within the Army under the heading THE ARMY BEGATS: "TAC begat OCOD . . . in 1945, which begat OTAC . . . in 1950, which begat both MOCOM and ATAC . . . in 1962. MOCOM died in 1967, and ATAC begat TACOM . . . which in 1976 begat both TARCOM . . . and TARADCOM. . . . In 1980 TARCOM and TARADCOM merged back into TACOM." Thus everything is brought into focus.

The ultimate state of maturity of an acronym occurs when it is finally written in lower case and everyone forgets that it is in fact an acronym . . . such as "radar" and "laser" . . . and almost no one remembers what it stood for in its original form.

Financial managers as well as bureaucrats and technologists have excelled in the exploitation of this powerful means of increasing confusion among the unwashed. Consider the world of federal finance, where the unpronounceable "FNMA" simply becomes a Fannie Mae or "GNMA" a Ginnie Mae, both related to a Freddie Mac. Other mortgage instruments closely parallel in terminology some of the expressions already discussed pertaining to defense matters, such as SAMs, RAMs, FLIPs, and ARMs. Most ominous in the world of mortgages is something called a GPAM, occasionally pronounced "Gyp 'em."

Acronyms can in fact convey important messages in their own right—consider the Washington Public Power System's (WPPS) bonds which were the Waterloo of so many investors. The acronym for these bonds, WPPS, was widely pronounced "woops"!

In summary, simply stated, it is sagacious to eschew obfuscation.

10

A Lawyer in the House

"The first thing we do, let's kill all the lawyers."
—*Henry VI*

The Securities and Exchange Commission had ruled that depreciation must be based upon the replacement value of an item in order to give the stockholding public a true indication of corporate worth. Simultaneously, the Internal Revenue Service had ruled that depreciation cannot be based on replacement value in order to give the tax collector a measure of actual cost (and, surprise of surprises, the maximum tax receipts possible). As the regulators sought to cover every contingency by aiming regulations to surround every possible problem, many at Daedalus were reminded of the proverbial three regulators who had gone rabbit hunting. It seems that after the first had fired a shot that passed one foot in front of a rabbit's nose and the second had launched a round passing exactly one foot behind the rab-

bit's tail, the third threw his rifle in the air exclaiming, "We got 'em." The principal effect of such bureaucratic illogic had been that Daedalus's legal department was now the second fastest growing segment of the organization, surpassed only by the public relations department which was besieged by investigative reporters from the media looking into product liability suits and by requests for charitable donations from wealthy benefactors of various local charities. In fact, the only groups which were no longer growing in the burgeoning company were the engineering and manufacturing departments—but amid all the excitement of law suits, countersuits, tax cases, and marketing conventions, hardly anyone even noticed. Besides, the new executive dining room was about to open.

"The exact date that professional attorneys came into existence is unknown, although the first complaints about them were recorded in the twelfth century"—at least that is what David Oppenheim, himself a lawyer and bankruptcy analyst for the U.S. Trustee's Office, reports. He goes on to note that the licensing of lawyers was introduced in England in 1402: "That act was dictated because there were too many attorneys. There were about 2000 of them. Laws were passed to limit them and they stayed on the books almost 400 years, but were never followed."

In more recent eras, lawyers have actually been declared illegal in a variety of locales, including early Salem and, just a decade or so ago, in China. Today, however, there seems to be no bar to the bar, at least not in the United States. The American Bar Association reports that 622,000 lawyers are alive and presumably very well in the United States—one for every 418 persons to be exact. Meanwhile, the country's law schools, like human geysers, are spewing forth another 30,000 lawyers each year. The United States thus can claim more lawyers to its credit than Iceland can claim people. In fact, according to a Colorado Court of Appeals Judge, two-thirds of the world's lawyers are located right here in the United States. This has led, in some quarters, to occasional suggestions for a new export product. The Appeals Judge went on to note the complexity of the legal issues faced in the world today and advised a group of new lawyers, "If you aren't confused, you aren't thinking clearly."

The federal government alone has 17,000 full-time lawyers on its payroll, some busy writing new laws and some hard at work trying to interpret what the first group meant. Others are occupied as lobbyists because they didn't agree with what *either* group said. This latter army has burgeoned from 3400 registered lobbyists in 1976 to 7200 in 1985. "Why are there more flies in Cairo than lobbyists in Washington?" Answer: "Cairo got first choice."

Almost 37 percent of the U.S. House of Representatives and 53 percent of the U.S. Senate are comprised of lawyers. It's like buying chicken wire from the fox— a Full Employment Act for lawyers. As noted on the T-shirt worn at a 1984 softball game by former President Jimmy Carter, "Politicians Are Always There When They Need You." And, as Abraham Maslow has observed, "If the only tool you have is a hammer, you tend to see every problem as a nail."

Figure 12 examines the apparent contribution of this large and growing body of lawyers to the efficiency of the industrial base of various nations throughout the world. A striking correlation is observed between the number of attorneys per capita and the productivity improvement of a nation. The problem, however, is that the relationship is exactly what one would expect rather than what one would hope—that is, the more lawyers, the *worse* the nation's productivity record. And the correlation is incredibly accurate. Thus, another truly disappointing finding emerges from the world of business. This leads to Augustine's Law of the Law:

LAW NUMBER X

> Bulls do not win bull fights;
>   people do.
> People do not win people fights;
>   lawyers do.

Only the United Kingdom departs significantly from the trend line noted in the figure, evidencing a productivity record far worse than that to which it should be entitled based on its supply of barristers. One must apparently conclude that England's lawyers are about four times as effective as their counterparts in other, legally less mature countries.

John Naisbitt, writing in *Megatrends,* asserts that "Lawyers are like beavers: They get in the mainstream and damn it up."

It should be noted that Figure 12 also provides a very useful predictive device. For example, having obtained the productivity growth rate for France but lacking the requisite data on the density of lawyers in that country, it was possible to interpolate from the productivity data

The Weight of the Law

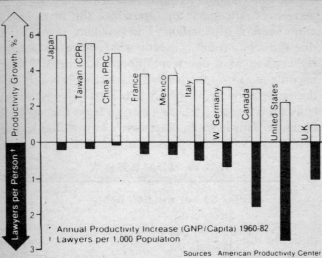

Figure 12. There seems to be a strong underlying relationship between the number of lawyers in any country and the productivity of that country. The evidence in the figure is presented without comment. Harry Truman once said, "I never give anyone hell. I just tell the truth. They think it is hell."

in Figure 12 to ascertain that France should have about 17,000 lawyers. (The author's General Counsel, when asked to confirm this figure, reported that there were actually 16,600 "avocats" in France and inquired "How did you know?" Upon having had the procedure duly explained, the author's very own counsel promptly threatened a class action suit.)

It may be that Japan graduates nearly twice as many engineers as the United States—although having less than half the latter's population—and has been ravaging U.S. industry in the competitive marketplace, but Japan will encounter considerable difficulty matching America's strength in the preparation of legal paperwork. This is a consequence of our lead of twenty to one in the number of lawyers per capita, not to mention seven to one in accountants. Few if any nations present a serious challenge to us in terms of the number of suers and suees present in our litigious society.

Thus the very system which was invented to settle controversy has itself become one of the greatest sources of conflict. Even the construction of the Jimmy Carter Center—dedicated to resolving international disputes—has been bogged down by disputes; in this case in the form of interminable court suits to block construction of a four-lane access highway.

So much for the past. What of the future? Figure 13 presents one considered projection of what lies ahead . . . and disconcertingly reveals that we probably haven't seen anything yet. The closest rival to lawyers in terms of *relative* internal growth rate in U.S. industry seems to be public relations practitioners. Narrowing the focus of this inquiry somewhat further, one finds that at the top of the corporate ladder, according to Golightly and Company, over a recent twenty-five-year period the number of corporate presidents with a technical background dropped 12 percent, those with a manufacturing background declined 25 percent—and those claiming as their specialty the "legal/finance" category increased by 50 percent. This may, however, be appropriate given the changing character of business. In the 1984 space rescue mission wherein an astronaut flew a "Buck Rogers" back-pack to capture an errant spacecraft and load it into the Space Shuttle for return to Earth and eventual repair and relaunch, literally the

Leaping Backward?

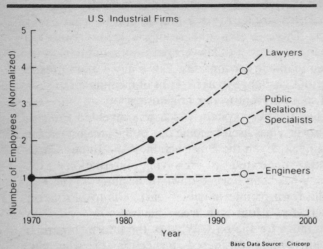

Figure 13. The fastest growing segments in U.S. industry are, on a relative basis, the legal and public relations departments. In Japan, the fastest growing segments are evidently the factory and the shipping departments.

most challenging aspect of the mission was not the engineering task but rather was the matter of overcoming legal impediments such as resolving ownership rights, liability exposure, and insurance coverage.

Somehow, the law does not always seem to serve those who created it, becoming at times a Frankenstein's monster of sorts. *Forbes* magazine only recently reported an incident whereby a man attempted to kill himself by jumping in front of a subway car in New York; however, having failed, he won a $650,000 judgment from New York City because the train hit him. The genie clearly seems to be out of the bottle.

Mickey Rivers, the baseball player, is quoted in *Sports*

Illustrated as saying, "We'll do all right if we can cap-
italize on our mistakes." That seems to pretty well sum
up the corporate legal situation as well.

In fairness, one should perhaps note the possibility
that the number of lawyers, as shown in Figure 12, is
in fact merely a surrogate for the broader, more diffuse
ailments which sometimes afflict mature, relatively staid,
overly comfortable societies. One hopes, however, that
this is not the case . . . or at least that if it is, the af-
fliction is more recognizable and curable today than it
was in Roman times. It is sobering to realize that there
are only about two countries (Great Britain and Thai-
land) which have had a longer uninterrupted period of
the same form of government than has been enjoyed
by the two-century-old United States.

Nonetheless, the business of law is booming. Annual
expenditures by U.S. corporations for legal services have
now sunk through the $40 billion mark, growing at a
rate of 14 percent per year when last seen. Commen-
surate amounts are annually extricated from private
citizens, as well.

The Denver Post may have been on to more than it
realized when it reported, ". . . the former Deputy Attorney General said the bar has never been so successful
in serving the poor."

11

Meetings Dismissed

"No more good must be attempted than the
people can bear."

—Thomas Jefferson

*The celebration which took place on the occasion
of hiring Daedalus's hundredth employee (a lawyer) was tempered somewhat when it was discovered that for some unknown reason both the
factory and the engineering department had begun
to fall seriously behind the schedules which had
been imposed upon them by the sales and marketing departments. It was decided to hold daily
status meetings wherein all the engineers and
factory workers would be afforded the opportunity to stand before an assembled throng of
managers from each of the other departments
and report at length on reasons behind their lack
of progress the previous day. In addition, separate meetings were scheduled on a daily basis
to review budgets, planning, and personnel assignments. A Master Meeting, conducted early*

each morning (which came to be known as the Sunrise Service) coordinated the scheduling of all the other meetings. Finally, a cost-control meeting was scheduled for each evening to discuss how overtime could be reduced. The workers themselves conducted periodic informal meetings to discuss what they might be doing if they weren't sitting in meetings. This led to meetings on how to reduce the number of meetings. Everyone at Daedalus seemed to be working so hard that no one had time to do any work.

Herm Staudt, president of Government Systems Operations of the Eaton Corporation, during his service as a senior government official once observed at the outset of an arduous thicket of briefings, "I always come to these meetings with a problem. I always leave with a briefing and a problem."

The first fifty-six minutes of a meeting (all meetings require one hour) are, in fact, relatively innocuous and pass with little being accomplished other than the presentation of routine and generally peripheral background material. It is during the remaining four minutes, however, that The Bombshell will invariably be dropped squarely on the center of the table. For example, the first fifty-six minutes will be devoted to heated debate among all participants as to the color the sign in front of the new oil refinery should be painted. Only during the final four minutes will it gradually emerge that earlier that morning the plant had been destroyed in an explosion.

Upon revelation of The Bombshell, the harried decision-maker, already late for the initial fifty-six minutes of the next meeting, is presented with three options.

Based upon the anatomy of decision-making, the first of these options will, unfortunately, require totally abandoning the hard-sought goal being pursued. The third, on the other hand, will demand funding of slightly over one gross national product. The middle option, then, will offer a course that has as its sole redeeming virtue that it is the choice the staff, which has prepared the options, wants the decision-maker to select. This is known as managing the management.

In the late 1960s, an admiral once contacted a top civilian official in the Secretary of Defense's office and strenuously objected to a decision paper that had been prepared for the Secretary of Defense's signature on the grounds that the paper contained only *two* options. Upon further discussion it emerged that the admiral's own preferred option was, in fact, one of the two alternatives presented. The resulting enigma was clarified only when the exasperated officer blurted out in a moment of candor, "You *know* the Secretary always selects the middle option."

The "middle-option" approach presumably derives from the school of thought that you can fool some of the people all the time and all the people some of the time . . . and that's enough.

But meetings to discuss such profound matters as schedule problems should not be demeaned: Recognition must be given to the fact that a great deal of effort is required even to *schedule* the schedule meetings. The first step in this process is for the chairperson to place a long-distance telephone call to the person who is to be the briefer to schedule a time for the proposed meeting. This call will usually prove abortive because the briefer will be away at another briefing. The briefer later returns the chairperson's call only to learn that the chairperson is out of the office, chairing another briefing. An average of 3.8 long-distance calls transpire (according to the author's actual sample) before contact is finally made. This process is known as Telephone Tag. Telephone Tag is not all bad. It helps make possible AT&T's contribution to the tax base and everyone's secretaries become very good friends.

Once a date is finally settled upon, the chairperson and briefer discover that the third requisite attendee cannot be available at the agreed-upon time. The process then starts anew. The probability of finding a time when six people, each of whom already has a half-filled calendar, are simultaneously available is only about one in *thirty-two tries* and each "additional person" implies an exponentially increasing number of telephone calls. It can thus be demonstrated that meetings with more than about ten busy people are mathematically impossible. The fact that many meetings take place with more than ten individuals present is not, it will be recognized, necessarily inconsistent with the above observation.

It should be noted that the United States, while at a handicap with regard to Japan, possesses a major strategic advantage over the Soviet Union in the field of meeting-scheduling. This stems from the fact that one of the major impediments to telephonically coordinating meetings is the three-hour time difference between the east and west coasts of the United States. This time disparity effectively reduces the available telephone-day to about five hours. The Soviet Union, faced with not just four but eleven different time zones, is virtually precluded from scheduling meetings which involve attendees from throughout the land. Many of these disappointed individuals are thus left with no alternative but to remain home and work. In this regard, it is instructive to recall that Webster traces the most favored type of meeting, the symposium, as stemming from the Greek for a drinking party.

In spite of these impediments, meetings, symposia, conventions, and forums flourish—clearly a case of talk around the clock. Among the most popular of these events are gatherings far from one's place of work, since, as everyone recognizes, there are so many distractions where one works that no one can get any work done there. Figure 14 presents evidence collected over two centuries which addresses the trend toward ever more meetings. The explosion of meetings in distant parts of the world reflects the growing need to hold events on neutral turf, so as not to unduly inconvenience anyone. In this manner, *everyone* can be inconvenienced equally.

Once a meeting finally takes place (prior to which it must necessarily be rescheduled yet another time because one of the principal attendees unexpectedly revises his vacation plans), protocol requires that the senior dignitary present be seated in the position of honor: at the head of the table—directly behind the large elevated reflector affixed to the viewgraph projector that permanently resides on the center of the table. This reflector thus effectively blocks from the decision-maker's view some forty-two percent of the projection screen, including that portion in the immediate center. This very likely accounts in part for the reason senior officials always select the middle option. The first and the last ones are too dreadful to contemplate and the middle one can't be seen.

In spite of such systemic limits passively accepted by most decision-makers, one Air Force general with the Tactical Air Command actually had the audacity to seek

Meeting Obligations

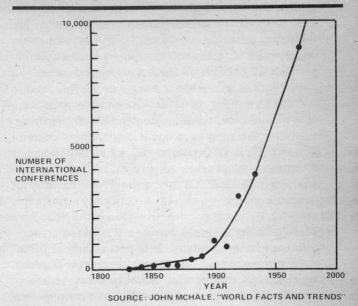

SOURCE: JOHN MCHALE. "WORLD FACTS AND TRENDS"

Figure 14. The social acceptability of holding meetings as a mechanism for consuming management's time is expanding on all fronts. This is particularly true of international meetings, which bear the additional burden of absorbing large amounts of travel time and disproportionate amounts of money.

to *control* the meetings conducted for his benefit. Displaying ultimate disregard for the Code of the Briefer—"Power lies in the possession of the chalk"—he had the signal button for changing the viewgraphs placed *not at the podium but at his own seat!* Briefings thus took on an altogether new excitement, with the last four minutes—people now actually listened to them—sometimes lasting a full hour. This also provided fodder

for a new form of wagering among the general's staff—
"handicapping" briefers.

But as has been noted, virtually all meetings are
scheduled to consume exactly one hour—or, at the very
"least," integral factors of one hour. Further, in ac-
cordance with Parkinson's Law, meetings can never end
early. In fact, as incredible as it may sound, there seems
to be no such thing as a fifty-five-minute issue or a
twenty-minute issue. All issues demand exactly one hour.
Thus, during an eight-hour day it is possible to contend
with only eight basic decisions, independent of whether
the matters at hand relate to survival or to trivia.

One might assume that this optimal meeting interval
is the consequence of years of evolutionary refinement,
or at least is based on intensive studies by efficiency
experts, decision theorists, business school researchers,
and human-factors analysts. It is particularly regretta-
ble, therefore, that one must conclude that the duration
of meetings has nothing whatsoever to do with the content of the material at hand, but rather is a consequence
of the speed with which the Earth rotates about its axis
(and, of course, the arbitrary decision to divide this
interval into twenty-four equal segments). If, for example, the Earth would rotate not in twenty-four but
in eighteen hours, meetings would almost certainly be
scheduled to occupy the resultant "new hour," now
forty-five "minutes" long. Nearly eleven meetings could
then be scheduled each day and a 33 percent increase
in management productivity automatically realized, assuming the basic *real* workday remained unchanged.
Not only does this suggest the excitement of an engineering undertaking that would dwarf the Apollo Moon
project—it would use millions of rockets fastened around

the Earth's equator to speed up the Earth's spin—but also it would extend everyone's life expectancy (in days) by one-third.

Thus is derived Augustine's Law of Meeting Objections, which recognizes that managers tend to move freely throughout their realms whereas workers are more nearly fixed to their tasks:

LAW NUMBER XI

If the Earth could be made to rotate twice as fast, managers would get twice as much done. If the Earth could be made to rotate twenty times as fast, everyone else would get twice as much done since all the managers would fly off.

The above law, it will be observed, is in contradistinction to the well-known Broadway show *Stop the World, I Want To Get Off.*

Some organizations, of course, do little *other* than hold meetings. This suggests that the utility of meetings as a business artifice could perhaps somehow be deduced in the limiting case from an examination of the output of these particular institutions—which count among their numbers the U.S. Senate, the House of Representatives, and the United Nations. On the other hand, such an examination may not be a particularly good idea.

The fundamental fallacy of the ubiquitous meeting is epitomized in the observation of the chairman of the Board of Directors of SpaceTran Corp., Bill Sword, who reminds us that meetings last hours but are documented in minutes.

Nonetheless, according to the trade magazine *Meetings and Conventions*, this year alone over 60 million people will attend over 900,000 off-premise corporate and association meetings.

12

The Secret of Quality

"It was the loudest noise they ever seen."
—Brooklyn expression

Although the Daedalus Model Airplane Company had continued to prosper, there was a growing number of frustrations plaguing management and workers alike. (Note that "management" is always distinguished from "workers" and "work" . . . what George Kaufman may have had in mind when he wrote, "Two men were killed in the construction work in Panama. One was English, the other a laborer.") People just didn't seem to realize how much fun they were having. It was found that meetings dragged on interminably as the attendees heatedly debated issue upon issue. It was also during this time frame that the company's president, who had fallen ill, received at his hospital bedside a copy of a resolution by the Board of Directors wishing him a speedy return to work—on which the cor-

porate secretary had dutifully albeit indiscreetly recorded "Approved by a vote of 6 to 4." But in spite of a number of such unfortunate incidents, the entire management had been drawn together by the realization that they would have to improve productivity. There was, however, concern expressed that it might not be possible to assemble the needed funds to take on such a project. The few skeptics were nonetheless silenced when it was pointed out that this was no time to be asking fundamental questions—certainly not in the formative stages of a project.

There are few subjects that seem to provoke philosophical speeches, slogans, banners, and flag waving so much as the subjects of quality and productivity. However, once one cuts through the fog it turns out that there *is* a great deal of meat to be found; it is just that it has been corn-fed too long.

Not too many years ago, the "Made in U.S.A." label was considered to be a symbol of desirability. Similarly, the descriptor "Japanese copy" was a pejorative term. But times have changed. A 1980 *Consumer Reports* survey of 257,000 automobile owners in the United States found no U.S.-built vehicles in the "much better than average" category, and no Japanese-built vehicles in the "much worse than average" category. American industry has since gone to work to rectify this problem: One U.S. automaker, for example, reports it has substantially reduced defect rates over the last few years while increasing output from ten vehicles per employee per year to nearly twenty.

Most if not all businesses would obviously prefer to produce a higher quality product—i.e, one which does what was promised, and does it *every* time—but they are often curiously inhibited by the presumed high cost of achieving such a degree of quality. It is in keeping with the abundant myths addressed in this literary tour through the business world that such a belief should be so rampant in these informed times. The truth, ironically first discovered some years ago by an American, W. Edwards Deming, and exported to Japan when *American* industrialists wouldn't listen to him, is that higher quality begets *not* increased cost but *reduced* cost. This is the miracle of productivity and quality.

In 1974, for example, one Motorola facility was said to be producing television sets averaging 1.5 defects per set, despite employing seven inspectors for every twenty-five workers—a very low "tooth-to-tail" ratio. When the facility was taken over by Japanese management, however, the defect rate dropped to 0.05, the number of inspectors was reduced to one for twenty-five, and costs dropped as well. The work force was basically unchanged. Similarly, a few years later at a Sony plant in San Diego, product quality was not achieving the expected level despite a ratio of one inspector per fifteen workers. U.S. management was again replaced by Japanese management but no change was made in the work force. Soon, with a ratio of one inspector to fifty workers, the plant set a worldwide record for Sony production—200 consecutive defect-free days.

Quality and productivity, like much else both good and bad, start with management.

A highly illuminating study of the cost of quality has been reported by Professor David Garvin of the Harvard Business School who has conducted an in-depth examination of the U.S. and Japanese room air-conditioning industries. Restructuring somewhat the basic data collected in his assessment, one can produce the graph contained in Figure 15. The conventional wisdom would argue that as more and more resources are expended in order to achieve high quality, the cost line in the figure should veer upward to the right. But the observed trend is exactly the opposite, sloping downward to the right. That is, the higher the quality that is achieved (within limits, undoubtedly) the *lower* the total cost. So much for the conventional wisdom.

Garvin observes that "The shocking news, for which nothing had prepared me, is that the failure rates from

The Cost of Quality

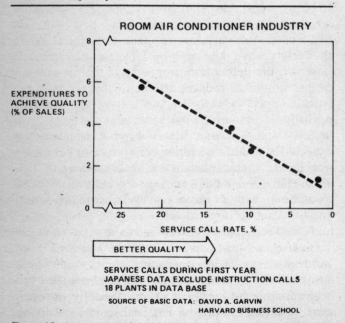

Figure 15. As greater quality is built into a product, the cost of achieving quality does not increase but rather decreases.

the highest-quality producers were between *500 and 1,000* times less than those of products from the lowest. . . . There indeed is a competitive problem worth worrying about." He goes on to explain that with regard to the *lower* "costs of quality" assignable to the more demanding high-quality manufacturers, "The reason is clear: failures are much more expensive to fix after a unit has been assembled than before . . . (and) field service costs are much higher than those of incoming inspection."

Thus, we have derived Augustine's First Law of Counterproductivity:

LAW NUMBER XII

It costs a lot to build bad products.

The knee-jerk reaction of a bureaucracy trying to solve a problem is often to hire more auditors to try and catch the wrong-doers. Similarly, the instantaneous textbook solution to achieving better quality has for too many years been to hire more quality inspectors. Unfortunately, it is simply not possible to "inspect-in" or "audit-in" quality. Quality must be designed-in and built-in.

Apropos of this conclusion is the experience at one large U.S. manufacturer with one of its Quality Circles, a now well-established concept wherein groups of employees meet to seek to better the products they produce. This particular Quality Circle conceived a superb idea involving the use of a special optical instrument for inspecting electrical connectors the company had been purchasing in large quantities. A resulting savings of $817,000 per year at a single plant was projected. When questioned as to just how many of the connectors received from suppliers were defective, the answer indicated a 40 percent rejection rate. Although the new inspection technique proved very effective, the real problem was that the supplier was building shoddy merchandise—and the purchaser was tolerating the practice. *That* was the problem that needed to be attacked. The principal task at hand was not one of more efficiently finding the bad parts (although that in itself was useful); rather, it was one of producing fewer bad parts in the first place.

Quality Circles have proven to be a very effective means of attacking problems. As usual, this breakthrough in business methodology seems rather obvious in hindsight: Who could possibly know more about the work being performed than the workers themselves? But the process is not easy. One General Motors manager has described the four stages of an employee Quality Circle as "griping, groping, grasping, and growing."

At the Martin Marietta plant in Michoud, Louisiana, where the large orange fuel tank is built that helps loft the Space Shuttle into orbit for NASA, Quality Circles were established which led, as expected, to substantial cost reductions. An unexpected benefit was an accompanying 58 percent reduction in employee grievances, a 45 percent drop in lost time, and a 59 percent decrease in hardware nonconformities among those individuals participating in the Quality Circles.

Perhaps the greatest impediment to the achievement of high quality—and productivity—is, as discovered two chapters ago, burgeoning bureaucracy. Every job and every externally imposed regulation needs to be challenged on a basis of value added, the "Where's the beef?'' test. The value-added can of course be measured in terms of intangibles as well as tangibles—such as quality of work life—should one wish. But absent such a disciplined cost-benefit analysis and a corporation or even an entire economy can descend into a businessman's never-never land, such as that which *The Wall Street Journal* attributes to Portugal. A classic article by Barry Newman sums up what sounds like the ultimate well-meaning but nonproductive society:

> Nobody gets fired in Portugal unless the boss has a very good reason. That is the law set down a decade ago after the radical left took over the government. . . . Bosses hate this. They want to consolidate, modernize. They are aching to fire people. Lucky for them, the radicals who wrote the law to protect jobs forgot to write a law to protect salaries. So Portuguese bosses have devised a new way to increase cash flow. They don't fire workers; they just don't pay them. . . . Yet almost everybody keeps on working. How come? Well, according to the law, if somebody doesn't show up for work just because he isn't being paid, he could get fired. . . . A worker could become officially unemployed if his company goes out of business. But Portuguese companies try to avoid that. If a company shuts down it has to pay severance. And it loses the state subsidies designed to keep people working. . . . If you lay people off you have to pay them. . . . It would be very expensive.

> According to one Portuguese employee, Frotuoso Santarem, who has been paid only nine months out of the last eighteen, ''We're used to

working, so we work. . . . If I left or the yard closed I'd have to look for a job." And Mr. Santarem does gain one advantage . . . (his company) used to subtract 15 cents from his salary for a midday meal. As long as he doesn't get paid, the company can't do that. He gets a free lunch.

That's why America must take productivity, and its counterpart, quality, seriously. Everyone knows that there is no such thing as a free lunch.

13

Malice
in Wonderland

"But Benjamin's mess was five times so much
as any of theirs."

—Book of Genesis

On the fourth anniversary of the company's cre-
ation the founders looked out upon their domain
of nearly 200 semihappy employees and won-
dered why they themselves were not happy.
Somewhere, somehow, something had gone awry.
They were now working half-days (7 a.m. to 7
p.m.), were more in debt than ever before, and
enjoying it all less. They had been so busy caring
for Daedalus's finances that their few remaining
personal assets were still stagnating unattended
in fixed-rate savings accounts in an era of run-
away inflation. It seemed that it was time they,
as chairman and president of Daedalus, should
begin to reap the rewards of building so suc-
cessful an enterprise. Thus was chartered the
study which would reveal how executives of other

*corporations were remunerated for their contri-
butions. After months of anticipation it was with
considerable excitement that the results were finally viewed. They showed that managers who
produce exceptional results can expect the rewards they receive to be increased. Unless, of
course, they stay the same. Or decrease.*

"Call it what you will, incentives are the only way to
make people work harder." The words of Andrew Car-
negie? The creed of John D. Rockefeller? Or perhaps
of Henry Ford? No, as it happens, these are the words
of none other than that old capitalist Nikita Khrushchev
speaking on the benefits of the incentive system. And
judging by the trend in today's China and the European
Satellite Nations, such thinking in the Communist world
is not confined to the Soviet Union.

Having thus established the manner in which incentives are viewed in the Communistic part of the world,
it is instructive to examine their use in the system extant
in the United States, for which incentives form the very
foundation: the Free Enterprise System.

Figure 16 displays the ranking of the fifty most profitable firms in the United States in one recent year as
compared with the rank according to pay received of
the individuals who led those companies the prior four
years.* The question of course arises whether there
should not be a strong correlation between the prosperity of a company and the prosperity of its leaders.
As shown in the figure, however, this is like asking, Is

*For the occasional instances where the leadership changed during the period
examined, the data for that company are not included in the figure.

Executive Wages and Company Performance

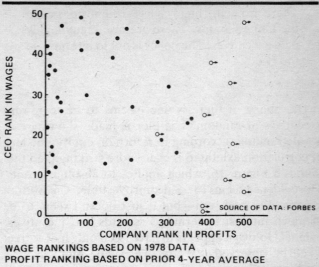

WAGE RANKINGS BASED ON 1978 DATA
PROFIT RANKING BASED ON PRIOR 4-YEAR AVERAGE

*Chief Executive Officer

Figure 16. It is difficult to detect any relationship between the wages of key executives and the performance of the firms they lead.

it colder in the winter or in Wyoming. There appears to be no discernable relationship *in the aggregate* between the parameters examined. Performance and rewards are unrelated.

The following law, known as the Augustine-Dozier* Law of Distributive Rewards, explains the available evidence (with apologies to P. K. Wrigley of baseball fame, who first framed the concept):

*Susan Dozier, Operations Intern, Martin Marietta Aerospace.

LAW NUMBER XIII

There are many highly successful businesses in the United States. There are also many highly paid executives. The policy is not to intermingle the two.

The policy, if there is one, seems to be to reward executives at random. If a plot is made showing corporate rankings according to return on equity, the lack of correlation exhibited is even more striking than that found in Figure 16, which applies to absolute profits. The evidence seems to be incontrovertible: The Bottom Line is alive and well—but it just doesn't seem to be of much interest in terms of rewards and incentives. Samuel Goldwyn appears to have been only half correct when he observed, "We're overpaying him, but he's worth it."

One might erroneously fall into the trap of thinking that executives merely take the viewpoint, "If it weren't for the honor, I'd just as soon be paid more and make less profit." Sort of like Bear Bryant, the only man honored by having an animal named after him. But even this theory cannot be sustained. For example, the chairman of AT&T holds what many would assert is one of the most honored and prestigious positions in corporate America. But when, a few years ago in a survey conducted by a polling organization, the name of AT&T's chairman was listed and the public was asked to identify him, only 2 percent of those surveyed could even associate him as a corporate official—which was about one-third as many who thought he was a cabinet officer and considerably fewer than those who identified him as a labor leader. There were nearly as many people who thought he was an astronaut or a TV journalist as thought of him as a corporate official. So much for prestige.

Although one could never confuse the operation of the U.S. government with the operation of the free enterprise system, it is no less striking that an overt effort at *demotivation* has been practiced for many years whereby the top five layers of government management have often all been fixed at the identical pay level due to the imposition of arbitrary wage ceilings.

General Dave Jones, a former chairman of the Joint Chiefs of Staff, describes the implications of these management practices by drawing the following fascinating view of the Joint Chiefs' organization as it would appear through the eyes of an industrialist:

> [The Corporate Board of Directors] consists of five directors, all insiders, four of whom simultaneously head line divisions. . . . [The Board] reports to [both] the chief executive and a cabinet member . . . [and is] supported by a corporate staff which draws all its officers from line divisions and turns over about every two years. . . . Line divisions control officer assignments and advancement; there is no transfer of officers among line divisions. . . . The Board meets three times a week to address operational as well as policy matters, which normally are first reviewed by a four-layered committee system involving full participation of division staffs from the start. . . . At seventy-five percent of the Board meetings, one or more of the directors are represented by substitutes. . . . If the Board can't reach unanimous

agreement on an issue, it must—by law—inform
its superiors. . . . At least the four top leadership
and management levels within the corporation receive the same basic compensation, set by two
[congressional] committees consisting of a total of
535 members . . . and any personnel changes in
the top three levels (about 150 positions) must be
approved in advance by one of the [congressional]
committees.

Nonetheless, there is no need for discouragement,
since the incentive system is, in spite of the above evidence borrowed from the U.S. government, still alive
and well: "People who show the best example in their
work must receive greater material benefit"—according
to a speech before the Supreme Soviet by the Premier
of the Soviet Union.

And right here at home it was recently pointed out
that "the challenge for American capitalism in the '80s
is to bring the entrepreneurial spirit back to America.
Depressed areas especially need enormous investment
of capital. Individual entrepreneurship can create the
new work ethic that is so desperately needed in America." So said Jerry Rubin, Yippie leader of the 1960s
and a defendant in the Chicago Seven trial—speaking
in the 1980s as a security analyst on Wall Street.

*"The budget included funds for the new executive tennis court
adjacent to the plant."*

PART III

MINOR
OVERSIGHTS

14

All Started by
a Spark

"Pro football isn't what it used to be and it
never was."

—Don Meredith

*The solution to the leveling sales trend, an-
nounced the breathless vice-president of engineering, was to upgrade the entire product line.
Daedalus, he said, had within its grasp the opportunity to become the first firm ever to offer
a fully microprocessor-controlled model airplane
containing a laser command link, a miniature gas
turbine engine, and internal fiber-optic communication paths between a distributed network
of adaptive digital controllers. The Board of Directors (which by now had grown to three bankers, a professor, five lawyers, the head of a local
PR firm, the two founders, and the chairman's
brother-in-law) listened with intense excitement.
Yet there was a degree of skepticism to this sud-
den new proposal. This concern was finally laid
to rest when it was explained that electronics was*

the wave of the future. One of the older board members told a story about a bear who, displaying a $5 bill, had entered a bar and ordered a beer and how the owner of the bar had directed the bartender to give the bear the beer, saying that since the bear didn't look very smart to only give it 25 cents in change. Having done as he had been instructed, and having watched incredulously as the bear placidly sipped the beer, the bartender finally could no longer contain himself and sought to engage the bear in conversation. "You know," he said to the bear, "we don't get many bears in this bar." To which the bear is said to have replied, "At $4.75 a beer, it's no wonder." Everyone laughed a lot, and the meeting was adjourned so the engineers could get back to their laboratories and begin work on the new project.

General of the Army Omar Bradley often quoted an old Signal Corps maxim that Congress makes a general, but only communications can make him a commander. In their zeal for technology, many civilian executives have placed themselves in a business environment where if all computers were to go on strike not only would the executives be unable to communicate but no paychecks would be written and few machines in the factory would function. We would be unable to drive to work because our highways would gridlock without computer controlled traffic lights and our banking system would grind to a halt. Nearly one trillion dollars changes hands each day in the form of the zeros and ones that move around inside computers and electronic communications systems. One of the most feared expressions in modern times is "the computer is down."

It would appear that the nation to win the worldwide trade war will be the one with the last robot standing. Recently, an incident in Japan actually resulted in the first recorded case of a robot killing a fellow worker. Paraphrasing the caution of Dr. Bob Everett, president of the MITRE Corporation:

> The American Worker,
> His strength is as the strength of ten,
> 'Cause he has LSI.

LSI, Large Scale Integration, a forerunner of the technique whereby a million electronic circuit elements will be placed on a single postage-stamp–sized "chip," is indeed important. But one suspects, as Everett hints, such intangibles as skill, motivation, and leadership may still be worth more than their weight in silicon—the material of which most such chips have been made.

Nonetheless, *The Washington Star* has reported that "If past wars were won or lost in places like the playing fields of Eton, future wars will be won or lost on computer terminals." The magnitude of the computer explosion was recently illustrated in a session at MIT where Michael Dertavzos noted that, in the next few decades, it will be feasible to store the world's knowledge in a computer for about half a billion dollars per LOC. But, in this case, an "LOC" is not the pedestrian "Line of Code" so well known to software developers, but rather is a "Library of Congress." The spread of electronics has been such that a recent issue of *The Wall Street Journal* felt obliged to point out that the scaffolding which was to be seen surrounding "Big Ben" in London did not foretell of the installation of a digital clock.

The trend toward proliferation of electronics could of course be either productive or counterproductive, depending on how it is harnessed. In the civilian world, our lives revolve around electronic boxes more than most realize or perhaps care to realize. Consider the ubiquitous television set. According to The Nielsen Index the average American youth spends almost twenty-six hours a week engaged in one-way communication with what is often perceptively referred to as a boob tube. Children ages two to five log some twenty-seven hours and nine minutes each week. The total hours accumulated in front of the tube by the average American youth far exceeds the time he spends in a school classroom.

In the military sphere, the notion of computers fighting one another is *already* a reality. Much has been written about giant data processors developing codes to protect the secrecy of messages while enemy computers simultaneously seek to decipher those codes. On a smaller scale, computers controlling countermeasures devices in electronic warfare operations fight enemy computers managing the enemy's counter-countermeasures equipment, and friendly computers assign countercounter countermeasures, and . . .

Each application of electronics seemingly leads to still another in an almost endless chain, raising the danger that electronics may indeed dominate the world before it can itself be controlled. Giant computers are at work designing their own offspring, the ultimate in electronic perpetuation. One example of the extent of this prolific trend borrowed from the aeronautical sphere is ex-

An Electrifying Experience

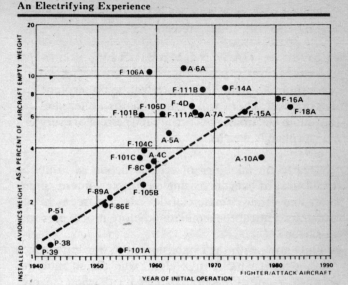

Figure 17. The fraction of many military systems which is comprised of electronics has grown like lightning for several decades, whether measured in terms of cost, weight—or problems.

amined in Figure 17, in which is presented the fraction of an aircraft's weight that is comprised of electronics. It has been observed that airplanes today are no more than trucks in which to carry electrons around the sky. The trend with time is, unfortunately, unmistakably supportive of this viewpoint. Extrapolating undauntedly, certain characteristics of the airplane of the future can now be derived. Namely, it will be made entirely of electronics.

Augustine's Law Number XIV, the Law of Unrelenting Electrification, predicts that:

LAW NUMBER XIV

After the year 2015, there will be no airplane crashes. There will be no takeoffs either, because electronics will occupy 100 percent of every airplane's weight.

Clearly the makings of science fiction . . . but the trend toward ever-increasing electronic content of aircraft and other commercial devices does seem to deserve a skeptical reexamination before it becomes cast in silicon.

Only now, with the establishment of this Law, can it be explained what Lord Kelvin, who did so much to advance modern science, had in mind when he predicted more boldly than wisely that "aircraft flight is impossible!" All those snickers over the years can be seen to have been undeserved; he was simply ahead of his time. Law XIV would certainly indicate, however, that it was not his finest hour when he also predicted that "Radio has no future!"

In fairness, it should be noted that, as pointed out by Dr. George Heilmeier, vice-president of Texas Instruments, "If the automotive industry had progressed during the last two decades at the same rate as the semiconductor industry, a Rolls-Royce would today cost only three dollars and there would be no parking problem because automobiles would be one quarter of an inch on a side!"

There remain those cynics who even in that bastion of electrification, the space program, would point to instances wherein had a human not been on board there would have been no one available to repair the failures which were encountered in the life-support system—which is needed to keep the human alive. There are, equally, those who might irreverently note that if it were not for the radar display screens in the cockpits of modern aircraft, there would be no place to affix all the caution and warning stickers which remind the pilot of all the things that might go wrong with the electrical equipment. The rampant use of computers is such that there are now those who refer to an airplane and its associated engines as "peripherals." The same is becoming true of automobiles.

This trend is nowhere better represented than in the case of the military bomber aircraft. The World War II B-29 contained about 10,000 electronic component parts, the B-47 approximately 20,000, the B-52 50,000, and the B-58 nearly 100,000—or a factor of two each generation. But this rate of growth has been eclipsed by the B-1, which is packed with microcircuits containing as many active elements on a single quarter-inch chip as were carried in an entire B-58 a few years earlier.

A modern jetliner has 4.5 million parts, 100 miles of wiring—and 12,000 pages of maintenance manuals. The typical space satellite in 1967 had some 5000 parts. In 1977, this had grown to 100,000. By 1987, it will be well over one million. Of course, their capabilities have increased enormously as well. In the case of communication satellites the standard in 1965 was 250 circuits per satellite. In 1970, this had grown to 4000—which in turn increased to 30,000 by 1985. It is projected that each satellite in the year 2000 will provide one million circuits.

Dr. Allen Puckett, chairman of Hughes Aircraft

Company, comments, not too seriously, that "the real miracle of the Wright Brothers flight was that they accomplished it without the use of any electronics at all." He explains, "The only electrical devices in the Wright Flyer were the magneto and the spark gap in each cylinder of the engine." Today, an International L-1011 contains $4 million of avionics, roughly the worth of a DC-7C some twenty years earlier. In fact, about one million dollars in 1960 would have bought every microcircuit then in existence.

Not only have military airplanes succumbed to the electrifying experience of embracing high technology, but so too have the missiles they shoot. The Phoenix missile, for example, contains 538,000 active circuit elements, contrasting markedly with its forebear of a dozen years earlier which suffered through its existence on a mere 118 active elements. Fortunately, great strides have been made in increasing the reliability of electronic circuitry; however, correspondingly great discipline must now be exercised not to negate this gain by the unbounded introduction of more and more circuits.

In the civilian world, only the mind of an electronics specialist, when called upon to come up with a simple way for the average person to keep track of the time of day, would think of designing a device that oscillated 4,190,000 times every second and then constructing an electronic counter which counts each and every oscillation until it reaches 4,190,000 when it announces that one second has passed—and then starts all over again to get ready to count to 4,190,000 for the next second. This is, of course, exactly the way the commonplace quartz wristwatch works, which is, in fact, perhaps the second most accurate electrical timepiece ever made— next, of course, to the automobile battery, which miraculously knows to fail within days after the expiration of its warranty.

One wonders how we could survive without voices in our cars that keep reminding us that "the door is open" even when we *want* the door open to get some fresh air in a parking lot, or how we could have become so quickly inured to the sound of burglar alarms crying wolf around our neighborhoods, or how we will escape the hassle of our offices when every car has a telephone and thus becomes a mobile office that we cannot escape, or why we obediently accept the explanation that airline service has temporarily collapsed because "the computer is down." As noted, a robot in Japan has killed a man, computer fraud is becoming one of the more commonplace crimes, and answer-phones carry on incoherent conversations with automatic-dialing advertising services. In at least one instance in America, a computer laid off a fellow employee—a discovery which cost the employee's company a 20 percent salary increase to get the employee to turn down the new job he had found before his supervisor became aware of the error. Even greeting cards carry electronics to sing out a message hopefully appropriate to the occasion.

When an Internal Revenue Service computer went berserk and sent 100,000 companies a letter threatening to seize their property, an IRS spokesman, Dan Seklecki, was forced to note, "It obviously caused a lot of frustration and anxiety to taxpayers, for which we apologize." A better idea might have been to pull the culprit's plug.

The confidence the creators of marvels of electronic wizardry themselves hold in their progeny can be gleaned from a recent issue of *Lockheed Life,* an internal company paper of the aerospace/electronics giant. It is therein dutifully acknowledged that Lockheed employs a squadron of carrier pigeons to carry messages between its Sunnyvale plant and its Santa Cruz test site in California. So much for high tech.

There are a few other remaining bastions of resistance to rampant electrification. One is the famous insurance underwriter, Lloyd's of London. At Lloyd's center of operations a modern computer drives a display screen and maintains constant contact with a worldwide network of high-speed communications which in turn flash key happenings from the four corners of the Earth. Closely monitoring the display screen, an official record-keeper then carefully copies the messages . . . using an eighteenth-century quill pen.

James McNeill Whistler, the renowned American artist, seemed to have had a premonition of just how different our world would become had it not been for advancements in microelectronics. Late in his career, he looked back upon a less than successful experience as a cadet at West Point during which he is said to have failed a course in chemistry. He lamented, "If silicon had been a gas, I might have been a major general."

If not a gas, semiconductors have nonetheless been accurately dubbed, at least from an economic perspective, the crude oil of the 1980s. How, for instance, could one survive without electric toothbrushes, 23-function digital wristwatches, and voice-synthesized robots which inform one over the telephone that one's last quarter has just been used to dial a number which is no longer in service?

Technology *has* produced some wonderful things, but it is also important to decide whether electrons or humans are to set the path for humanity. Sometimes there is a tendency to forget what technology is all about—

as in the case of the subway cars for the new Washington, D.C., Metro. When first installed, the cars had a habit of flexing when filled with passengers, with the result that the doors would jam and hold the people prisoner. The director of engineering for the Metro put this all in perspective in the following quote from *The Washington Star:* "We'd have great cars if it weren't for the passengers."

15

Very Marginal Costs

> "Live within your income even if you have to
> borrow to do it."
>
> —Josh Billings

*"We know of not a single case where the enemy
has successfully used camouflage against us." At
least that's what the World War II placebo
boasted. One could then presumably rest at ease—
Daedalus's competitors did not seem to have
caught the scent and started responding to the
fantastic new development underway. But to some
it appeared that the enemy had perhaps been
glimpsed and, in the words of that immortal pos-
sum's friend, "He is us." Nonetheless, how could
anyone doubt that the enormous technological
sophistication of the new line of model airplane
products would assure instant success in the marketplace? To believe otherwise would be to for-
sake the flag, apple pie, and personal computers
all at once in this high-tech world. The task was*

*to squeeze the last little bit of performance out
of each and every product. Clearly, to compete
in this modern world one must venture out onto
the very precipices of the state-of-the-art. But
none of this seemed to raise much concern among
the firm's executives since everyone was occupied in what was widely referred to as the Space
War—a conflict that had broken out upon the
completion of the first module of the modern
new office building.*

Lord Kelvin once observed, "Large increases in cost
with questionable increases in performance can be tol-
erated only for race horses and fancy women." It therefore appears worthwhile to examine in some detail the
proposition that "the best is the enemy of the good"—
a precept which has had its heritage variously traced to
the Russians, the Chinese, and the Arabs. Whatever
its origin, there is considerable present-day evidence to
attest to its relevance. This is not to say that in terms
of personal and organizational attainment there can never
be any goal other than to be the very best. The problem
arises when this perspective is applied too broadly to
things rather than people. Lee Iacocca, writing about
the small car mystique, has observed, "The American
car buyer wants economy so badly he'll pay almost anything to get it!"

In times of rapidly advancing technology, by waiting
until tomorrow to begin a project it will always be possible to incorporate a little more advanced technology
and presumably to make the item being sought still a
little bit "better." But come tomorrow, there will be
yet another carrot just over the horizon. Thus, the sur-

est way to get nothing is to insist on waiting for everything. The result is that many companies tend to view their competitors' products with some condescension because they are clearly inferior . . . to that which their own company does not yet have.

The process of generating requirements or performance specifications for future products basically consists of enthusiastic engineers in industry promising to deliver "all the capability you want for a dollar" and a customer which generally responds, "I'll take two dollars' worth"—at least, until time to pay. This is particularly true in the case of purchases by the federal government. It seems that some people just won't take "yes" for an answer. The dilemma is worsened in the case of governmental procurements by the fact that the customer's "requirements" are frequently viewed as sacrosanct, even though initiative and imagination are, of course, always highly encouraged in responding to the government's purchase orders. Experience has shown, however, that winning contractors can offer anything they want—as long as it is what the government's employees wanted in the first place. There are in fact three criteria for winning competitions held by the government: responsiveness, responsiveness, and responsiveness. In that order. It is useful to recall, when considering whether to disregard something someone has written into a customer's specification for a product—even when it seems superfluous—the hard-learned truism that the same individual will undoubtedly participate in evaluating the contractor's proposal. Thus, when it comes to requests for proposals, there is truly a career in every paragraph.

Congresswoman Pat Schroeder, speaking at a House

Armed Services subcommittee hearing, expressed her exasperation at the inability of government officials to make difficult choices and thereby eliminate costs in the following terms: "If those guys were women, they'd all be pregnant—they can't say no to anything!"

The temptation to flirt with the edge of the state-of-the-art does appear irresistible to many engineers and their would-be customers, yet often results in the would-be developers finding themselves in circumstances wherein they are ill-equipped to work their way out of problems. They then must face a very skeptical Congress or other set of customers listening to their excuses. It is much as if these technological pioneers were following the course of an inmate at the Butte County Jail in California, who recently explained his brief absence from the jail to skeptical sheriff's deputies in the following manner, as reported by a national wire service: "I was playing pole vault and I got too close to the wall and I fell over the wall. When I regained my senses I ran around to try and find a way back in, but being unfamiliar with the area, got lost. Next thing I knew I was in Chico." Clearly this gentleman must have been a research and development manager in some earlier incarnation.

Not only does operation near the edge of the state-of-the-art often greatly increase cost and risk, but worse yet it can have a seriously deleterious effect on reliability. One might ask Mario Andretti for his views on this subject, in recognition of his being intimately familiar with the process of squeezing the last ounce of performance from high-technology machines: in his case, the Indianapolis Formula One auto racer. Andretti's record over the years gives insight into the hazards of operation near the edge of the state-of-the-art, particularly, once again, when it is not altogether clear which side of the edge one is on. The evidence:

In the words of Rick Mears, himself an Indianapolis 500 winner, "To finish first you must first finish." Such is life in the fast lane.

Even when dealing with established technology, the best can still be inordinately expensive. Sometimes its cost is, of course, very appropriate in that it provides the winning margin—that narrow edge between victory and defeat in a military context or a sale and a loss in the commercial sense. But other times, particularly in times of fixed overall budgets, the practice of seeking that last little bit of capability from hardware can be not only very costly but also very counterproductive.

Consider the matter of seeking to increase reliability

Mario Andretti's "Indianapolis 500" Experience

Year	Percent of Race Completed	Outcome
1965	100	Finished Third
1966	14	Engine Exploded
1967	29	Lost Wheel
1968	1	Burned Piston
	(42)	Replaced Another Driver, Burned Piston Again
1969	100	Won Race
1970	99	Engine Smoked
1971	6	Crashed into Wall
1972	97	Ran Out of Gas
1973	2	Burned Piston
1974	1	Broken Piston
1975	25	Crashed into Wall
1976	5	Engine Smoked
1977	—	Did Not Race
1978	93	Oil Leak
1979	—	Did Not Race
1980	36	Engine Seized
1981	100	Finished Second
1982	0	Crashed at Start
1983	42	Crashed
1984	76	Engine Failed, Crashed

through the provision of redundancy, a policy often employed, and appropriately so in most cases. But when the part most likely to fail is also the dominant cost contributor—which is occasionally the case—this practice merely serves as a convenient example of the high price of truly maximizing performance. For instance, increasing the reliability of an element with an *inherent* reliability of 80 percent by just sixteen more percentage points will double its cost if achieved through duplication. The next 3 percent will *triple* the cost . . . and so on. But from the seller's standpoint it is simply a confirmation of Mae West's assertion that "too much of a good thing can be wonderful."

That this phenomenon is not totally unique to hardware reliability is shown in Figure 18, which presents the cost of obtaining ever-increasing performance for items ranging from optical components to baseball players. The difference in market price between a .250 hitter and a .300 hitter is marked, even though the actual performance difference is merely that one will get a hit just one more time than the other every twenty tries. Similarly, the price of a normal investment grade diamond jumps from $6,800 per karat to $44,000 per karat when the demand is made that it be flawless (Grade D). Much the same is true of airplanes, inertial reference systems, and so forth.*

Some very astute soul is alleged to have remarked, "Never try to teach a pig to sing. It just wastes your time and annoys the pig."

For the more mathematically inclined manager, if one

---

*In the case of inertial reference unit precision, smaller is better. To accommodate this the available data were spread across the ordinate of the plot in linear fashion. The grade of diamonds has been treated in the same manner, a practice which probably understates the cost of increasing quality.

The High Cost of That Last Little Bit

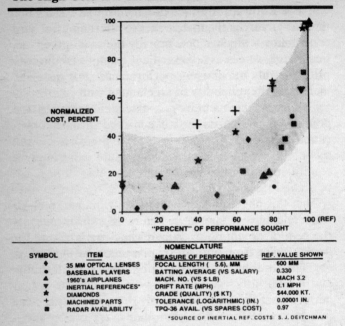

*SOURCE OF INERTIAL REF. COSTS: S. J. DEITCHMAN

Figure 18. A disproportionate share of the cost of most purchases is concentrated in a very small fraction of the features sought. So-called "extras" are particularly flagrant contributors to cost in both the commercial and government marketplaces.

equates the cost scale in Figure 18 to the "agony" of a project, a bit of graphical analysis reveals that "agony is proportional to ecstasy cubed."

That "nice to have" features can be costly is certified in the answer given by a recent million-dollar-lottery winner to a question about what he had done with all the money. His answer: "To be honest, I spent half of it on liquor, gambling, and women. The rest I wasted."

Once costly features are designed into a system they are very, very difficult to remove. Bert Fowler, vice-president of the MITRE Corporation, observed that one can learn a great deal from a graph of the increase in cost of a system versus the system's total capability as each successive feature is added—or, correspondingly, the decrease in cost as features are eliminated. The "Fowler Hysteresis Law," as it has become known, states, "When each element of capability is successively *deleted* until a systems capability is *altogether gone*, 30 percent of the cost still remains!"

Fowler has also pointed out an interesting contagiousness associated with asking for more and more of some item until costs are driven to unaffordable levels. It seems that when the cost of that item is allowed to rise, it drags the cost of other items along with it. Thus, for some reason, a mess table on a nuclear submarine costs substantially more than a mess table on a conventional submarine. Similarly, a clock in a Mercedes Benz costs a great deal more than a clock in a Volkswagen. So it goes with the ashtrays, the horn, and each other component until the capability and cost of the entire system rise to the threshold of intolerance. This is in spite of the fact that a clock simply tells time no matter what car it is located in, an ashtray collects ashes, and so forth. As the fried chicken commercial says, "Parts is parts"—at least for peripheral functions.

These observations comprise the foundation for Augustine's Law of Insatiable Appetites, which traces its origin to automobile salesmen and the omnipresent "extras" with which they make a living—and may be stated as follows:

LAW NUMBER XV

The last 10 percent of performance generates one-third of the cost and two-thirds of the problems.

The price of the ultimate is very high indeed. Sometimes it would seem that one might be better served by having more of a little less. If not, the ultimate outcome seems to be to have nothing, albeit of the *very* highest capability. Watson Watt, speaking of the British radar used during World War II, noted that ". . . the best design had to be rejected because it would never be achieved, and that the 'second best' would be achieved too late to be used by the armed forces when they needed it. The third best would be adequate and was available in time, and it was what won the Battle of Britain."

Econo Lodges' president, Ben Douglas, evidences a solid understanding of this principle: "When you turn the lights off," he says, "we like to think you can't tell the difference between an Econo Lodge and a Hilton."

The temptation to ask for more and more until there is nothing left to seek leads to the philosophical dilemma of life once described by a well-known cartoonist: "There is nothing left to do that I want to do because if there were I would have done it."

The secret, if there is one, to controlling the costs which are added by the pursuit of peripheral, albeit impressive, capabilities is actually quite straightforward and can be seen in the workings of a sculptor creating a statue of a hippopotamus. How does one make a statue of a hippopotamus? Very easily; one obtains a large block of granite and chips away every piece that does not look like a hippopotamus.

16

The High Cost
of Buying

"I was expecting this, but not so soon."
—Tombstone, Boot Hill

Being novices in the model airplane business it was only natural to view the builders of large modern jet aircraft with a certain awe, much as Little Leaguers might view, say, the Mets or the Oilers. It was therefore only natural to conduct the investigation into historical cost trends using real airplanes as the case study, particularly since over the years technology had been poured into them by the bucketful. The results of the study turned out to be devastating. The only good news to be found was that at least in the case of military aircraft, warfare seemed to be pricing itself out of existence. Sadly, these same findings seemed also to apply to a wide spectrum of products. What then would happen when a model airplane cost more than a Model-T had once

*cost? Or when the excitement of flying a model
airplane consisted of sitting in one's living room
and pushing a button to initiate a completely
automatic takeoff, flight, and landing sequence
totally out of sight and out of control of the flying
enthusiast? Could it be that something was being
missed somewhere?*

It can be shown that the unit cost of certain high-technology hardware is increasing at an exponential rate
with time. Figure 19 shows, for example, the historical
trend of rising unit cost in the case of one category of
military aircraft. From the days of the Wright Brothers'
airplane to the era of modern high-performance fighter
aircraft, the cost of an individual airplane has unwav-
eringly grown by a factor of four every ten years. This
rate of growth seems to be an inherent characteristic of
such systems, with the unit cost being most closely cor-
related with the passage of time rather than with changes
in maneuverability, speed, weight, or other technical
parameters. The same inexorable trend can be shown
to apply to commercial aircraft, helicopters, and even
ships and tanks, although in the last two somewhat less
technologically sophisticated instances, the rate of growth
is a factor of two every ten years. Automobiles, houses,
and certain other commercial products more nearly approximate this latter case. The point is not, of course,
that new technology is inevitably more expensive than
old technology; the opposite is often the case. But what
happens is that, as has been noted, new technology
opens vast new capability vistas which are then crammed
into each new generation of a product.
The cost of high-technology military hardware can

Cost of Tactical Aircraft: Taking Off

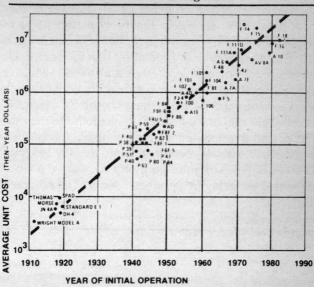

Figure 19. The unit cost of tactical aircraft has increased in a very consistent manner ever since the beginning of the aviation age. The rate-of-climb is a factor of four every ten years. There is no ceiling in sight.

then be accurately expressed in terms of an increase by a factor of four during each sunspot cycle, which happens to be about eleven years, independent of anything else.

The significance of this observation does not, however, lie in the mere fact that cost growth is, in itself, predictable. Rather, it lies in a comparison of the rate of growth of, say, aircraft unit cost contrasted with the rate of growth of other seemingly relevant parameters, such as the nation's defense budget. This particular comparison is presented in Figure 20, wherein the identical data points shown in Figure 19 pertaining to the cost of aircraft are reproduced, but to a smaller scale in order to facilitate extrapolation into the future. Objection might of course be raised as to the validity of any such extrapolation; however, it is noted that the above-mentioned trend has faithfully prevailed throughout the entire history of aviation. On the other hand, one is reminded of the economic forecaster in Washington who was ecstatic to learn that his 280-pound brother-in-law had gone on a diet and had announced he would be losing five pounds a week. The economist

Calvin Coolidge's Revenge

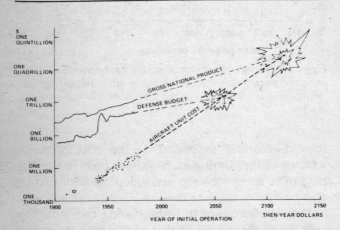

Figure 20. The cost of tactical aircraft built throughout the recorded history of aviation, as represented by the dots, can be accurately projected in a manner which points to a singular problem in the not-too-distant future.

quickly figured that he would be altogether rid of his brother-in-law in just a little over a year.

When the trend curves for the national budget for defense and the unit cost of tactical aircraft are, in fact, each extended forward in time, as shown in Figure 20, a rather significant event does occur in the not-too-distant future: namely, the curves *intersect*. And they intersect within the lifetimes of people living today. This observation has led to the formulation of what is known in some circles as the First Law of Impending Doom and in other circles as the Final Law of Economic Disarmament:

LAW NUMBER XVI

In the year 2054, the entire defense budget will purchase just one aircraft. This aircraft will have to be shared by the Air Force and Navy 3½ days each per week except for leap year, when it will be made available to the Marines for the extra day.

One can only imagine the difficulties that such an arrangement will entail. There will be, for example, the advocates of helicopters who will point to the corresponding plot for their devices, noting with pride that due to successes in cost control a "fleet" of *rotary-wing* aircraft would not dwindle to the quintessential machine until the year 2064—a full decade later.

It should be pointed out to those who take solace in challenging the validity of the above extrapolation of the defense budget that, were a plot of the gross na-

tional product to have been used instead, the aforementioned singular event would have been delayed a
mere sixty years. In this latter era the cost of aircraft
will no longer be measured in dollars but a new unit
will be introduced, the Gross National Product, or
"GNP," pronounced, "nip." Hence, an aircraft in the
year 2100 will cost about half a nip.

Dr. John Wall of McDonnell Douglas has pointed
out that this law demonstrates that

> all the military might of the U.S. will be concen-
> trated into one grand vehicle in the latter half of
> the 21st Century. But this is just the *Battlestar
> Gallactica* which we all know so well, with perhaps
> a few smaller ships such as the *USS Enterprise*
> preceding it by 50 years or so. And in the mid-
> 22nd Century we find: Darth Vadar's planet-size
> *Death Star*! One single grand fighting machine
> encompassing a whole nation—or perhaps a whole
> planet!

Seldom has the power of extrapolation been so ma-
jestically stated!

Interestingly, if not surprisingly, the trend shown in
Figure 19 is independent of the amount of funds available. Even though, for example, the defense budget of
the United Kingdom is substantially less than that of
the United States (but growing rapidly), the aircraft cost
trend line for the United Kingdom almost exactly rep-
licates that of America. With its smaller budget, the
Royal Air Force and Navy will thus be reduced to a
single airplane two years before the United States reaches
that milestone. There have been many proposals
throughout history that international disputes be settled

by one-on-one duels between heads of the contending nations. Technology may be contriving to make that a reality.

This particular law might, perhaps, more accurately be remembered as "Calvin Coolidge's Revenge" as a tribute to the prescience of that gentleman. It will, of course, be recalled that it was Calvin Coolidge who in 1928 asked, in a moment of budgetary frustration over paying $25,000 for a *squadron* of aircraft, "Why can't we buy just one aeroplane and let the aviators take turns flying it?" Calvin Coolidge, like Lord Kelvin, was ahead of his time.

Turning to the commercial arena, such has been the pace of progress that the passengers' seats in a modern jetliner cost more than an entire airliner of the late 1940s. In fact, a modern airliner costs five times the market value of the entire airline industry as it existed in 1938. A daring extrapolation of the spectacular growth rate in airline passenger-miles flown (5 percent increase per year) and of the U.S. population growth (1.4 percent per annum) leads to the astonishing conclusion that in a mere 250 years it will be necessary for the *entire* citizenry of the United States to be airborne twenty-four *hours a day, every day*. Anyone doubting the validity of this projection need only visit the airports in New York, Chicago, Denver, or Atlanta some Friday night in order to be reassured of its truth. Although this will unarguably reduce freeway congestion, the concept of a nation's populace continually flying around with an airplane of some sort strapped to its posterior somehow seems extraordinarily nonproductive.

Figure 21 shows the corresponding trend in unit cost for commercial airliners and Figure 22 presents the corresponding data for bomber aircraft as opposed to

Cost of Commercial Airliners: Up, Up, and Away!

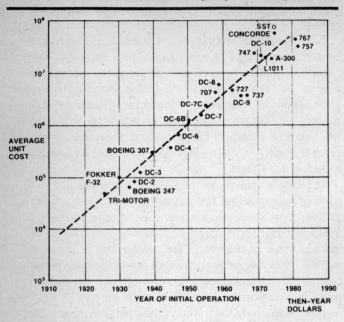

Figure 21. The trend of increasing cost with time has been basically the same for commercial aircraft as for military aircraft. In both cases major performance advancements have been achieved, but not without a price.

smaller, tactical aircraft considered in the previous figures. This chart culminates in the B-1 phantom data point which, for the sake of consistency, can be referred to as "Jimmy Carter's Revenge" (B-1 canceled) or "Ronald Reagan's Re-revenge" (B-1 revived) or "Walter Mondale's attempted Re-re-revenge" (a revenge that never quite venged). But in spite of the fact that as a project the B-1 seems to have left more people dis-

Cost of Bomber Aircraft: Bombing Out

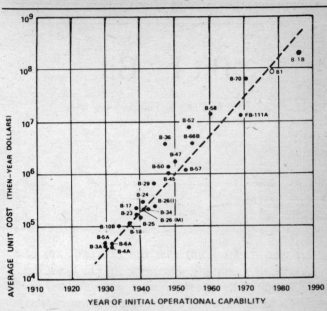

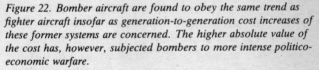

Figure 22. Bomber aircraft are found to obey the same trend as fighter aircraft insofar as generation-to-generation cost increases of these former systems are concerned. The higher absolute value of the cost has, however, subjected bombers to more intense politico-economic warfare.

gruntled than gruntled, it nonetheless serves as a powerful example of the use of this particular law. Simply waiting for things to settle down to abnormal has been very demanding in this case.

But somewhere lurking in the background there remains the echo of that troublesome warning by Lenin, "Quantity has a quality all its own."

17

Bit by Bit

"We look at it and do not see it."
—Lao-tzu, sixth century B.C.

It was at this point that the Daedalus Model Airplane Company unexpectedly ran headlong into one of the most ethereal, abstruse, and recalcitrant substances ever to challenge managers: software—a substance that creeps into systems to an ever-increasing extent whether it is wanted or not. The words attributed to Louis Armstrong about jazz seemed to apply equally well to software. When asked to define jazz, Satchmo is said to have replied, "If you got to ask, you ain't never goin' to know." And, in this case, there seemed to be a lot of managers who weren't never goin' to know. For instance, at the very same time that one of the software lead engineers was advising senior management not to worry because the software effort was not in any trouble, one of his colleagues was telling them not to worry because they were already halfway through the trouble. Little did the ancient Greeks realize that the universe actually consists of earth, fire, water—and software.

Considerable strain has been building within the business community as engineers and managers seek to produce useful products while complying with the plethora of laws that have come into existence, both natural and man-made. Indeed, laws, especially the unnatural ones, seem to grow like weeds. Complicating the effort required to comply with all these constraints is the often contradictory guidance given by customers or other official bodies. As but one example, in several recent instances the U.S. Congress has gone so far as to legislate as part of the Appropriations Act the initial availability dates for new high-technology systems it was having developed. This is like scheduling invention— but nonetheless the dates are *law*. It is not yet clear what the exact liability might be for managers of those projects should they fail to meet the prescribed end dates, especially in instances where the Congress subsequently cut their projects' budgets, but it is clear that this has not significantly reduced the stress within the process of supplying the federal government.

The dilemma faced by those involved in producing high-tech products is typified by the difficulty of complying with both Augustine's Law XIV (page 124) and Augustine's Law XVI (page 143) simultaneously. The latter of these laws of course ordains that the cost of hardware (e.g., airplanes) increases *rapidly* with time. To comply with this stringent requirement in the time period when there will be no additional space or weight left in an airplane (since the entire volume will, according to the former of the above Laws, already be filled with electronics) places severe demands on the designer. Optimally, what is needed is something that can be added to airplanes and other systems which weighs *nothing*, is *very costly*, yet violates none of the physical laws of the universe, such as the law of gravitation or the laws of thermodynamics. This might appear to be an insurmountable challenge. However, as a result of the traditional ingenuity characteristic of American engineers it can be reported with confidence that such an ingredient has already been found.

It is called . . . *software*.

A principal property of software, the phantom of modern technology, a "riddle wrapped in a mystery inside an enigma," to borrow Churchill's words, can be seen in Figure 23, which illustrates the trend toward ever-increasing quantities of software in any given family of systems.*

There are actually three separate growth modes evidenced by software. The first two of these are from generation to generation of new items of equipment and from version to version of a given item of equipment, respectively. The third growth mode, an internal growth mode, reflects the increase in quantity of software from the time the magnitude of a given job is initially scoped until it has actually been completed. This is the most exasperating mode of software growth. In this regard, it has been accurately stated that if you automate a mess, you get an automated mess. In software parlance, this can be typified by a costly and un-

---

*The groupings of the data shown in Figure 23 into the categories of unmanned and manned systems is interesting, but is most likely a figment of the rather modest data base available with which to treat this topic—although there can be little doubt of the reality of the growth trend within a given class.

Software: A Growing Concern

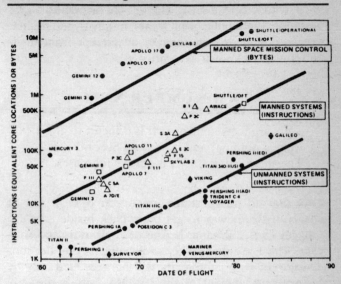

Figure 23. Software, almost nonexistent a few decades ago, is rapidly becoming the dominant element in the design of most major high-tech systems.

desirable type of computer code which has been descriptively named, "spaghetti code."

Figure 23 addresses the former two modes and suggests a growth rate on the order of a factor of ten every ten years.* Computers themselves have been found to obey a form of Parkinson's Law, namely, the amount of computing to be done expands until it fills the available capacity.

Augustine's Law Number XVII, the Law of the Pi-

*The author is indebted to Stephen L. Copps for his assistance in collecting the data presented in Figure 23.

ranha, has its origin in the fact that many contractors are devotees of the "Big Bang" Theory of Software Development, a policy which eats money by the bushel. For its explanation it borrows a concept from high-school physics known as "entropy":

LAW NUMBER XVII

Software is like entropy. It is difficult to grasp, weighs nothing, and obeys the Second Law of Thermodynamics; i.e., it always increases.

As the old adage states, once you open a can of worms, the only way to get them back inside is to use a bigger can. The same is true of computers and software. There are those who would suggest that the contribution of such complexity will be exceeded only by the projected advent of the "WOM," the write-only memory. Such a computer memory is of absolutely no use since once information is entered into the memory it can never be recovered again. The Black Hole of the information business!

Various studies have been conducted which suggest that over the last twenty-five years the hardware/software portions of the cost of major systems are shifting from an initial 80/20 hardware/software ratio to a ratio approaching 20/80 in the decade ahead. It can be safely reported that the problems encountered in development programs have managed to stay abreast of this trend. Further, it has been reported that the net effect of the computer revolution may turn out to be no more than that we will have the capacity to create errors more efficiently.

It has been estimated that in 1980 there were already 275,000 programmers in the United States, as contrasted with none in 1950. The choice thus seems clear: managers either need to learn to manage software tasks more efficiently or start learning to program! Software is eating our lunch, a byte at a time.

Actually, software exhibits many of the same properties as hardware. For example, it imposes high penalties for failure to discover problems early. Dr. Barry Boehm of TRW has collected data which show the cost of correcting software errors at various points in a development activity relative to the cost incurred if the error is discovered in the initial coding phase. The cost of repair is a factor of five greater when not discovered until the acceptance test phase and a factor of fifteen greater when uncovered in the operational phase.

A sobering realization is that the total number of lines of software code extant in the United States doubles every fourteen months. It is left to Weinberg's Second Law to observe that if builders built buildings the way programmers wrote programs, then the first woodpecker that came along would destroy civilization!

A classic example of the perversity of software was encountered in the Mariner program which was conducted by NASA to develop a spacecraft to fly to the planet Venus. On the Mariner 1 flight the lack of a single dash over a symbol in a little-used routine (the guidance module for failed doppler radar) resulted in a multimillion dollar spacecraft striking out on its own to explore the distant universe instead of observing Venus as its human masters had in mind. But if software is perverse, it is not without some redeeming virtues. The next Mariner flight was saved when the same set of equations (with the dash safely in place) managed to keep Mariner 2 on target in spite of an uncontrollable roll in the launch vehicle which caused loss of ground contact seventy-five times before full lock was reestablished.

In one report on software released by the federal government, note is made of the fact that "some problems" do remain in the area of software management—and then an *abbreviated* list of eighty-six examples is presented!

But if the state-of-the-art in managing software development is in some respects primitive, the acronymical language used to cloud the art from those managers necessarily thrust onto the periphery of such activity has reached a high degree of maturity indeed. This language is laced with a veritable core-dump of bauds, bits and bytes, MIPs, MOPs, BOPs, and nibbles (half a byte). On a still larger scale, there are megabytes, megacycles, megatrends, and megacontracts. But the unquestioned greatest semantical contribution of the software art is the term originally coined to describe one million floating point operations but which can be seen herein to have much broader applicability in describing entire products or even entire groups of products—i.e., the "megaflop." Unfortunately, descriptors from the software world have even led to confusion among some workers whether discussions pertain to software or to management as a whole—involving such jargon as "Artificial Intelligence," "Fault Tolerant," and "Bubble Memories."

18

The Reliability of Unreliability

"Adde parvum parvo magnus acervus erit."*
—Ovid

There had been concerns intermittently expressed by several individuals, who were admittedly already recognized for their propensity to "view with alarm," about the probable cost of the new high-tech product line. But these complaints were ameliorated when it was pointed out that the impending high cost would make it possible to build a much more reliable model airplane than had ever before been produced, and if there is anything that pilots of all scales dislike more than simultaneously running out of sky and ideas it had yet to be invented. It had already been learned that in balance the cost of a high quality item of a given type was less than a lower quality item, but now they were addressing the

---

*"Add little to little and there will be a big pile." Quoted from *The Mythical Man Month*, by Fred Brooks.

> *quality of various* types *of items. It was clearly worth spending a lot of money to have a product that could be relied upon.*

George Santayana observed: "All living souls welcome what they are ready to cope with; all else they ignore or pronounce to be monstrous and wrong . . . or deny to be possible."

Consider the crucial matter of producing more reliable products or, to take a specific case, electronic products. Everyone knows such products are comprised of components whose individual reliabilities have been improving at a rate of about 15 to 20 percent per year for nearly two decades. Further, with size decreasing dramatically and the aggregate cost of integrated circuits consistently decreasing since 1963 along a 75 percent learning curve, it should be possible to achieve extraordinary system reliability through careful component selection and built-in redundancy, and thus to eliminate what has been one of the most troublesome problems for electronic equipment users for many years: unreliability.

Now, if one were not privy to the anachronistic behavior of business management activities as they have been dissected herein, one might unwittingly conclude that as more and more money is spent on *various types* of items, their reliability would get progressively better and better. Surely no one would spend more to get *less*. The initiated would of course never fall into such a logical trap and would recognize immediately that quite the opposite must be true. That this latter situation indeed prevails is verified in Figure 24, which exhibits field reliability data on a number of categories of airborne electronic systems. It is seen that the items ex-

The High Cost of Failure

Airborne Electronics Equipment

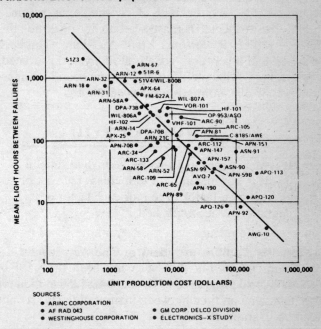

Figure 24. The more an item of electronics costs, the less reliable it is likely to be. As successive generations of technology evolve, the overall reliability curve shifts parallel to its predecessor and in a favorable direction, but the trend of decreasing reliability with increasing costs tends to remain inviolate.

amined range from relatively simple devices such as marker beacons and glide-slope indicators which aid pilots in navigating and landing, to completely automated multichannel airborne intercept systems for advanced military aircraft. The specific cost and reliability factors change over the years with increases in inflation and growth in technology, but the trend at any given time remains unwavering. Whatever the spectrum of equipment and technologies involved, the conclusion is unmistakable. As the cost of various items within a family of products increases, reliability does not improve; rather, it worsens. Frank McKinney Hubbard advised half a century ago, "If at first you do succeed, quit trying." This philosophy is summarized in Augustine's Law of Undiminished Expectations:

LAW NUMBER XVIII

It is very expensive to achieve high unreliability. It is not uncommon to increase the cost of an item by a factor of ten for each factor of ten degradation accomplished.

Dr. Eb Rechtin, president of The Aerospace Corporation, points out that such has been the pace of technological progress that by spending $250 million for an item, a mean time between failures of thirty seconds can be guaranteed.

Although great care must, of course, be taken in interpreting the meaning of a "failure" (all failures are not created equally, nor do they have equal consequences), data released on the mean flight hours between failure for twelve different types of Navy and Air Force fighter and attack aircraft are illuminating. Nine of the twelve aircraft experienced a "failure" at least once every thirty minutes. Of those, five experienced failures every fifteen to twenty minutes. This would seem to be conclusive proof of the correctness of those who have argued that the next strategic bomber must be supersonic rather than subsonic, if for no other reason than it had better get its job done *fast*—before it breaks.

In any event, it can be understood why there are those who argue that an airplane is merely a collection of spare parts flying in close formation, or, for that matter, an automobile is merely a collection of spare parts traveling in close proximity.

What, of course, is happening—as was already observed—is that as component reliability improves, more components are crammed into each system to provide more and more capability—or, more precisely, more capability during those interludes wherein the product is not broken. A modern jetliner, for example, has about 4.5 million parts including 100 miles of wiring. If a system has one million single-string parts, each with a reliability of 99.9999 percent for performing some specified mission, the overall probability of the mission failing is over 60 percent. The foreman of an automotive plant perceptively explained the *solution* in the following terms: "The part you engineers don't put on the machine ain't going to cause no trouble."

Even such unsophisticated items as solder joints can become a source of major problems when, as for example is the case for the new Patriot missile, there are two million of them.

Thomas Paine summed it all up in the 1790s when he counseled, "The more simple anything is, the less liable it is to be disordered, and the easier repaired when disordered." Sadly, it has become commonplace to view high technology and simplicity as contradictory terms. The two are not, in fact if not in practice, antonyms. The challenge is to use technology in a fashion which engenders simplicity. Who could argue, for example, that today's pocket calculators are less reliable than their 18,000 vacuum tube predecessor, the ENIAC, which completely filled a room as recently as the 1940s.

The Law of Undiminished Expectations, Law Number XVIII, which states that expensive systems won't work, will be seen to pose a particularly serious dilemma to equipment designers when it is applied in conjunction with Law Number XLII (page 380), which will note that inexpensive systems are not possible (they require infinite testing). This may all be academic, however, since it has already been established (in Law Number XVI, page 143) that before long it will not be possible to afford any new systems anyway.

19

Too Late Smart

"Yesterday I was a dog.
Today I am a dog.
Tomorrow I'll probably still be a dog."
—Snoopy the dog

Although most of the components making up the new design were now failing their initial tests, there was little reason for concern since the reliability experts were successfully demonstrating that the performance which would be experienced in actual use by the consumer would be near-perfect. Their method for accomplishing this was simply to list each failure which had been encountered during the test program and indicate the redesign which had been incorporated to preclude its recurrence; ergo, future failures were impossible. To most of the workers in the test laboratory this was just one more example of management's prowess in the field of artificial intelligence. Ironically, at the same time that this logic was gaining widespread acceptance, another major effort was getting underway within

> *a different department to write the large number of detailed instruction books which would be used to explain how to repair the product. This latter effort grew at such a pace that it became necessary to increase its manning by shifting large numbers of engineers off the effort which had until then been devoted to redesigning the hardware to make it reliable.*

A great deal of ink is devoted in advertising brochures to extolling the simplicity of operation and ease of maintenance of newly introduced products. In cases where high complexity is incorporated into the item, the canonical reassurance given to purchasers is that all the complexity is "user transparent," meaning, presumably, that the user doesn't need to be very smart to operate or fix the item in question. The fact is, however, that everyday twentieth-century life, in stark contrast with the life of citizens existing a mere century earlier, is rife with encounters with broken hardware which its user has no idea whatsoever how to fix. How many homeowners, for example, can pull out their trusty tool kit and repair a radar oven, an automobile's digital fuel controller, the synchronization on a color television, or even an electric razor. Children's toys, generally and appropriately presumed particularly susceptible to damage, require for their repair a working knowledge of microcircuitry as used in video games, as well as of speech synthesizers, laser shooting galleries, tape decks, fiber-optic table decorations, and liquid crystal game and watch displays. Whatever happened to good old Mickey Mouse?

But if this is the situation for items merely intended

for household use, what of high technology, state-of-the-art-challenging items designed to fly at Mach two, travel through space, or swim deep under the ocean? Or for that matter, how does today's young volunteer GI learn to maintain his Army tank?

The solution, as observed with concern by General Paul Gorman, has been to provide ever more detailed instructions for the use and repair of each successive generation of new hardware. Consider as but one example the page count of technical manuals provided to various generations of GIs with their tanks:

Tank	Year	Number of Pages in Users Manual
M-26	1940	8,000
M-47	1950	9,000
M-48	1960	12,000
M-60	1970	15,000
M-60A3	1975	23,000
M-1	1980	40,000

No wonder that today's soldiers need to be PhDs while their fathers got by as PFCs.

The trend indicated in the above table can be shown to have rather general applicability to automobiles, lawn mowers, bicycles, dishwashers, and many other devices. In the case of the newest Hewlett-Packard pocket calculators, the instruction manuals are considerably larger than the calculators themselves. According to George

Gendron, Editor of *Inc.* magazine, Lotus Development Corporation published a $22.95 textbook on how to orchestrate their Symphony software system. The weight of the manual was 7 lbs. 3 oz.—about three times the mass of James Michener's *Hawaii*.

The solution might at first appear to be simply to develop more reliable and more easily used equipment; but this will be shown herein to be altogether impossible. The real solution, the more straightforward one, the one apparently being pursued, is to place greater demands on the intelligence and ability of the operators and maintainers of modern products—in short, to develop a breed of superhuman humans.

Unfortunately, it is one more testimonial to the fact that nature is not simply indifferent but is actually belligerent that at the very moment such increased capabilities are most needed the intelligence of humans is beginning to decline. This is indicated in Figure 25, which illustrates that, although the information which must be absorbed in order to use space-age machinery is increasing markedly, the intelligence of the humans who must use it, as measured by that indisputable standard, College Board scores, is actually deteriorating.* We thus have a situation wherein man has been progressively evolving upward from the ape for nearly 14 million years and just at the very moment when his utmost intelligence is needed, at the dawn of the electronics age, what should happen but his intelligence peaks out in 1956 and begins the long process of devolution back toward the ape.

*The author is indebted to General Paul F. Gorman for pointing out the connection noted in the figure.

The Rise and Fall of Human Knowledge

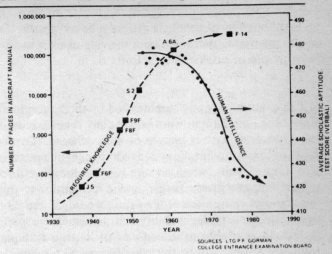

Figure 25. At the same time that the information which is required to use and maintain modern products is increasing dramatically, the human ability to comprehend that information is decreasing catastrophically.

It seems that those individuals who have long been proclaiming that we should conduct a search for intelligent life in the solar system may not have been guilty of any oversight.

But still another problem yet remains to be confronted: Law Number XVI stated that hardware will soon cost so much that none will be affordable. How can this square with the evidence shown in Figure 25? The answer lies in the Law of Mind Over Matter (If no one minds, then it doesn't matter):

LAW NUMBER XIX

Although most products will soon be too costly to purchase, there will be a thriving market in the sale of books on how to fix them.

The situation is aptly summarized by the apocryphal story of the gentleman who, lacking any cheese, baited his mousetrap with a *picture* of some cheese. To his acute disappointment, he is said to have caught a picture of a mouse. Thus, when no one can any longer afford to purchase any products (giving due recognition to the fact that the equipment of the future would in actuality be of extremely high capability and sophistication were in fact anyone able to afford any of it), the thriving trade of the time will be the sale of *instruction manuals* for nonexistent products. A best-seller list at that time might contain such provocative titles as "Do-It-Yourself Repair of Your Imaginary Rolls-Royce," "How to Fix Your Model T-422A Light-Emitting Diode," "Bubble Memory Repair Made Easy," "Self-Diagnosis for Your New Automatic Test Equipment," or "Robot Repair—Self-Taught."

But the most discouraging piece of evidence is the now well-established decline in human intelligence. Modest extrapolation of the College Board scores in Figure 25 reveals that, if the trend of the late 1960s and 1970s prevails, in just 142 years there will be no perceptible intelligence left whatsoever. This is why computer experts are already at work on something called artificial intelligence—but they had better hurry. Widespread discussion takes place even today in industry about the necessity to write maintenance manuals at the level of a sixth-grade reader. This desire for simplicity, reaching its zenith in the case of children's products, is presumably why the instructions provided for one well-known electric train set are replete with passages such as the following:

> The reversing switch changes the polarity of the main line. The polarity on either side of the upper insulated rail joiners now agrees so the locomotive can move off the reversing loop section and back onto the main. Note that the loop direction switch was never thrown, only the reversing switch. The loop direction switch is thrown when a train is on the reversing loop only when it is desired to make that train back up. Obviously if it was desired to run around the reversing loop clockwise, the loop direction switch and the track switch would be set opposite to the position shown before the train approaches the reversing loop.

Or why the assembly instructions for a widely marketed doll house direct: "Insert friction spring in right groove of bottom sash and hold with forefinger; insert spring in left hand groove and hold with thumb. Tip sash and place into frame removing forefinger slowly and push spring against right side joint. . . . Place header in corner of jig, smooth side down. . . . Assemble mitered casing in jig as shown and apply to inner frame using sill and apron."

Kid stuff!

Murphy knew this all along. "When all else fails," he counseled, "read the instructions."

20

Small Change

"A billion here and a billion there. Pretty soon
it adds up to real money."
—Senator Everett Dirksen

*Following the special internal review which had
been conducted at one of the nation's more attractive watering holes, top management concluded that Project X, as it was now called, was
still generally under control. The overrun was
increasing at a decreasing rate and the company
was losing money less rapidly than at any time
since beginning work on the new design. Euphoria thus prevailed once again. Even the component test program was encountering occasional
random successes. Attention therefore turned to
preparation of the budget request for the following year, a process which all confidently presumed would recognize the growing needs of
Project X and, correspondingly, the decreasing
needs of Daedalus's other undertakings which
were nearing economic maturity. Further, the*

> *budget included funds for the new executive tennis court adjacent to the headquarters.*

Former Ambassador to Portugal and now Chairman and Chief Executive Officer of Sears World Trade, Frank Carlucci, was once asked how he could tell, as he moved from one to another in a long series of high-level government posts, who were the constituent pressure groups and what were their specific objectives. His answer: "No problem. The constituent groups will find you and will be quite vociferous in what they want. And 98 percent of the time, whether it's poor people or defense manufacturers, the issue is money, and their position is that they want some of it."

Similarly, certain patterns can be established for most allocaters of resources, whether they be corporate boards of directors or the U.S. Congress, as to what sort of undertakings will be looked upon favorably and which rejected out of hand. Fundamental in this regard is that the budgeting process resists change. It is very difficult to establish a large budget for a social security system, but once established it will tend to plod along and become very difficult to reduce. It is very challenging to introduce a new item in a corporate budget for, say, advertising, but once included it will subsequently change by only a few percent each year. This is, of course, the *real-world* antithesis of zero-based budgeting.

Perhaps the most instructive place to begin an investigation of this momentum phenomenon is to start right at the top, with the U.S. Congress itself. It appears to be possible to predict with very good accuracy what the impact of the congressional approval process will be on the major segments of the federal budget. That is, the result of month upon month of debate and de-

Predicting Executive Behavior

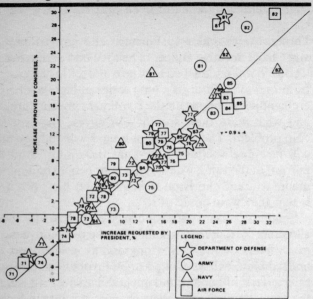

Figure 26. Executives have a compulsive tendency to change whatever has been proposed—just enough to have had an impact but not so much as to risk unraveling what the staff has recommended.

liberation can, in the aggregate, be reduced to a simple equation.

As an example, Figure 26 displays the effects of congressional actions on the administration's budget requests over a substantial interval of years. It is seen that a trend line can be quite accurately drawn which will predict the outcome of the congressional review process. This would suggest that the administration's efforts to gain approval of its budget requests have about the same impact year after year, independent of the political parties involved or the magnitude of the budget change requested, the latter even over quite large excursions.

These observations are summarized in Augustine's Law of Infernal Revenue as it applies to the defense budget:

LAW NUMBER XX

In any given year, Congress will appropriate the amount of funding approved the prior year plus three-fourths of whatever change the administration requests—minus a 4-percent tax.*

This Law has accurately applied over a range of year-to-year changes in the requested funding level extending from minus 7 percent to plus 24 percent. Thus, one can replace Congress with an equation—just as one could the inertia-driven budget allocation processes of too many other organizations, whether they be giant corporations or PTAs.

---

*Data for years subsequent to the original formulation of this law (1971) would suggest that as concern increased over the growth in Soviet military capability in the latter part of the decade, the tax was gradually eliminated.

21

You Can Bank on It

> "Banks will lend you money if you can prove
> you don't need it."
>
> —Mark Twain

*It was becoming increasingly evident how Dae-
dalus's prosperous wholesale customers had been
maintaining so attractive a Return on Investment
as they sold Daedalus's wares to the consumer.
As it happens, there are not one but two ways
to achieve a large positive ROI. Other than the
conventional method, even when suffering a
negative profit ("loss," as it is sometimes intem-
perately called) one can still post a very respectable ROI simply by paying one's bills so late that
not only is R negative but so too is I—thus a
positive ROI. And the bigger the loss, the bigger
the ROI, a case of two bads making a good.
Stated less mathematically, it is better to ship
than to receive. Although such pathological cases
are seldom studied in business schools, Daedalus
was now faced with this situation right there in*

the real world. Its business had been so successful that more and more money had to be pumped into new factories and inventories, yet its customers were paying their bills so slowly that a major cash flow crunch had developed. It seemed that the company had been so successful that it was in danger of bankruptcy. They appeared to have on their hands the corporate equivalent of the Rio Grande river—one of the few rivers in the world said to need to be irrigated. They had discovered that there was not one but there were two ways to do business: one was for profit—the other was the way they were doing it. The solution, when one needs money? Why, go to a bank, of course—to the Big Green Machine. In fact, through a stroke of good fortune, just that very week one of the founders had received a letter from a local lending institution which, citing his fine reputation, his important role as a pillar of the community, and his solid financial status, offered to loan substantial funds at a very attractive rate. It wasn't until later, much later, that it was discovered that the letter had been addressed, "Dear Occupant."

Some unidentified sage once noted that bankers understand three things: money, makin' money, and not losin' money. Although recent events have cast at least a shadow of doubt upon the latter, the intent and perseverance of most bankers in these regards is clearly beyond reproach.

Correspondingly, fledgling businesses quickly become familiar with three things: shortages of money, difficulties in getting money, and problems of paying it back. Ironically, the more successful such companies are, the more money they will need to float their growing inventories and provide new plants. If they are so very successful that they are unable to borrow sufficient funds from banks or other more conventional lenders, they may even have to turn to the equity market and give away a share of the very company they themselves have built in exchange for the needed infusion of life-sustaining capital. If they have been *extremely* successful and need *very large* amounts of money, they may have to give away most all of the enterprise they so painstakingly built, and thereby become simply another employee in their "own" company. Such is the price of success . . . and what is called the velocity of money.

Jerry White, an expert in entrepreneurial activity at Southern Methodist University, states: "You can absolutely go broke being successful." Of course, it should be noted herein that you can also absolutely go broke being unsuccessful. In fact, there are *many* ways of going broke. The Penn Square Bank found one way to do this. Continental Airlines found another. Braniff still another. According to White: "Growth consumes cash and cash is what you use to meet the payroll." Braniff, he says, ran out of cash. Simple enough.

A related malady struck Comtek Import/Export Ltd. Cofounder Bruce Gilman has explained that in spite of unimpeachable credit, Comtek was suddenly and unexpectedly "invited" by their bank to take their business elsewhere. The problem, it seems, was their bank's loan officer; "He was scared by our growth. So they told us to go find another bank . . . . It was a devastating blow." Gilman's partner, Robert Tracht, continues, "We called thirty-five banks and they all gave us the same answer.

Everyone said, you have to have been in business for at least two years and have $100,000 in working capital." Needless to say, this makes it a bit difficult to get started. In the words of Nelson Rockefeller, "The chief problem of the lower income farmers is poverty."

Variations on this theme reverberate daily throughout the business community. From the health care industry there is the case of Home Care Service, a company whose partners were forced to sell out when, according to one of them, Louis Esposito, "My best effort was done in by my own success." Home Care's financing was based on accounts receivable (because it had no assets). When the company grew and accounts receivables began to stretch out, insufficient working capital remained and the partners had to bail out.

In a letter to the editor in *Inc.* magazine, Wesley Batten, vice-president of finance for Inmed Corp., commenting on an earlier article which had addressed the relative ease with which wealthy firms are able to borrow money from banks, wrote, "It is comforting to know . . . that they'll be begging to lend us money as soon as we are big enough that we don't really need it anymore."

Figure 27 quantifies the problem. As can be seen, cash-rich companies like AT&T and General Motors have enormous lines of credit available to them (which they don't need). As Willie Sutton said, "It is a rather pleasant experience to be alone in a bank at night." On the other hand, struggling firms like Osborne Computer Corporation and the Manville Corporation, which could have used a little cash, have only a negligible chance of raising substantial funds. (Osborne and Manville both went broke to varying degrees, albeit gracefully.)

Gary Edman, seeking to purchase Chambers Belt

Being Helped Out

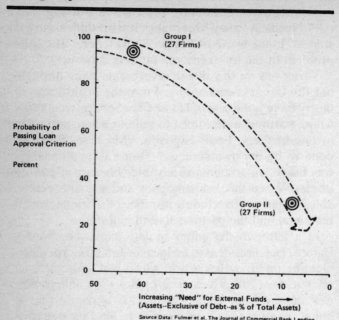

Figure 27. *The greater one's need for money, the lower the likelihood one will be able to borrow any.*

Company from the financial conglomerate which had assumed control of it following a "period of financial distress," ran into the *triple*-whammy when he and his partners sought to borrow money. First, the bank wouldn't consider a loan application until the partners produced a half million dollars of new equity. Second, according to Edman, "We were told it would be impossible to get a loan approved without going through several layers"—and then came the third whammy— "of *committees*" (see chapters 26 and 31). This is what Willem de Kooning had in mind when he said that "the trouble with being poor is that it takes up all your time."

Even when the owners of a burgeoning firm succeed in finding a bank that will do business with them they should leave it promptly if they are at all successful— at least that's the advice of Robert Kahn of Robert Kahn and Associates. "Change banks whenever your credit line has increased fivefold," he cautions. "No matter what you do, someone will always remember the borrowing level at which you started at the bank, and will then be able to persuade himself that your bubble is bound to burst."

All of which compounds into Augustine's Law of the Piggy Bank, based on the concept originally espoused by Mark Twain:

LAW NUMBER XXI

It's easy to get a loan unless you need it.

There are, of course, the hordes of venture capitalists to whom an aspiring businessman can turn. Duane Meulners, founder of Dymek Corp., dismisses that option outright: "In the last few years, it's gotten so venture capitalists felt they couldn't just invest in Joe Schmuck. You have to be a celebrity. Good solid growth isn't enough anymore. The venture capitalists are looking for wild, rampaging weeds."

The effort to appear as a wild, rampaging weed can, unfortunately, lead to what might be called "creative accounting" on the part of needy firms. A provocative headline in *The Wall Street Journal* recently reported, "Comserv to Switch Accounting Methods in an Effort to Return to Profitability." R. Lee Taylor II, president of the Federal Co., observes, "You can take any company's cash flow and, with the right kind of accounting, make it into whatever earnings you want." He concludes that strength on the balance sheet and in the margins is what really counts.

But in the arcane world of corporate finance sometimes the only thing worse than *not* getting a loan is *getting* a loan. Steve Birnbaum of Oxford Partners explains, "You have to understand this is an industry where people are not used to having a lot of money. Then somebody gives you $150 million, and you start to feel you can walk on water. You read in the paper that you're a genius, and you start to believe it." But the sword cuts both ways. Elizabeth Taylor (the other one) sought a loan from the Small Business Administration to open a restaurant. The SBA gave her only about half the amount she sought. Promptly running short of money, the business went belly-up. Taylor is quoted as remarking, "I can't tell you how it would have helped my life so much [sic] if they had never given me the damn money." It would seem to have potentially been the smartest thing they ever didn't do. But in the words of one Merrill Lynch executive quoted in *The Wall Street Journal,* "When you have them by the credit, their hearts and minds will follow." It's simply one more case of the golden rule attributed to business: "He who's got the gold makes the rules."

A perspective of another quarter in the strange world of borrowing has been offered by a number of economists who have proffered the thought-provoking notion that once you are successful in borrowing money from a bank the last thing in the world the bankers want is for you to pay it back! This argument, it turns out, is not without logic. If you pay the money back, the economists explain, the bank simply must undergo the considerable inconvenience and nontrivial expense of finding someone *else* to whom the same money can again be loaned. The only reason the bank wants you to pay them back is to demonstrate that you are *capable* of paying them back. It's not the money they want. It's the reassurance.

Incidentally, many financial wizards make an equally compelling argument that most corporations, ideally, should not pay dividends. When an investor selects a firm as the place he *wants* his funds, it is counterproductive for that firm simply to keep returning portions of those funds to the investor—in obvious contravention of his wishes. The shareholder, in spite of having already indicated a preference for the particular firm as his investment medium, must then go through the effort of reinvesting in new shares—all after paying taxes . . . and a broker's commission.

Although a bit heretical, this logic is certainly a lot more logical than much of the illogic that permeates the world of economic logic. Consider the following actual examples of economic logic borrowed from recent radio and printed commentaries on the health of the economy:

• Media report: "The dollar is strong." Good News? No. *Bad* News. Explanation in subsequent portion of media report: "A strong dollar hampers exports and bolsters imports, costing the U.S. tens of thousands of jobs and squeezing many companies." (So much for the strong dollar. Bring on the weak dollar.)

• Media report: "The economy grew considerably

beyond expectations during January." Good News? *Wrong—Bad* News. Media explanation: "Rapid growth in the economy may lead to increased inflation with an adverse impact on the bond market, push interest rates upward, and result in an end to the recovery." (Conclusion: Avoid growth at all costs.)

- Media report: "Reducing the deficit could have certain adverse consequences for the economy." Media explanation: "Easing the deficit with increases in taxes or reduced federal spending could slow the recovery." (Conclusion: Long live the deficit.)

- Media report: "Unemployment dropped markedly during the past month." Good? No—wrong again—*bad*. "Too fast a recovery could drive prices upward again and lead to another cycle of inflation." (Conclusion: The solution to unemployment is employment . . . or something like that.)

To paraphrase the title to Ben Wattenberg's book, the bad news is that the good news was wrong.

No wonder the world of economics is peppered with such terms as "stagflation," "revenue enhancement," and the likes. Revenue enhancement, incidentally, as attractive as it sounds, is of course just another pair of words which add up to higher taxes! Monte Gordon, writing in the *Dreyfus* newsletter, sums it all up: ". . . the so-called 'strong dollar' can have a weakening effect on the U.S. economy—reflecting, once again, the perils of semantics." And, it might well be added, economics. In the world of economics, it seems, *everything* is bad.

An article in *USA Today* tells of two Republican members of the Colorado State House of Representatives by the name of Bird: "Both Birds are men of faith," the article confides. "The one from Denver is a former clergyman; the one from Colorado Springs is an economist."

A student-produced guide to courses at Harvard, according to *The Wall Street Journal,* reports that "Jocks flock to the Ec department. . . . Some of the courses are fun; some are not; but they all . . . demand almost no intellectual background."

One of the fundamental underpinnings of the financial world is the concept that the greater risk in an investment, the greater the return. This is of course obvious; what investor would put his money at greater risk for a lesser return? Answer: Lots of them, according to the data in Figure 28 borrowed from the Colorado National Bank's *Bond and Money Market Observations* newsletter.

Then there is Uncle Sam's debt, a morass wherein a great deal of imagination has been sunk over the years. Want to prove the federal debt is bursting out of control? Just quote the federal debt in current dollars as it has been recorded over the years. Want to prove the federal debt is decreasing? Just quote the federal debt in terms of Uncle Sam's ability to pay—analogous to what one does for any individual mortgage holder's personal debt—as a fraction of the gross national product. Want to show that the federal debt is not changing? Just quote the debt in deflated (constant) dollars. All legitimate calculations. The comment has been attrib-

Risk vs Return

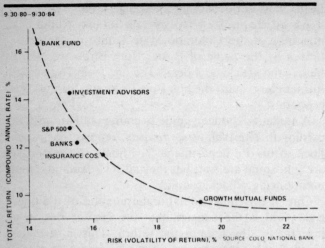

Figure 28. For a fairly extended period of time, many investment mediums have been violating the principle that the greater the risk the larger must be the return.

uted to George Bernard Shaw that if all the world's economists were laid end to end, they would not reach a conclusion.

Nonetheless, the financing community may sometimes be less perfect than it would have those believe to whom it gives the business. To borrow once again from United Technologies Corporation's advertising series,

An irate banker demanded that Alexander Graham Bell remove "that toy" from his office. That toy was the telephone. A Hollywood producer scrawled a rejection note on a manuscript that became *Gone with the Wind.* Henry Ford's largest original investor sold all his stock in 1906. Roebuck sold out to Sears for $25,000 in 1895. Today, Sears may sell $25,000 of goods in 16 seconds.

The one fundamental truth in the money-borrowing business seems to be that it is tough, very tough indeed, for the fledgling company that badly needs funds to obtain those funds. Wealth, on the other hand, seems to make all things possible. *The Denver Post,* quoting a well-known prize fighter by the name of Larry Holmes, sums it up eloquently, although in an altogether different context. The *Post* quotes Holmes, speaking on being black, as remarking, "It's hard being black. I was black once, before I got rich."

22

Buying High

"If it looks like a duck and if it walks like a duck and if it quacks, then it's a duck."
—Senator Edward Kennedy

The effort to get a loan from a bank had been like putting the milk bucket under the bull. In the words of Samuel Goldwyn, "The banks couldn't afford me. That's why I had to be in business for myself." And if schedule control problems in the daily operations had been proving resilient, cost control problems were proving utterly intransigent. It was the first anniversary of starting testing for the third time and Project X was now under open attack from its critics at the Corporate Headquarters. The local management's seemingly brilliant stroke of launching an intensive advertising campaign when first inundated with technical problems appeared to have failed abysmally. Somehow the problems persisted in spite of this enlightened technique. It nonetheless spoke highly of the firm's manage-

184

ment that they seemed to be going out of business in an orderly fashion. The cash-flow situation, however, was worsening—with, of course, the banks' having failed to produce any money. It looked as if it might be necessary to sell stock to the public. It was ironic: Here was Daedalus Model Airplane Company, grown to over 500 employees in just six short years, and the founders—because of their success—were now in danger of losing control of their very own company. Had they not grown so fast and needed money for expansion they would not be suffering this indignation. In fact, it appeared that they were now even to lose their identity: The brokers had insisted that if the offering was to sell to the public, Daedalus Model Airplane Company must be renamed "Daedalus Aircraft, Inc." to give it a more solid sound. The founders did manage to resist the brokers' recommendation to insert "Lasers" into the corporate title, even though the market experts had assured them such a change would in itself double the multiple at which the stock would sell because of the magnetism of high-tech in the market. But in this case reason prevailed, if for no other reason than that multiples don't make much sense when you are losing money. Nonetheless, in most all other matters the founders took the advice of the experts on the stock market. How can a mere novice argue with individuals having the expertise of the world's principal financial centers at their very fingertips?

It has been wisely stated that amateurs should stay out

of the stock market. It can equally wisely be stated that so should professionals. At least that is what much of the evidence seems to suggest. But what else should one expect from a group which divides the dollar into eighths as its unit of measurement—thus leading to such convenient measures as a 0.875th of a dollar? Or quotes the price of U.S. Treasury bonds in 1/32 of a percent? Some anonymous soul once described Wall Street as a thoroughfare that begins in a graveyard and ends in a river. This is certainly factual, although the directions may be reversed.

The preponderance of available data indicates that the advice given by high-priced financiers is no better than that generated by good-for-nothing novices. In fairness, it must be conceded that although the advice provided by the experts may not be very useful, it *is* very expensive. In fact, the principal discriminator between the amateur and the pro when it comes to financial prognostication appears to be that the former loses his own money and the latter, someone else's. But that in itself is not unimpressive.

Figure 29 compares the performance of leading stock funds over the most recent one-year period. These include the larger, established load- and no-load mutual funds as well as several unestablished funds: the Dart Board Fund, the Random Rice-Dropping Fund, the Matchstick-Dropping Fund, the Pins and Needles Fund, and the Monkey Market Fund, the latter five especially formed for the readership of this book. The results are disappointing. Consider each fund's performance one by one as displayed in the figure.

First, an Index Fund is shown, which is an investment medium intended merely to keep even with the market as a whole. In other words, its aspiration is to be average

A SINKING FUND (1984 Performance)

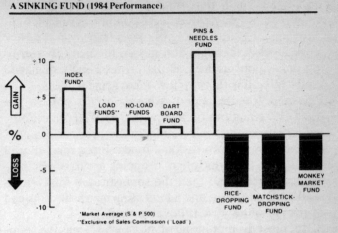

Figure 29. Stock funds managed by financial experts have a difficult time keeping up with the market averages and often fall short of funds based on such scientific principles as dart throwing and dropping pins and needles at random.

and, as can be seen, it was entirely successful by that inspiring standard (except for deductions due to fees, of course). Conventional Load- and No-Load funds, on the other hand, are presumably intended to beat the market averages. In the year studied, they too performed in a less than spectacular fashion and were not entirely inconsistent with the trend over the years that funds which charge no sales fee ("load") do about as well as those which do charge a commission. It will also be noted, regrettably, that these managed funds did little better during the particular year examined (1984) than would have been done by keeping one's money in a coffee can.

The five special-purpose funds created especially for this study were certainly not guilty of consistency. The

Dart Board Fund, employing a selection process founded upon the sophisticated aerodynamic principles of throwing darts at a listing of issues traded on the New York Stock Exchange, also missed the mark, performing only about as well as the professionally managed funds (albeit with very low management costs). The Pins and Needles Fund, wherein sharp objects are dropped at random on a copy of *The Wall Street Journal*'s stock listing, was pointedly the best performer— far excelling the professional funds. But a related fund based upon the principle of dropping grains of rice performed even worse than the sophisticated funds managed on Wall Street, and a fund using matchsticks instead of rice absolutely went down in flames.

But most disappointing of all—by far—was the Monkey Market Fund, with a portfolio personally selected by the fund's director of research, Boomer N. Buster, shown in Figure 30, which did not even do as well as the professionally managed funds of New York.* This of course represented a considerable blow to what was to have been the primary thesis of this chapter. Nonetheless, facts are facts. It simply turns out that the New York financial experts are in fact superior in performance to some primates who seek to ape them. However, in fairness to the fund's top banana, Boomer, it must be recognized that he was altogether inexperienced in the world of high finance—and furthermore evidenced a willingness to work for peanuts. Mark Twain

---

*The author first met a friend of Boomer's in the friend's native Tanzania . . . although most of the fund's research is performed by a relative of Buster's who resides at the Washington National Zoo. He makes his selections by generating a stream of binary digits from turning his head one way or the other; right for "zero," left for "one"—much as is done in a modern computer. The numbers thus generated are keyed to alphabetical listings of all stocks on the New York Stock Exchange.

may have been correct when he concluded, "I believe that our Heavenly Father invented man because he was disappointed in the monkey."

It can be concluded that, at best, the quality of advice available to investors bears no discernible relationship to what one pays for it. In short, if you want it bad, you get it bad. Augustine's Law of the Bulls and Bears states:

LAW NUMBER XXII

If stock market experts were so expert, they would be buying stock, not selling advice.

During the year examined in Figure 29, according to SEI Funds Evaluation Services, fully 74 percent of the fund managers failed to outperform the Standard and Poor 500 Index. Apparently it is standard to be poor— or something like that.

It should be noted that 1984 was not simply an anomalous period to be disregarded insofar as the investor's plight is concerned. Over a ten-year span, 56 percent of the fund managers still failed to keep up with the S&P 500 average. It is obviously not easy to be wrong for so sustained a period of time. As Larry Cole, the Dallas defensive end remarked defensively upon learning that the touchdown he had just scored was his first in eleven years, "Anybody can have an off decade."

Fixed-income fund managers fared no better, with 71 percent of them failing to keep up with the Shearson Lehman Government/Corporate Bond Index for the same year considered above. Over the ten-year period, 60 percent of these experts fell short of the "dumb-

Figure 30. The director of the Monkey Market Fund has a financial record even worse than many Wall Street experts, but works for peanuts.

Gregory Augustine

luck" averages. Apparently, when picking investments, it is very, very difficult to be average. It can also be very costly to the recipient of such advice. But, fortunately for the pros, the competition is becoming easier. Whereas in 1965 the experts were forced to compete nose-to-nose with individual investors from Dubuque, Sheboygan, and Skokie—who accounted for 85 percent of the stocks traded on the New York Stock Exchange— today, 89 percent of the activity merely involves other professionals.

Not to be left ahead, the publishers of market newsletters have also been falling all over themselves to fall short of the average. "About half of the newsletters published since 1980 have underperformed the T-bill rate," according to the *Hulbert Financial Digest*. Perhaps it was a foretelling Freudian slip when the editor of *Changing Times* magazine discovered that his occupation was listed on his credit record as "changing tires."

Looking at the big picture, forecasters have, in the last four years, according to *Investment Outlook* magazine, "failed to call the 1981–82 recession, predicted a recovery that never materialized, and then did not foresee the magnitude of the strongest business expansion to occur in more than 30 years." Uncharitably, one cannot help but be reminded of the market forecaster who tried to scratch himself and missed.

Perhaps it has not always been thus.

On the other hand, perhaps it has.

One unarguably cataclysmic period to examine in the history of the market would be the crash of '29. What were the experts saying then? In the book *The Experts Speak* by Christopher Cerf and Victor Navasky, one learns that Irving Fisher, a professor of economics at Yale, assured on October 24th (exactly one week before the crash) that "Stocks have reached what looks like a permanently high plateau." Seven days later, at the close of the initial day of the crash, a joint statement released by thirty-five of the largest wire houses in the country reassured investors that "The worst has passed." Not to be outdone, the Friday, October 25, headlines of the *New York Journal* had proclaimed, "Experts Predict Rising Market." Giving the benefit of the doubt, the experts of course did not say *when* the rising market would occur. Patience has always been considered a necessary virtue in the market.

Only the political experts seem to rival the financial

forecasters when it comes to evidence of malpractice—as in the *Newsweek* headline of October 11, 1948, which noted: "Fifty political experts unanimously predict a Dewey victory." "President" Dewey must have been very pleased to know that the experts were in his corner. But once in a great while there is a silver lining to such predictions, as in the case of the projection of a pragmatic Henry Luce, publisher of *Time, Life,* and *Fortune:* "I think the world is going to blow up in seven years. The public is entitled to a good time during those seven years!" Right on.

The truly bad news, however, is that insofar as the market is concerned, people actually *listen* to the advice for which they pay. When Joe Granville, publisher of the *Granville Market Letter,* exclaimed on January 6, 1981, "Sell everything!" the public did exactly that. The next day the market lost three times the dollar amount lost on Black Thursday in 1929, with the Dow Jones Industrial Average declining twenty-three points on record volume.

But one could never deny that such turbulence is good for business—the stock trading business, that is. How often does one hear on the evening news the enigmatic report "100 million shares traded hands today. Prices remained unchanged."

Returning to Figure 29, which presented not one but several scientific methods that matched or surpassed the experts' performance, the puzzling question remains, "Where *did* we go right?" This is, of course, not an altogether new question for amateurs in financial wonderlands. Methods for accurately predicting the market's behavior have in fact been available for some time. For starters, there is what might be called the Pigskin Prognostication. This projection simply states that if one of the *pre-merger* National Football League teams wins the Super Bowl, the bears (*not* the Chicago-type) will be routed in the market the forthcoming year. If one of the *original* American Football Conference teams wins, the bulls will instead be gored. Looking at the record, one finds that in seventeen of eighteen years the Pigskin Prognostication was correct. The apparent founder of the method, Hugh Gee, who publishes the market letter *Money Power,* is quick to explain away the one fumble on the grounds of extenuating circumstances. In 1984, it seems, when the Standard and Poor Index—exhibiting undue belligerency—climbed a tiny 1.4 percent when it should have dropped, in reality there was a split decision. That very year the Amex, Dow, NAS-DAQ, and Value Line all went the other (correct) way by a small amount.

Actually, the market has more in common with pro football than most people realize. One of the 600 traders occupying the "pit" where T-bonds are bought and sold in an area the size of a medium-sized house is John Dwyer, a former running back in the Canadian Football League. Another is Barney O'Doherty who, according to *The Wall Street Journal,* ". . . was knocked to the floor one day and another trader fell on him. In the time he could scramble back to his feet, prices had moved sharply and Mr. O'Doherty had gained $1,250."

In a valiant effort to be average, so-called Index Funds have been established which are intended to "merely" match the market averages and thus require no brainpower at all. These funds, in less than a total vote of confidence for the professional money managers, grew to $60 billion in assets in less than a decade. Such investments are, according to Seth Lynn, president of Great American Core Investors Inc., ". . . like a heat-seeking missile on the tails of active equity managers."

With such an overwhelming proliferation of advice available, what is needed are advisers who can tell the public whose advice to take. As luck would have it, this service is available too. At a price. These are, of course, the funds put together by professionals who simply assemble a fund made up of other funds. Judging by the problems of even these funds, what may be needed is a fund made up of funds made up of . . .

Still another approach to being no worse than average on the long haul is simply to call upon an oracle, much as was done by the ancient Greeks in their visits to Delphi. One such network of psychic consultants is available through Delphi Associates, managed by Anthony White, holder of an MBA from Stanford. White confides, "In the past, many people may have consulted Madame Zsa-Zsa on the corner for personal guidance. We're doing the same thing, but we don't come along with all the metaphysics, mumbo jumbo and props like crystal balls." This, it would seem, might be the worst approach there is—except, of course, for all the others.

Yet another avenue for the acknowledged novice might simply be to monitor the track record of the financial experts advising the nation's 790 stock and bond funds, identify with the proven winners, and adopt the policy "If you can't beat 'em, join 'em." In the year just completed, for example, income funds performed better than most other types of funds, which were mauled by the market. The problem with simply joining forces with these proven winners is that of the prior year's ten top performers, four are now firmly ensconced in the bottom fifty. A "proven" performer can thus have proven a variety of things. According to the *Toronto Globe and*

Mail, "One way to stop a runaway horse is to bet on him."

It was this sort of logic that allegedly caused John Kennedy's father to answer the question why his son had not sought the advice of experienced political consultants for the 1960 election by noting, "Hell, they're all experienced in losing."

But perhaps the most imaginative approach is simply to take the "contrarian" view and do just exactly the opposite of whatever the experts are advising. This appears to be the best approach—other than to adopt the 20-20 hindsight perspective of the Monday morning quarterback and just *talk* about how well you *could* have done. This formula does at least possess an interesting existence theorem: William Baldwin, writing in *Forbes,* examined one recent ten-year period and found that an investor with perfect foreknowledge who switched monthly between stocks and cash could have increased his assets by a factor of 22, excluding transaction costs. The problem, of course, is that thing called foreknowledge—and the experts are so inconsistent they can't even be relied upon to always be wrong.

The truth of the matter *is,* of course, that there *are* some better-than-average bargains to be found in the stock market, as a number of prosperous investors have convincingly demonstrated. It simply takes better-than-average performance to find them. This in turn demands better-than-average competence and perseverance—and a bit of luck does not hurt.

The trouble with most investors seems to be that they are willing to settle for whatever advice or results happen to come along first. George Rogers, formerly of the New Orleans Saints and now with the Washington

Redskins, may be an example of an individual who is spending too much time with his financial consultants. Rogers was quoted on his goals for the forthcoming season as saying, "I want to gain 1500 or 2000 yards, whichever comes first."

Patience with the market, however, has its limits. As former Congressman Chet Holifield, then eighty-two years old, told his broker who was pushing ten-year maturity bonds: "I don't even buy green bananas."

Damian Strohmeyer, *Denver Post*

"Unexpected impediments . . . tugged them backward at the most inopportune times."

PART IV

THE
GATHERING
STORM

23

The Reality of the
Fantasy Factor

"We're really gonna get 'em this season. Last year we were
too overconfident."

—Greg Augustine, age 15

*The annoying trickle of schedule slippages which
had previously been suffered had, it must be
reported, grown to avalanche proportions. This
was exacerbated by the fact that the most experienced 40 percent of the engineers had been
reassigned from the project to work on the audit
team which had for several months been seeking
to discover why the project was falling behind
schedule. Although the supervisors were encouraging everyone to try faster, master schedules were being reissued on a weekly basis and
updated hourly. Even the effort to find a more
accurate method to estimate schedules was running late. It seemed that the 99-percent-complete
point had been reached in no time at all, but the
last 1 percent was taking forever. Friends at more*

*experienced firms pointed out that one should
always expect that this should be the case—"that
is," they said, "sort of the meaning of 99-percent
complete." That these problems were taken seriously at Daedalus, however, was suggested by
the fact that the members of the marketing department were now staying around until two or
three in the afternoon and were even considering
going to a five-day week. And there were more
lawyers assigned to Project X than engineers.
Management's motto seemed to be, "Don't follow me . . . I'm lost." But things finally began
to move when the threat of help from headquarters was received.*

In 1798, Eli Whitney contracted to deliver 10,000 mus-
kets to the Continental Army within twenty-eight months.
As things worked out, they delivered them in thirty-
seven months, or in about one-third more time than
had been anticipated.

In 1978, and most every year since, a number of new
systems were delivered to the U.S. military forces by
major industrial firms. On the average, according to the
reports submitted to the Congress, these systems were
delivered in one-third more time than had been projected.

The fraction one-third seems to have enduring scientific significance in determining the schedule error
associated with predicting major events in business undertakings. Some say the correct number is actually
more nearly equal to one over pi, which may explain
why the Indiana Legislature in 1897 came within a few

"The Earliest We've Ever Been Late"

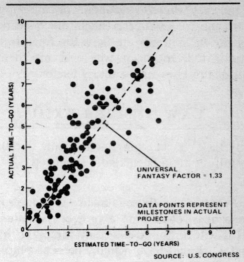

Figure 31. Like cost, the prediction of schedule involves uncertainties and risks. When the time actually required to complete a task is compared with the time which had originally been projected, a quite consistent correction factor can be empirically derived.

votes of declaring pi to equal exactly 3.2.* Figure 31 presents data on how promptly various schedule milestones were met in a large sample of major development projects. The points shown happen to have been drawn from the aerospace industry; however, the results seem to be applicable to a variety of commercial enterprises ranging from housing construction to shipbuilding—ex-

---

*Actually, things might have been worse: It is recorded in *Facts and Fallacies* by Morgan and Langford that the Indiana General Assembly decided that same year to make pi equal 4.

cept for those pathological cases such as the nuclear power industry where the grouping of data points is the same but the trend-slope is much, much steeper. The data in the figure form the basis for Augustine's Law of Unmitigated Optimism, which, in turn, defines the concept of the Universal Fantasy Factor:

LAW NUMBER XXIII

Any task can be completed in only one-third more time than is currently estimated.

Unfortunately, as those familiar with Zeno's Paradox will recognize, each time a project's schedule is reviewed it will be found that only three-fourths of the planned work will have actually been accomplished—leaving one-third more to do, and so on ad infinitum, this verifying the impossibility of completing anything. This represents the limiting case of the maxim stated by Bill Curra, an expert in corporate personnel development, "Things take longer than they do."

A former coach of the Washington Bullets used to dismiss the frequent and premature burials of his team by the local media with the remark, "The opera ain't over till the fat lady sings."

It is a fundamental property of human character to be able to believe in all earnestness, after having missed twenty-two consecutive monthly schedules, that there is no reason whatsoever to question that the next month's schedule can be met. The same principle applies to family budgeting. And to sports. Denver Broncos defensive coach Joe Collier, recognizing such human failings, approaches the resulting problem with pragmatism:

"Our goal," he says, "is five missed tackles a week." The upper-left-hand data point in Figure 31, whereby the manager's official estimate was that the project was eight months from completion when in fact another eight *years* were required, is something of a record. Presumably this manager is now somewhere teaching a course in schedule management at a business school.

Yogi Berra summarized the schedule-prediction situation eloquently: "It isn't over till it's over," he noted with his usual sagacity.

The vice-president and general manager of the division of The Boeing Company, which produces the 767 commercial jet airplane, may have had this law in mind if he was referring to the fraction of work previously accomplished when he remarked, as reported in *Aerospace Daily,* that the development of the 767 "is further ahead at the halfway point than any new airliner program in Boeing history."

Similar reassurance was once offered to a senior project review group by a manager of a troubled undertaking to develop a new airplane engine: "Even though we have admittedly fallen behind on the engine development," he confided, "I feel confident that we will have the airplane's engine there for the first flight." As it happened, this turned out to be one of his few correct predictions. It was only later that it was realized this individual was an adherent to the James J. Walker school of management: "If you're there before it's over, you're on time."

Little consolation can be derived from the fact that nearly all programs report "99 percent schedule compliance." This generally means that every weekly letter report in two years was submitted on time . . . and merely the hardware deliveries fell hopelessly behind schedule.

Anyone who has ever built a home will understand this phenomenon—wherein the only thing that the general contractor ever manages to get out on time are the bills.

Seemingly the last frontier of optimism for that body of managers who lead multiyear programs which invariably miss each individual cumulative deadline by "only a few days" lies in participation in the effort to explore the solar system. By a happy coincidence of planetary kinematics, a *day* on the planet Venus is actually longer than a *year* on Venus, making it exceedingly difficult to continually miss deadlines by the proverbial "few days." A few years, yes; a few days, no.

If there is a single causal thread in the web of program slippages, it would seem to be that plans are too often made on the basis that nothing in the future will ever go wrong—a "success-oriented" plan, in the vernacular. And if nothing will ever go wrong, there is no need to provide resources such as time, funds, manpower, or facilities for contingencies. The problem is, of course, that something always does go wrong. Will Rogers, it seems, never met Murphy.

When it comes to schedule adherence, everything seems to be relative. Relatively bad. Or, to once again quote the anachronistic view expressed by Yogi Berra when asked what time it was—"You mean right now?"

But then, as some wise soul has said, "The sooner you start to fall behind, the more time you will have to catch up."

24

Buying Time

> "The cause is hidden—but the result is well known."
> —Ovid

Project X truly seemed to be descending deeper and deeper into a morass. It had been a bad day for nearly a month now. Incessant changes in objectives, funding, people, and even the design itself plagued the project; all initiated either under the guise of reacting to budgetary pressures or of "leapfrogging forward." This prompted a number of employees to quip that they might have been better off had they just kept the first frog. The apparent solution was to once again revise the schedule so as to save money. But debate broke out this time over the question: "In which direction should the schedule be revised?" It was a dilemma paralleling that encountered by the young man who was running for political office and asked the established but controversial local politico for his support. The pol answered, "Sure, I'll support you. Do you want me to endorse you or your opponent?" Somehow, Daedalus's leaders needed to decide which approach to schedule control they would endorse, and in this instance it simply became a matter of management making the wrong mistake.

It is widely recognized that if projects are stretched out *ad infinitum*, their costs, even in noninflated dollars, will increase substantially. Conversely, as most production efforts are accelerated within limits, their costs often decrease due to the efficiencies attendant to higher rates of throughput. This is presumably no more than a restatement of the observation that most existing production programs are operating at far from an optimal rate due to budgeting limits or built-in overcapacity due to excessive optimism in the original sales forecasts.

Correspondingly, if stretching the schedule increases the cost of product *development* activities, then it follows that accelerating the schedule must decrease the cost. Right?

Wrong.

An examination of the data in Figure 32 reveals two things. First, that there are precious little data on programs that have been accelerated . . . although an unhealthy abundance exists pertaining to programs that have been decelerated. Second, that not only does stretching a development program increase cost but so does accelerating it. Somehow the status quo, whatever that may be, seems to be the best of all possible worlds. Or at least the most comfortable.

The argument goes that once a schedule is established, accelerating it is disruptive, may demand over-

Schedule Changes: One Positive Effect

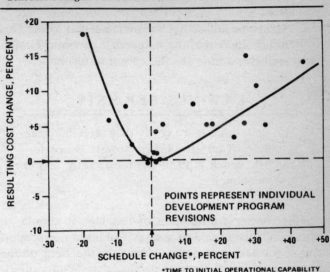

Figure 32. Although evidence relating the impact of schedule changes on cost is sparse, that which does exist indicates that accelerating or decelerating the schedule of an established development program has the same impact on cost: They increase it.

time payment to workers, increases the strain on facilities, and exacerbates concurrency risks caused by overlap between development and manufacturing activities. Decelerating the schedule, on the other hand, increases the cumulative effect of fixed costs and introduces inefficiencies associated with operating with less than a critical mass. Although many decry prolonged schedules and plead for acceleration, the limited record available suggests that for established development programs, accelerating, as is the case for decelerating, produces one predictable consequence: The developer will send you a bill.

Clearly some additional phenomenon is at work. This is identified in Augustine's Law of Economic Unipolarity, which summarizes the empirical results:

LAW NUMBER XXIV

The only thing more costly than stretching the schedule of an established project is accelerating it, which is itself the most costly action known to man.

This specific formulation of this law, it should be noted, is attributable to a small Colorado newspaper, which warned in a news column, in the heat of the commercial nuclear power debate, that "Plutonium is even more dangerous than americium, which itself is the most dangerous substance known to man."

In the words of Yogi Berra, "When you come to a fork in the road, take it."

25

Just in Time

"Always remember that this whole thing was
started by a mouse."

—Walt Disney

*The first annual company picnic was the only
event at Daedalus that had never missed its
schedule. It was a rousing success—even though
the event reminded some of the attendees more
of a convention of retired kamikaze pilots. Furthermore, the extra hour recently recovered in
the move away from daylight savings time had
afforded the management at least a morsel of
good schedule news it could provide to the shareholders and customers in the monthly progress
report. This report, some said, would be more
appropriately named a "Regress" report—just
as people in the factory were no longer speaking
of a learning curve but were instead focusing on
what they called a forgetting curve. Some means
seemed to be needed to get everything back on
track so that the employees could quit spending*

*so much time trying to explain why they were
behind schedule. That alone, it was estimated,
would save every manager at least five hours a
week. At this point the harried executives adopted
the approach of the legendary politician who had
once promised, "We will spend whatever time
it takes to solve this problem even if it takes ten
minutes." Ironically, the solution to the schedule
problem was found totally unexpectedly—in the
world of politics. A true case of serendipity. But
that is perhaps what should have been expected,
in retrospect, when one is in a managerial sense
seeking to leap out of the fourth century.*

Sir William Gilbert, standing forlornly on a train station
platform overlooking an empty track, once observed,
"Saturday afternoons, although coming at regular and
well-foreseen intervals, always take this railway by surprise."

In competitive, time-sensitive markets, managers are
simultaneously challenged on three fronts. Not only
must they produce a desirable product at a reasonable
price, but, in addition, they must deliver their output
to the marketplace in a timely manner. This urgency is
characteristic of a large variety of products, irrespective
of whether the aforementioned pressure arises from
perishability of the product, the need to rapidly exploit
some temporal market advantage such as a technological breakthrough, or merely to keep up with demand.

However, in environments wherein only one source
of an item is available, an altogether different set of
dynamics prevails. This has in the past been the case
for such organizations as the post office, the phone
company, the railroads, the utility companies, and the

public schools—to name but a few. As so often seems
to be true, the U.S. Congress itself provides an excellent
case study, not so much because it is fundamentally
dissimilar to other organizations but because of its pen-
chant for doing things with great flair in terms of documentation and publicity. Consider, as but one example,
the problem faced by the Congress as each year, while
in addition to its myriad of other crucial tasks it pursues
the matter of approving a budget for each of the federal
departments. For one reason or another, the Congress
has apparently found it increasingly difficult to complete
this task prior to the beginning of the fiscal year in which
the money is to be spent. There have even been attempts to organize task forces to deal head-on with the
problem of legislative procrastination, but thus far such
efforts have themselves been deferred.

The data in Figure 33 display how in each fiscal year
the date at which funds are finally appropriated has
tended to slide further and further into the year for
which the funds are intended. This problem recently
culminated in a circumstance wherein the appropriation
act did not become law until the year for which funds
were being appropriated was more than half over! The
challenge posed to those charged with executing that
budget can barely be imagined—particularly those unfortunate managers whose requested budget was halved
midway through the year!

What the future portended for those same managers
could be glimpsed by projecting forward in time the
trend line in Figure 33 for the period just prior to 1975.
The inevitable conclusion seemed to be that it would
be only about a decade until the situation reached crisis
proportions; that is, the budget would not be approved
until the year was altogether a matter of history. As

Falling Further Ahead

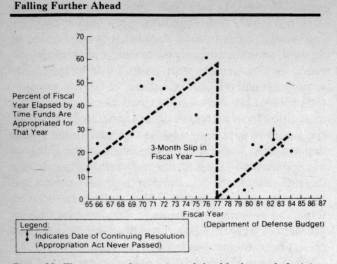

Figure 33. The process of preparing a federal budget and obtaining its approval used to consume an increasing period of time each year until a drastic and clever step was taken at the end of fiscal year 1976—after which the process continued to consume an increasing period of time each year.

Perkins McGuire said, "With the past coming down the road so fast, we are going to have to address it in the future."

Fully recognizing this dilemma, the Congress proceeded to rectify the intensifying problem with both alacrity and decisiveness. Less imaginative managers in private industry, which is generally rich in competitive pressures, given the same circumstances might have resorted to such conventional techniques as eliminating some of the eighteen repetitive votes taken each year by Congress on large segments of the budget (an outgrowth of the old "vote early and vote often" school of politics), or even to expediting the budget cycle by combining various steps in the review process (such as the now-separate authorization and appropriation actions), or perhaps even by resorting to multiyear budgeting as almost all other nations on Earth have adopted.

As it turns out, no such pedestrian approaches were needed—they would have demanded an uncommon amount of common sense. The obvious solution, and that seized upon by the Congress, was to pass a new law changing the definition of the year, starting it (for fiscal purposes) in October rather than July as had been the case for two centuries, thus slipping the budget process neatly into compliance with the time it was actually taking to complete the task. "Know the right timing"—in the words of Diogenes Laërtius.

The Congress actually may not have originated this general concept but instead may merely have emulated the practice of the official U.S. Observatory which occasionally adds a second to a day to keep clocks in synchronization with the Earth's movement. Such a "leap-second" was added on the last day of January 1983 and was reported in the media as "stopping the clocks to allow the Earth to catch up." It must be noted, however, that even in these modern times the Congress has continued the practice of unplugging the wall clocks in the meeting chamber whenever a new fiscal year is about to start and the enabling spending resolution has not yet been enacted. This lends credence to the view held by many that Congress could not bring tomorrow in on time.

Alas, as shown in Figure 33, immediately upon slipping the fiscal year into conformance with the time consumed in the budget process in the past, things again began to slip even with respect to the *new* baseline. It may be that it will soon be logical to slip the fiscal year one more time into neat compliance with the calendar years—although this has the disadvantage of seeming logical.

In the case of fiscal year 1983 the process fell so far behind even the new calendar that, faced with the arrival of the 1984 budget request before the FY83 budget had been acted upon, the lame-duck 97th Congress *never did* produce a complete set of FY83 appropriations acts. Rather, some departments proceeded under a year-long series of continuing resolutions. The Congress simply missed the year by about a year—equivalent in effect to a passenger missing an airplane flight by only ten feet.

Hence, although budgets are still being approved after the fiscal year is well underway, they nonetheless—at least for a time—turned out to be the earliest they had ever been late.

The *Orlando Sentinel* found a sports-world analogy to the above practice when it reported that a Florida State offensive guard, "a muscular 5'11" 240-pounder with powerful legs—recorded the fastest time in his weight division in the 12-minute run."

This methodology pioneered by the Congress has now been adopted by industry. One firm, which had widely advertised amid much fanfare that the first flight of a new commercial jet aircraft would take place "before the end of the year," later announced that the goal had indeed been met—the successful flight "took place on the 32nd of December." Close only counts in horseshoes and hand grenades.

One problem with setting new baseline schedules is

that it is much like establishing a new accounting system—namely, all traceability is lost. Under these circumstances everyone merely settles back into the same old routine of missing schedules except that in this case the schedules missed are the *revised* ones.

The essential element that made this resolution of a nasty problem possible in the case of the Congress was, of course, the fact that there is only one Congress available, and if this one does not produce a budget by some particular time, there is no danger of another competitive Congress stepping in and producing one of its own. It can be safely inferred that such latitude for problem solving is suitable for use by virtually any entity functioning in an environment which is generally free of competition. There is nothing profound in such an observation; it is only one more manifestation of the Golden Rule: He who has the gold makes the rules.

Professor C. Northcote Parkinson, in the well-known law which bears his name, examined the amount of effort which is devoted to activities which are *time-constrained*. Augustine's Law Number XXV is the reciprocal to Parkinson's proposition and considers the case wherein the work to be performed is constrained. Parkinson's Law pointed out, in essence, that work expands to fill the time prescribed. In contradistinction, the Law of Inconstancy of Time points out:

LAW NUMBER XXV

A revised schedule is to business what a new season is to an athlete or a new canvas to an artist.

In noncompetitive situations, time expands to fit the work prescribed. Or, as John Lowenstein of the Baltimore Orioles suggested when asked for his views on how to improve the game of baseball, "They should move first base back a step to eliminate all the close plays."

26

Piled High

"This is the saddest story I have ever heard."
—F. M. Ford, 1915

It must regrettably be reported that as the technical effort moved forward haltingly when at all, a few alarmists began to appear—even in the sales and marketing organizations. The burst of enthusiasm that had followed the decision by the site survey team to locate the new Long Range Planning Center in Hong Kong had long since dissipated. Nonetheless, the task of providing a new management structure for the beleaguered project was proceeding unimpeded. What was necessary, it had been concluded, was a means of providing each task with more supervisory oversight. In addition, there was the need to find positions on Project X for all those individuals who had been displaced now that Daedalus's original project lines were phasing out in preparation for the new family of products. This im-

proved management approach of increasing the amount of supervision provided each worker also proved to be a great boost for management's sagging morale, since the large number of new high-level positions which were opened made wholesale promotions possible with attendant increases in salaries and country club memberships, and business trips to some of the world's most renowned watering holes. Only the workers were reluctant—having already noted that each new improvement seemed to generate its own set of unexpected impediments which tugged them backward at the most inopportune times. But all things considered, they were in pretty good shape, considering the shape they were in.

Professor C. Northcote Parkinson would not be disappointed were he to apply his now famous studies, which revealed a shore contingent in the British Admiralty growing by 5 to 6 percent a year in spite of a steadily decreasing number of ships at sea, to U.S. management practices in industry and government. Similarly, Parkinson found a 5 to 6 percent growth rate in the British Colonial Office "during a period of manifest decline in . . . colonial activity." The present law expands modestly on Parkinson's work so as to examine the organizational or structural consequences of operating with heavily-peopled administrative overheads.

In the words of Czar Alexander, "I did not rule Russia; ten-thousand clerks ruled Russia." The more recent Western analogue of the Czar's frustration was summarized in the words of President Truman speaking on Eisenhower's future as President (as reported by

Richard Neustadt): "He'll sit there and he'll say this! Do that!' And nothing will happen. Poor Ike."

Lee Iacocca, chief executive of the Chrysler Corporation, has observed, "There are times when even the best manager is like the little boy with the big dog waiting to see where the dog wants to go so he can take him there."

That the extent of an administrative structure is largely an artifact of historical precedent and is in fact relatively insensitive to the amount of work to be performed is reaffirmed in Figure 34, which presents but one piece of the available evidence, in this case relating to the

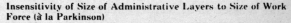

Insensitivity of Size of Administrative Layers to Size of Work Force (à la Parkinson)

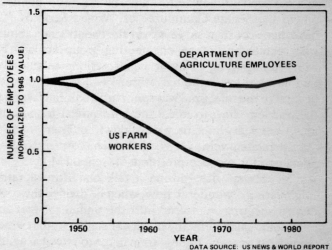

DATA SOURCE: US NEWS & WORLD REPORT

Figure 34. As the number of individuals involved in "touch-labor" decreases, the size of the supporting (overhead) labor pool expands to take up any slack.

agricultural industry. As will be seen, the number of farmers in the nation may be dropping precipitously, but the number of employees in the Department of Agriculture seems to hang right in there. An apocryphal story is told of a tour group in Washington visiting the Department of Agriculture and inquiring why one of the Department's employees, seated at an empty desk, was crying. The answer: "His farmer died." Fortunately, however, the Department of Agriculture also has in its official employment 144 full-time public-affairs staffers with a budget of $6 million to tell everyone how good things are.

That the same fundamental disorder is true of other industries is asserted by Kelly Johnson, former director of Lockheed's renowned Skunk Works, who pointed out to the Senate Committee on Armed Services, "I have made constant surveys over the twenty years about what percentage of an engineering group actually is engaged in putting a line on paper, writing an analysis that has to do with the hardware. . . . I found that 5.6 percent of the total time was spent in actually addressing the problem: how to make the hardware. I found out about ten years later they were down to 3 percent."

In a related vein, Dr. Bob Frosch, former NASA administrator and vice-president of General Motors Research Laboratories, during a talk on "Bureaucratic Engineering," wondered how, when he divided the cost per engineering man-year into the annual budget to build some small item, the hordes of engineers that were being paid were ever going to manage to crowd around the lonely piece of hardware that was being constructed. His conclusion: "From time to time I have been able to identify and demonstrate in a particular case that about one-tenth of the engineers involved were in fact doing engineering in any traditional sense—and the rest were writing each other memos."

The problem with the existence of large bodies of administrators is not solely a consequence of their numbers, per se, but rather is a result of the number of *layers* they constitute, with each layer having an opportunity to reject, deny, modify, filter, eliminate, reduce, stretch, or otherwise retard every suggestion that has the audacity to seek to wind its way through the labyrinth-like approval processes adopted by most large organizations and which would make even a Minotaur proud. The larger the organization, the bigger the probable problem. Unlike professional football, however, there is no penalty in U.S. management practices for "piling-on." The General Accounting Office, for example, reports that the Navy's Mark 48 torpedo project was at one time led by eighty-seven subordinate program managers.

This general situation is exacerbated by the fact that the populace at each layer, particularly the higher ones, inevitably concludes they need a staff to support them. Such staff positions are characterized by the lack of line authority, the absence of a charter to make decisions, no direct responsibility for meeting a payroll, and no premise to give orders. Staffs then serve as sources of reviews and as counsels of advice—with full authority to ask questions. When small and totally dedicated to being part of the answer and not part of the problem, such staffs can make significant contributions. Otherwise, they can be a speed-bump on the path of progress.

Although staff functions are widely employed in the private sector as well as in government, in few instances has such burgeoning success, at least in terms of size, been observed as in the case of—where else—the staff which serves the U.S. Congress. For example, since World War II the U.S. population has increased by about 59 percent while the size of the Congressional staff has blossomed by slightly over 700 percent.

It is interesting to note that as the size of the staffs increased, presumably to help expedite the tasks at hand, as shown in Figure 35, the time to produce the products of the Congress has grown steadily longer. With regard to the matter of approving a budget for national defense, only four times since 1945 has a budget been produced in time for the start of the year (and then

Helping Speed Things Down

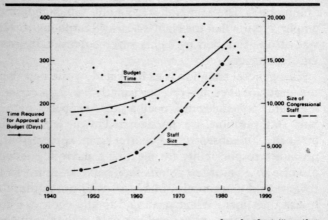

Sources: Payroll Records of House and Senate
Data of Defense Appropriations Act

Figure 35. As the size of a staff is increased to expedite an activity, the time required for that activity will also increase. Ultimately, everyone is working in a staff role with the result that nothing is produced.

only by an average of five days). As a staff grows in size, the volume of questions it can ask also increases as does the time to get the answers. This is akin to the law promulgated by Dr. Fred Brooks, professor of Computer Science at the University of North Carolina, which relates to the development of software. "Adding people to speed up a late software project," says Brooks, "just makes it later." He presents quite convincing evidence in support of his thesis and it would seem that his conclusion has applicability far beyond the realm of software.

Although widely recognized, solutions to this problem have been inhibited by the fact that where people stand on the subject depends on where they sit. It has been pointed out by Dr. Paul Berenson, executive secretary of a government science board, that *management* is what one does to provide sound leadership of those below one's self on the organization chart. On the other hand, he says, *micromanagement* is all that which takes place *above* one's self on the chart.

An individual working at the bottom level of, say, the Army's missile development command is looking up at forty-four layers through which must be gained support for any new idea before it can be funded. The view from such a valley can be demoralizing indeed. As one Canadian flatlander was once observed to remark, "Mountains are okay, I guess, but they sure do get in the way of the view."

The problem of layering of management permeates virtually all organizations—it is simply more debilitating for governments and large corporations because of their size. A typical Fortune 500 firm will have on the order of a dozen layers. Each layer of course represents one more "connection" which must be established in any effort to communicate from the top to the bottom of the organization—or *vice versa*.

There is, however, some reason for hope that high-level headquarters layers may be having less of an adverse impact than the above examples would suggest. In October 1984, for example, the national media carried a report of a major fire at the top headquarters of the Post Office Department in Washington, D.C., with damage "exceeding $100 million." The report was accompanied by an official statement presumably, if not altogether successfully, aimed at easing the concerns of taxpayers, noting that ". . . there will be no impact whatsoever on the nation's mail service." If nothing else, the statement is certainly provocative. A similar phenomenon occurs most every winter whenever a heavy snowfall strikes the nation's capital. On such occasions the media dutifully relates an official announcement to all government workers, "Only essential employees need report to work." The mentality of the city is such that no curiosity seems to be raised when hardly anyone shows up at the office. With minor geometric exceptions, the classical description of Washington, D.C., as a diamond-shaped city surrounded on all four sides by reality would seem to fit many other headquarters as well.

The statistical implications of the above assessment of managerial layers in business or governmental organizations are devastating. Consider the probability of obtaining approval of a project which must be agreed upon by forty different layers, each of which has almost a 99 percent likelihood of reaching an affirmative decision. As shown in Figure 36, despite the favorable individual odds, the chances of overall success in such a case are only about fifty-fifty. This is explained by Robert Massey's Law which, slightly paraphrased, notes that one vice-president, two vice-admirals, and three Congressmen wired in series produce near infinite impedance. *The Washington Post* on occasion has referred to the progenitors of this impedance as The Abominable No Men.

The examples shown in the figure for specific organizations count "deputies" as a layer as well as counting staff levels as layers. On the other hand, they neglect altogether the existence of multiple parallel channels in the approval process at any given level which must also somehow be hurdled. Further, for many actions, such as budget approvals, it is necessary to penetrate this thicket not once, but once each year. There are said to be some individuals alive today who believe it may be possible to get to heaven without transferring in Atlanta, but there can be none who would suspect that one can get funding in a large organization without traversing each and every passageway of the approval maze.

One Air Force general has defined a "yes" as "the requisite ninety-nine non-no's." Dave Packard, a former Deputy Secretary of Defense and currently chairman of the Board of Hewlett-Packard Company, cites the example of the Argon National Laboratory in Chicago. He notes, "Nineteen separate congressional committees act on line items before Argon's budget can be approved." But such statistics often merely address the federal government, which itself is simply the end in a system known to encompass 81,000 local governments, 3000 counties, 18,000 cities and villages, 17,000 townships, 25,000 school districts, and 18,000 special districts.

Double Jeopardy Would Be an Improvement

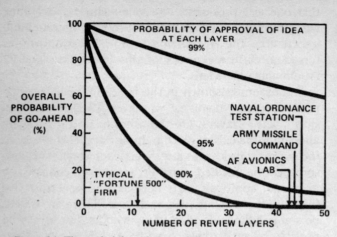

Figure 36. The probability of successfully accomplishing any objective declines in a very calculable manner as the number of layers in the approval process increases.

In all too many organizations in business and elsewhere, rare indeed is the individual who can do something or make something happen. Rather, the situation is as described long ago by Samuel Johnson: "To do nothing is in every man's power."

Actually, the probability of peeling one's way through the onion-like layers of the corporate or governmental approval process without obtaining a "no" somewhere along the way may be the least threatening aspect of the prevailing system. There is also a "Catch 22," the implications of which can be illustrated by a few simple calculations. Consider the federal government as the case in point.

Data gathered by G. D. Brabson reveal that prior to seeking program approval from the System Acquisition Review Council (a committee established to streamline the government's decision process), the program manager of the Army's new Patriot Air Defense system was required to present no fewer than forty briefings to intervening layers so that each could approve what he was going to say when he arrived in the streamlined management system. In the case of the Joint Tactical Information Distribution System, forty-two separate appearances were required not including Saturday matinees. The Air Force's F-16 aircraft necessitated fifty-six of these prebriefings, whereas the Navy's F-18, a best-seller, endured seventy-two. These data equate to fifty-three briefings on the average passage through the system. This proves to be an important number.

Now, since there are typically eighteen layers (Service Material Command, Service Staff, Service Secretariat, Office of Secretary of Defense staff, etc., each with its own strata) between a project manager and the senior body of streamlined decision-makers, it can be readily determined that par for a passage is 2.944 briefings per layer. (The precision of this number will become clearer later in Chapter 35.)

Consider an individual at the very bottom layer who happens to have an idea, the pursuit of which requires annual budget approval. It has been shown that this individual must pass through some forty-two layers with an impedance of 2.944 BPL (briefings per layer). Under the modest assumption that each briefing consumes two days for preparation, travel, presentation, and recuperation, the total approval cycle occupies 250 days—which is exactly the number of working days in a year!

The notion that managers should spend their time managing instead of talking seems to miss the mark in today's society about as much as did the remark by Harry M. Warner of Warner Bros. Pictures in 1927, "Who the hell wants to hear actors talk?"

And none of the above accounts for the special demands that take effect when any out-of-the-ordinary needs arise. For example, when the managers of the B-1B bomber and F-16 fighter projects sought to save money by seeking approval from the Congress for multi-year funding, about 100 *special* briefings were required of each project.

Thus ends, in mathematical rigor, the mystery of why new ideas seldom manage to bubble forth from many systems designed to encourage creativity.

But things get worse. Recall that the above-mentioned executive management forum was established to permit "face-to-face streamlined decision-making" among high-level officials. Records of the Navy's Ground Launched Cruise Missile program reveal that the average dry run in preparation for an appearance before the streamlined forum was attended by fully twenty-four individuals. Thus, recalling the average of fifty-three briefings prior to a high-level decision-making session, we have a total attendance at these intimate management gatherings of 1272—each with a charter to cast a "no" vote. This rivals the crowds drawn at some of the other sporting events which are held in Washington.

Further, according to official records, even after the high-level, streamlined meeting is completed, it takes an average of twenty-seven *workdays* to sort out what was actually concluded with sufficient clarity that it can

be documented in an official decision paper. Chrispher Columbus would never have made it through such
an approval process. And even if he had, the General
Accounting Office (the federal government's watchdog)
would have excoriated him after the fact. Not only did
he not know where he was going, when he got there
he didn't know where he was. Columbus would be a
cinch for the Golden Fleece award given for extraordinary ineptness. *Sixty Minutes* would crucify him.

Stratification also introduces profound problems in
the realm of titular engineering and heraldry, an area
where the United States has only recently been able to
challenge its longer established European counterparts
or, for that matter, the Soviet Union. This has led, for
example, to the creation in the United States of such
positions as the one listed in the telephone book for
the Department of State's Agency for International Development as the Associate Assistant Administrator in
the office of the Assistant Administrator for Adminisration. Similarly, when it was decided that the Under
Secretary of Defense for Research and Engineering,
who already had a layer of deputies who themselves
possessed a sublayer of assistants who were in turn buttressed by deputy assistants each of which had a staff,
sensed the need for still another layer, the rank of *Principal* Deputy Under Secretary was created. When it was
subsequently found that not one but *two* such individuals were needed, the system took right in stride the
creation of *two Principal* Deputy Under Secretaries of
Defense for Research and Engineering! It just turned
out, as one might have suspected, that one was more
principal than the other.

Augustine's Law of Propagation of Misery summa-

treatise on organizational layering and
derived from the data already presented

LAW NUMBER XXVI

If a sufficient number of management layers
are superimposed on top of each other, it can
be assured that disaster is not left to chance.

Trying to manage the operational *details* of an undertaking from the lofty strata of top management is
akin to herding chickens on horseback, and produces
much the same result. This is exactly what the Congress
is seeking to do and what is happening in commercial
organizations with unduly large headquarters staffs.

If Noah were alive today, he would find no need to
construct an ark; he would need only create a management structure of the above type and assign it responsibility for making rain. Or in the words of Damon
Runyon: "In all human affairs, the odds are always six
to five against."

27

Hail on the Chief

"Nuts."
—General Anthony Clement McAuliffe
Bastogne, 1944

The problems plaguing Project X were proving to be more intractable than should have been expected when so many enlightened management techniques were being applied. A widening gulf seemed to be growing between the company leadership and the rest of the work force, exacerbated by the amount of time consumed in the unsuccessful negotiations to sell Project X to the company's most antagonistic competitor. Clearly some further decisive step would be needed beyond the recent issuance of company cars to the headquarters staff if the morale of the project's personnel was to be recovered. Having abandoned the suggestion to cancel all vacations until morale improved, attention turned to the matter of providing still more management strength, and in this instance not one but two substantive techniques for resolution were found and promptly implemented. The first was to provide a more exalted title for each of the current managers—thus was created the position of senior vice-president, outranked informally only by the assistant to the president, the incumbent for which happened to be the president's cousin. There are major differences between "assistants to" and "assistants." It has been said, not always fairly, that assistants know something and assistants to know someone. The second action which was implemented was to have the company's top executive and founder personally assume command of Project X. Given his authority and prestige, it was apparent that it would be only a short time until all the remaining technological problems succumbed to the sheer intimidation of his presence. As he said on the day he assumed command of the project, "I am aware that this will not be easy, but I also know most of the obstacles." In fact, most of the obstacles were sitting right there in the room as he spoke.

It is widely believed in senior management circles that by assigning people of high rank to manage a task, the chance of problems occurring with that task will be greatly diminished. This is something analogous to the corollary to the Peter Principle promulgated herein, "Decisions rise to the management level where the person making them is least qualified to do so." That is, as various experts, each involved in narrow segments of an issue, find themselves unable to reach agreement, the matter is elevated for adjudication to a senior manager who has no particular expertise or currency in *any* of the factors under contention. This concept is frequently put into practice when a project suffering discomfiture is handed from, say, a manager to a vice-president in order to "straighten things out." But, as Air Force Lieutenant General Dick Henry explains, "Many companies are very loyal to their senior employees. Some even independent of talent."

The viewpoint of business executives who usurp the function of lesser managers only to discover that in the real world no improvement results has been well summarized by the baseball manager who yanked his centerfielder after he dropped three straight fly balls. Having decided personally to take the place of the errant fielder, the manager suffered the ignominy of himself dropping what proved to be the game-winning pop fly. Returning to the dugout and the penetrating stares of his players, the dismayed manager explained, pointing at his predecessor, "He has that position so fouled up that now no one can play it."

It seems to be hereditary for managers to blame others for their failings—as almost anyone who has ever been the purveyor of bad news to the boss will have discovered. For centuries it has been commonplace for kings to "shoot the messenger" conveying bad news. In one legendary instance a king having just received a messenger is reported to have concluded, "That message was *neither* good nor bad—just take him out and rough him up a bit." Not a great deal has changed over the years, to the eternal detriment of corporate communications.

The payoff from the escalatory approach in industry of blaming one's subordinates for all problems and then taking over the task oneself is, however, difficult to measure because the necessary data are once again, probably mercifully, unavailable. A rather good measure is, however, possible for government project managers working in the Department of Defense. This measure is very likely applicable to industrial managers as well, based on the theorem of Equal Escalation in Rank, whereby companion pairs of customer and supplier managers working on the same project must be of equal strata in order to satisfy the respective rules of engagement, elevation, and protocol.

Specifically, the theory of superior performance by organizational superiors demands that were a plot made of some measure of the occurrence of problems in a project against the rank of the manager involved, a steeply decreasing trend in problems would be observed as rank increases. Such a plot is actually presented in Figure 37, (wherein each data point represents a different project) except, that is, for the steeply decreasing trend. The results seem to verify the adage of unknown origin that in the industrial world, "Rank times IQ is a constant." What is seen is that the occurrence of problems (in this case, cost overruns) is altogether unrelated to the rank of the executive in charge.

This contemptuous behavior of hardware for the exalted, as reflected in the figure, has undoubtedly already been suspected by any practitioner of these unnatural laws. It will therefore be no surprise to learn that hardware has equal disdain for managers of *all* ranks. It can thus be reliably stated that in carrying out day-to-day management tasks the superior is frequently inferior. Coach Tommy Prothro described the situation very succinctly: "Our team is well balanced. We have problems

A Case of Rank Insubordination

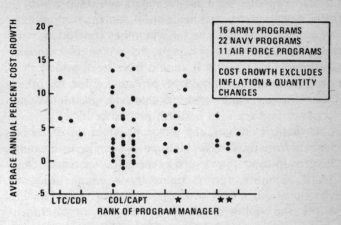

Figure 37. Project managers with the Department of Defense generally hold ranks spanning from Lieutenant Colonel/Commander to two-star Flag Officer, depending on such factors as the size and importance of the program they direct. Unfortunately, cost growth shows little respect for rank.

everywhere." Cost and technical problems are found to be woefully disrespectful of rank. Somehow, hardware is inexplicably not as impressed by who you are as by what you do.

Although it has been tried repeatedly, there is little evidence that one can simply anoint people as managers. A well-known baseball umpire was once asked if there is such a thing as a "natural" umpire. He responded, "Yes, but no one starts out that way." In this regard managers, umpires, and surgeons seem to have a lot in common.

238 · Augustine's Laws

The insensitivity of the occurrence of problems to the titular grandeur of the management would seem to suggest that Socrates and his faithful student companion, Plato, did not go far enough when they concluded, perhaps not altogether surprisingly, that *philosophers* should be kings. Apparently it should have been added that project managers should be privates, if for no other reason that privates cost less than vice-presidents and generals and seem to perform just as well.

Perhaps, however, the most important lesson to be learned from the Greek philosophers by those who would be progenitors of laws such as these was succinctly captured in more recent times by a young student, obviously enamored with the virtues of brevity, who wrote the following essay on the life of Socrates: "Socrates was a philosopher. He went around pointing out errors in the way things were done. They fed him hemlock."

Nonetheless, to return with undaunted vigor to the problem of senior managers being denied their due respect at the hands of complex undertakings, the argument will, of course, be made by higher-ranking officials that higher-ranking officials generally have more difficult projects to manage. But it can be equally argued that those higher-ranking individuals command more authority and enjoy access to more resources with which to *avoid* problems—and that the allocation of management assignments is made by none other than high-ranking officials themselves and, as such, complaints of this type might be suspect.

Augustine's Law of Equipartition of Misfortune (sometimes referred to as the Law of Rank Insubordination) is thus derived:

LAW NUMBER XXVII

Rank does not intimidate hardware. Neither does the lack of rank.

As has already been noted, no less a body than the U.S. Senate has recently taken to legislating into actual *law* the dates by which certain high-tech development programs being pursued by the government are to be completed. The failure by the Senate to recognize the above law would suggest that this august body is laying the groundwork for a profound lesson in humility. Meg Greenfield of *The Washington Post*, writing about the challenge of policymaking in the nation's capital, accurately observes, "The ordeal, the setting for failure, is the effort to make any of it happen."

The irreverence of hardware for officialdom has long been recognized by individuals working in factories, in customer service organizations, and at new-product test facilities. Among this latter group of enthusiasts it is an article of faith that the incidence of test failures is directly proportional to the square of the size of the crowd multiplied by the rank of the senior observing official.

Examples of this general phenomenon are rampant throughout history. There was, for example, the great sailing ship, *Vassa*, newly launched into the harbor of Stockholm in the witness of an enormous gathering of royalty, only to float tentatively a few hundred yards, overturn in full view of all present, and ignominiously become a sunk cost. This demonstrated conclusively, it should perhaps be pointed out, that the metacenter of a ship desires to be located in a certain relationship with the center of gravity irrespective of the amount of royalty, cannon fire, and band music brought to bear.

It was just such a phenomenon that led to the abort, viewed by literally millions of people on worldwide television, of the first attempt to launch the Space Shuttle. In this instance, a set of computers which had been repeatedly tested successfully turned out to have inherent in them a hidden malfunction mode which would preclude synchronization with the backup computer. The chances of the timing clock falling into this malfunctioning mode can be accurately calculated and has now been shown to be about one chance in a hundred. When, then, was this malfunction finally to be encountered in actual operation? Why, on the very first launch attempt, of course. That this could be explained on a statistical basis totally challenges plausibility. The explanation necessarily resides in the above law relating to the number of observers at test events—which makes clear that there *never was* a possibility that the computer could be expected to synchronize while three-quarters-of-a-million in-person spectators, including a gaggle of VIPs, surrounded the launch site. No reasonable observer could possibly be expected to arrive at any other conclusion.

Caesar Geronimo, upon striking out to Nolan Ryan to become Ryan's 300th victim one season after having been Bob Gibson's 300th some years earlier, explained, "I was just in the right place at the right time."

Another embarrassment similar to the one encountered in the Space Shuttle program occurred when the generally successful and very high priority cruise missile flight test program was visited for a launch event by the Secretary of Defense and, of course, the appropriate entourage. On this occasion, not one but *two* of the expensive missiles fluttered a few hundred yards and then plunged ignominiously into the ocean like wounded ducks, proving once again that having a reserve test item with which to guarantee success in reality only ensures the extent of the disaster (the Principle of Replication of Failures).

A similar series of events encountered some years ago during the development of still another cruise missile, the Snark, led during that period to annoying references to "the Snark-infested waters" around Cape Canaveral. Clearly, hardware exhibits an unfriendliness toward managers which is exceeded only by its innate sense of bad timing.

That this antagonistic behavior applies equally badly to hardware encountered in everyday life is suggested by the law promulgated by the author's daughter, René Augustine, then age fourteen, while observing automobile drivers in unfamiliar environs. "Attempting to read a roadmap while driving," she states, "causes all traffic lights to turn green."

28

The Amoeba
Instinct

"The meek shall inherit the earth . . . but the
strong shall retain the mineral rights."
                              —College graffito

*During the past twelve months, to paraphrase
Britain's Margaret Thatcher, things had been
looking desperate, but they were now becoming
serious. So great was the concern over the firm's
profitability—specifically its earnings before interest and taxes or "EBIT," as it is called—that
financial meetings were beginning to sound like
a group of frogs croaking. Each department head
now adopted a favorite color: green for the
Treasury, black for Accounting, and black and
blue for Legal. The headquarters (affectionately
known as the Mushroom Factory—"Keep 'em
in the dark and cover them with manure") was
even beginning to understand the problem:
namely, everyone was working alone together.
The independent auditing firm which surveilled*

Daedalus's books had been writing the company's name as "(Daedalus)." Problems were growing like bananas: in bunches, and the headquarters staff was busy doing its quarterly impersonation of Chicken Little. It was thus evident that if some incisive management action were not taken promptly the program would find itself in what the weekly project report had for months euphemistically referred to as "not inconsiderable difficulty." Fortunately, during the card game returning on the new company jet from the cost control meeting at the recently relocated corporate headquarters in Palm Springs, the appropriate step to take was recognized. It would be necessary to reorganize. Each and every element of the organization would be restructured independent of its past record, abandoning Bert Lance's advice, "If it ain't broke, don't fix it," in favor of Heraclitus's perspective, "Nothing endures but change." Thus began what actually proved to be merely the first in a long series of sweeping reorganizations. These eventually came to be disdainfully referred to by the workers as "redisorganizations."

A member of the President's Cabinet once signaled the demise of an elaborate reorganization of one segment of the government which was being enthusiastically espoused by the author of these laws, said endorsement being marked by a profusion of the classical organization charts showing all the requisite little squares and branches, with the four-word eulogy, "New tree . . . same monkeys."

The problem with reorganization was perhaps best summarized some 2000 years ago in the remark attributed to Petronius Arbiter:

> We trained hard . . . but it seemed that every time we were beginning to form up into a team, we would be reorganized. I was to learn later in life that we tend to meet any new situation by reorganizing. And a wonderful method it can be of creating the illusion of progress while producing confusion, inefficiency, and demoralization.

The popularity of reorganization might best be viewed from the perspective espoused in the advertisement placed in *The Wall Street Journal* by United Technologies Corporation, which dutifully notes: "When forty million people believe in a dumb idea, it's still a dumb idea."

Even the term "reorganize" is a semantic non sequitur. To "reorganize" implies that one must have been previously organized. But if one were organized, why then would one want to reorganize? John Lehman, the Secretary of the Navy, says that what we need is not reorganization but *deorganization*.

Playing with blocks nonetheless seems to be inherent in man. In fact, the proclivity to play with blocks may even be on the increase. One can draw this conclusion from studies of organizations at all levels in businesses, universities, and governments. In seeking a centerpiece of evidence to display, one may as well begin at the very top: The U.S. Cabinet. Figure 38 thus examines the frequency of *re*organization of the President's Cabinet throughout the history of the nation. The observed trend is one of an ever-increasing pace of restructuring

The Urge to Purge

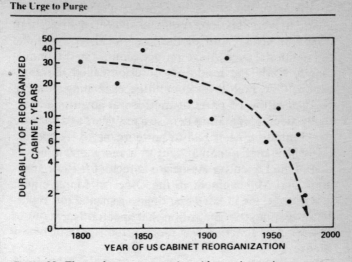

Figure 38. The tendency to reorganize with ever-increasing frequency is a phenomenon observed in organizations ranging from PTAs to the Cabinet of the United States.

moving inexorably toward a condition wherein the time-durability of any given organizational state will soon become negative. The meaning of this is presumably that it may actually become necessary to organize *before* reorganizing. That such a condition should come to exist is a sad testimonial to the great American tradition that if one reorganizes with sufficient frequency, it is possible to altogether avoid ever becoming organized. It has been said that this approach is a fundamental factor in America's historical record of dominance on the international political scene. Generally, in the midst of critical events, everyone becomes confused at one point or another. But our government is *used* to being confused. Thus . . .

Organizations of all categories, including government, universities, conventional industrial firms, and nonprofit firms (both of the intentional type and the unintentional type) have on occasion formed committees to study the mode of confusion called reorganization. One high-level committee examining possible reorganization of parts of the federal government actually met its premature demise a few years ago because the committee itself had to be reorganized. A specific job which met a similar fate in a reorganization was that of the Executive Associate Director for Reorganization and Management in the Office of Management and Budget, the ill-fated czar of governmental turf rights. In a sweeping reorganization that apparently got out of control, this function was reorganized right out of existence.

It is possible to visualize many graphic organization charts apropos to various types of bodies. For the less stable dictatorships in the world, an organization chart with various blocks crossed out in advance with a large "X" has been suggested. The United Nations would be represented with a set of boxes joined together in a circle; the U.S. Congress with a single horizontal chain of 435 separate boxes. In the case of U.S. industrial practice, it has been suggested that the system can be represented by the classical organization chart but with little stringers going to and fro from the bottom boxes directly into the top box. As noted some years ago by one Mr. Al Capone, to the dismay of those occupying the intermediate boxes, "You can get more with a kind word and a gun than you can get with a kind word."

Just as military commanders have known for centuries that battles are always fought on the edges of the map in use, contract disputes are almost always fought on the interfaces of responsibility of the respective participants. This in itself should be sufficient deterrent to wanton restructuring.

When an old block is retained on a newly reorganized organization chart, it is generally lauded as being indispensable. But all is not lost; when a block is deleted from the wiring diagram, it is duly announced that the incumbent was irreplaceable. All are thus winners. Clarence Darrow remarked, "When I was a boy, I was told anybody could become president; I'm beginning to believe it." The net result, however, is that we may be reorganizing ourselves right out of existence. Many modern managers would find irresistible the tendency to run around rearranging the ashtrays on the deck of the *Titanic* in the ship's final hours.

In summary, to paraphrase a comment by Dr. Clark Kerr, the former president of the University of California at Berkeley, most organizations are collections of loosely knit individuals bound together by a mutual fear of reorganization.

The bottom line, then, is recorded in Augustine's Law of the Nest, which is itself simply a restatement of Martin Luther's observation "It makes a difference whose ox is gored." The law therefore notes:

LAW NUMBER XXVIII

It is better to be the reorganizer than the reorganizee.

Nowhere has this been more openly recognized than on the organization chart of IBM's corporate office, wherein one finds none other than a "Vice-President for Reorganization." Sadly, however, it must be reported that this office was last seen on an IBM organization chart in November 1981. It was, to paraphrase Muhammad Ali, a case of "Sting like a butterfly; dance like a bee."

29

The Half-Life of a Manager

"We have a lot of players in their first year.
Some of them are in their last year."
—Bill Walsh, coach, San Francisco 49ers

Trying times had befallen Project X and, thereby, all of Daedalus. Neither the creation of a new organizational structure nor placing the president of the entire company in charge of the project seemed to resolve the technical problems. Schedules were now slipping at a rate slightly in excess of one day per day and talk of potential catastrophe was rampant among the work force. Just as there are said to be three solutions to a leaky fountain pen—buy a new pen, fix the pen, or buy a pair of rubber gloves—it was in this instance decided to go with the gloves. Five more robots were laid off and the entire second and third echelons of management were summarily resigned. Such was the tension created among the remaining four levels of management that when the president was overheard to casually ask

*one executive in the elevator "How are you?"
it created a whole series of rumors built upon
the issue "Why did he ask that?" And after each
group's staff meeting, hours would be consumed
by the water cooler with everyone trying to figure
out what management meant by what it hadn't
said. The entire place seemed to be imploding.
All the newly promoted executives stepping into
the vacuum which was created by the mass exodus began over time to open, one by agonizing
one, the three infamous envelopes which had
been passed down by generations of managers
to their successors to be used whenever disasters
occurred on the new team's watch. The first of
the apocryphal envelopes, of course, suggested
"Blame it on your predecessor"; the second advised, "Blame it on bad luck"; and the third
simply stated, "Prepare three envelopes." It has
been said that if you carry a torch when traveling
through alligator-infested swamps it will keep
you safe from the alligators. Of course, this depends to a certain extent on how fast you
carry it.*

According to former Dallas Cowboy guard Blaine Nye,
"It's not whether you win or lose that counts, but who
gets the blame." Will Rogers once pointed out with
respect to his business pursuits, "It is not the return on
my investment that I am concerned about; it is the
return *of* my investment." Perhaps within this philosophy lies the key to refuting the rather disappointing
thrust of the earlier law which examined management
incentives and the rewards for good performance.

Surviving in the Jungle

CHIEF EXECUTIVES LEAVING FORBES' 20 LEADING CORPORATIONS*

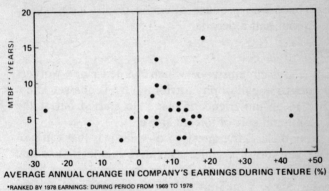

*RANKED BY 1978 EARNINGS: DURING PERIOD FROM 1969 TO 1978
**MEAN TIME BETWEEN FAILURE REPLACEMENT

Figure 39. Data which relate longevity of corporate executives to profitability of the firms they lead indicate only very subtle correlations—if any.

Possibly the significant consideration with respect to successful managers is not what they *keep getting* from their job, but rather that they are *getting* to *keep* their job. This possibility can be readily assessed using Figure 39, which displays the number of years the top executive in the twenty most profitable firms in the United States, in recent years, has been able to hold his job as a function of the success achieved by that executive in increasing the company's profits. Unfortunately, the results are doubly disappointing. Not only do they fail to refute the earlier law on rewards, but worse, they call for still another law. This new law is known as the Law of Infinite Mortality:

LAW NUMBER XXIX

Executives who do not produce successful results hold on to their jobs only about five years.
Those who produce effective results hang on
about half a decade.

It is this circumstance which has led many workers
to adopt the philosophy attributed by Tennessee Ernie
Ford to an old friend of his: "He started out at the
bottom, and sort of likes it there."

Nonetheless, the question of what it is that can pre-
serve the job of a senior executive is a legitimate one
which deserves an answer. For insight, one can begin
by turning to Yogi Smith, defensive end for the Atlanta
Falcons, speaking of teammate Jeff Yates's thirteen years
in professional football: "The thing that has kept Jeff
around," Smith explains, "is his longevity." Now the
secret is out.

It *should* be possible to fight this form of executive
apathy; but so far it has not been possible to find anyone
interested enough to do so. The essence of the above
law seems to be true over a wide span of profit growth
and even over severe profit "retrenchments" (as they
are gently referred to in stockholders' reports). The
correlation coefficient between profit growth and the
ability to retain one's job, on a scale where zero is purely
random and 1.0 represents perfect correlation, is calculated to be 0.1—just about random. The strongest
correlation observed between longevity and any other
parameter examined is found to be between the first
letter in the name of the company and the first letter
in the last name of the chief executive; as in "Ford, du

Pont and Brown (Cleveland-type)." As Prince Philip put it, "I'm self-employed."

A median survival duration of a little over five years for top executives may seem rather short at first glance.* However, it is really quite good when compared with certain other professions—such as, say, coaching football. Many practitioners of this latter art have had fine careers in a single afternoon. Consider the case of the Washington Redskins coach who, several years ago, was fired at half-time of the first exhibition game; or the situation that developed a few years later when the same team had three head coaches in twenty-four hours. A real-life case of "If my boss calls, get his name."

In pro football it is clearly a liability to be recognized for outstanding performance. Of the last fifteen coaches to be honored by the Associated Press as coach of the year, eleven were fired within the next twelve months. As Bum Phillips, coach of the Houston Oilers, noted, "There's only two kinds of coaches, them that's been fired and them that's about to be fired." Phillips has now been fired by Houston. But firing the boss is no panacea. Consider the case of the twelve National Football League teams who fired their head coach during or after the 1982 and 1983 seasons. The coaches who were fired had a mere 41.2 percent winning record whereas those who replaced them promptly improved this down to a 39.8 percent record the following season. To quote Jerry Tarkanian, basketball coach at the University of Nevada at Las Vegas (upon the loss of nine seniors

---

*The data sample considered in Figure 39 contains a slight potential bias since the available evidence covers only a ten-year period. The impact of this is to have relatively little effect on the median longevity addressed herein; however, the overall (arithmetic) average longevity would perhaps increase to seven or eight years.

from his team), "We probably won't feel the loss of them until they're gone."

Most owners, however, simply take the position that it doesn't matter whether you win or lose as long as you win. There is, incidentally, a certain generality to the remark by Ed Vargo, the major league baseball umpire, "We're supposed to be perfect our first day on the job, and then show constant improvement." As John McKay, former coach of the Tampa Bay Buccaneers, points out about his ballplayers, "They're paid to catch the ball."

It can, of course, be asserted that many of the individuals included in the data base of Figure 39 retired or moved on to more important jobs. But it can be equally accurately asserted that many of these individuals were yet relatively young at the time of their departure and had already enjoyed some of the better jobs in America.

Sooner or later the odds just seem to overtake most executives. The public approval rating of reelected American presidents is a case in point. The last four such presidents carried, according to the Gallup Poll, ratings of 69, 73, 71, and 51 percent, respectively into their final term. In periods ranging from fourteen to forty-six months they managed to drive their approval ratings down to 23, 48, 35, and 24 percent. Familiarity does seem to breed contempt. As Frank Layden, general manager of the then less than successful basketball franchise, the Jazz, remarked, "We formed a booster club in Utah, but by the end of the season it had turned into a terrorist group."

Billy Martin, the itinerant baseball manager, presumably understands all this, having been fired an average of once every 2.1 years during his long career, including several times from the same job—all the while compiling a winning record.

Casey Stengel has said that the art of management consists of getting credit for the home runs your players hit. He might equally have added that it includes getting credit for the home runs your players *don't* hit.

30

The Manager of the Year

When the going gets tough, everyone leaves.
—Lynch's Law

The newly anointed managers acted with dispatch and with confidence. Some even believed that the world was coming to a start. They had, as the saying goes, met the enemy and it was their predecessors. It had, in the new management's view, become increasingly conspicuous that many of the project's other participants were groping with jobs for which they were ill-suited. A decision was therefore made to shift positions among all the remaining members of management at all the firm's various locations in order to afford everyone a fresh start. A few were actually demoted, many promoted, but most just moted. Among the workers, the ever changing members of management were now simply referred to as UFOs. Daedalus thus became a member of one of the newest schools of business:

"No-Fault Management." The effect of the tur-bulence which resulted was magnified by the sud-den appearance of hordes of Head-Hunters, referred to in more dignified circles as executive search firms, all seeking to precipitate a game of musical chairs among the nation's management cadre—with commissions. The lack of a stable chain of command had, according to Daedalus's workers, led to the abandonment of such well established management precepts as MBO (Management by Objective) and in their place such novel techniques were sprouting up as MBR (Management by Rumor). But, in the case of management turnover, as in another area of business endeavor, most managers think they know their capacity but simply pass out before they reach it. One worker summed up his new boss by saying: "He is the kind of person who can walk into an empty room and fit right in."

It is a part of the great American tradition that when problems arise, you fire the boss. This has a secondary effect that many executives who are moving into jobs new to them have the additional handicap of doing so under adverse business circumstances. Stephen Wolf, president of Republic Airlines, says, "When I joined the company, our official name was 'Financially-Trou-bled-Republic-Airlines.'"

One of the greatest impediments to that fundamental precept of management referred to as accountability is the rapid turnover of individuals holding leadership po-sitions. Government managers of major high-tech proj-ects, for example, hold their jobs an average of only thirty months. Even this is a substantial improvement over the situation which existed a few years ago when in 1965 government managers retained their jobs an average of only fifteen months. Similarly, at the top echelon of officialdom, over the last two decades the tenure of secretaries of governmental departments as a group has been no better, also averaging about thirty months. In the case of industrial management, the turn-over in operating positions is not a great deal better, averaging about thirty-five months.

But the group most entitled to hazardous-duty pay are those brave souls who coach major league athletic teams. A brief search of the record books and a bit of statistical meandering leads to the following startling findings concerning coaches in major league baseball and the National Football League:

Probability (%) of Remaining As Coach of Team for Years Shown

Years	Football Coaches	Baseball Coaches
1	87	73
2	60	48
3	40	28
4	27	17
5	19	11
10	5	4

Such evidence of job insecurity makes all the more superhuman the records compiled by Tom Landry (twenty-five years) and Earl "Curly" Lambeau (thirty-nine years) in football or Connie Mack (fifty years—consecutive) in baseball.

Turning to the fledgling United States Football League, in its first three-and-one-third years ten of its fourteen teams changed owners, ten changed quarterbacks, seven dumped their coaches, and four changed cities.

Could it be possible that so important a tenet as leadership stability and accountability has been totally overlooked in managing so important an enterprise as, say, our nation's defense affairs—let alone athletic affairs? No, there is reason for optimism. Consider the following newspaper article quoting senior Navy managers: "By constantly changing our . . . director every two or three years, we have destroyed continuity." "If you had a million-and-a-half-dollar business, would you want to change bosses every three years for someone who didn't have any experience?" "Most directors come right from sea duty to this job, and it can take a full year to get to know the ropes. . . . How many people in the Navy do you think know things like scheduling problems?"

Encouraging indeed: The problem is recognized, presumably in an article from the pages of *The Wall Street Journal* discussing the management of an important Navy fighter aircraft, or perhaps even a new shipbuilding program. Alas, the article is from the sports page of *The Washington Post*, addressing the decision reached a few years ago to stop rotating individuals through the position of Athletic Director at the Naval Academy.

At least we have our priorities in perspective.

There is, of course, the viewpoint taken by one senior executive, "There is no problem with rotating people as long as they aren't doing anything anyway!" The consequences of this anonymity in responsibility once prompted an aggrieved Lyndon Johnson to remark, in response to a question by a reporter as to why he had not fired the individual who had scuttled one of the President's very favorite programs, "Fire him? Hell, I can't even *find* him."

Gilbert Fitzhugh, chairman of the blue ribbon panel which reviewed the management of one government department in the late 1960s, summarized the situation in the following terms: "Everybody is somewhat responsible for everything, and nobody is completely responsible for anything." A senior manager in Washington once commented in an outburst of candor in response to a question as to how he was going to work his project out of the seemingly untenable position into which it had descended, "Perhaps a miracle will happen, or else maybe I'll get transferred!"

Dr. Ray Cline, the former Deputy Director of the Central Intelligence Agency, reminds that the essence of planning is to be nearby when successes occur and far away when disaster strikes. The basic premise of successful management in Washington does in fact seem to be to always keep someone between you and the problem.

The dilemma of personnel turbulence, troublesome in virtually all management situations, is particularly acute in the case of major research and development undertakings for which a single project will not uncommonly consume from five to ten years. Added to this is the fact that studies of the frequency of reference to technical articles in archival journals held in libraries indicates that their utility falls off rapidly with time after their initial publication. Similarly, the rate of change of content in course catalogs in the scientific departments of various universities indicates rapid turnover in subject matter. Drawing an analogy to radioactive decay, the half-life of many technologies is today only about ten years and in such cases as electronics and space science it approaches three years.

This, incidentally, points to the enormous challenge faced by managers in high-tech markets to maintain themselves scientifically current. In such fields, without a conscious effort at continuing education, one literally becomes professionally middle-aged by age thirty.

Paraphrasing this inconsistency as once pointed out by the *Armed Forces Journal*, we are attempting to develop major new systems with ten-year technology, eight-year programs, a five-year plan, three-year people, and one-year dollars. At present there is much debate in Washington over multiyear procurement and multiyear budgets to produce at least some semblance of stability, but as Senator Bill Cohen says, what we first need is multiyear people! Tom Watson, Jr., from his vantage point as chairman of IBM, expressed concern when he learned "people began to say that IBM stood for 'I've Been Moved.' "

The pervasiveness of such continuing turnover is suggested by the following passage from the Farm Paper of the Department of Agriculture, as reported in *The New Yorker* magazine, "Sam Katz, once with USDA's kumquat division, later with the tung nut division and more recently with the mung bean division, may switch to the kiwi fruit division after the first of the year." *The New Yorker* concludes, editorially, "Ever onward, Sam."

Attendant to each change of management there is also likely to be an instant "virtual" cost increase as the new leadership offloads blame on the old management and builds shelter for itself with a new cost baseline. Executive mortality data would seem to suggest that one never wants to be the first manager in charge of a new project, the manager on whose watch all the promises which were necessarily made to obtain ap-

262 · Augustine's Laws

proval for and win the job in the first place come home
to roost. Just as in marriage it is said to be best to be
someone's second wife or husband, in management it
is clearly best to be the second project manager. In
effect, from here there is no way but up. Accountants
have a name for this: "FIFO" (rhymes with "Why
Throw"), which means First In . . . First Out. The concept seemingly applies to people as well as dollars.

A brief study of the cost reports of a variety of projects reveals a strong correlation between changes in
management and jumps in projected cost which appear
immediately after the changeover.

Thus, a long succession of leadership changes takes
place, but all too often with no accompanying improvement in results. A frustrated Casey Stengel once im-
mortalized this apparent shortage of talent in the
following words: "Two hundred million Americans, and
there ain't two good catchers among 'em."

Turning to football, Dallas, Miami, Pittsburgh, Minnesota, and the Raiders have mostly had but one coach
since the late 1960s—a maximum of two. These same
teams have had fifty-nine out of a possible sixty-five
winning seasons and made eighteen Super Bowl appearances. In contrast, Baltimore and New Orleans have
together cycled through no fewer than seventeen coaches
in the same time period—while suffering losing seasons
77 percent of the time. Although cause and effect can
be debated, few would argue that the coach-of-the-month
approach is to anyone's advantage except possibly the
media. Perhaps the answer resides in Washington Irving's observation that "There is a certain relief in change,
even though it is from bad to worse; as I have found
in travelling in a stage-coach that it is often a comfort
to shift one's position and be bruised in a new place."

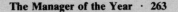

Changing Times

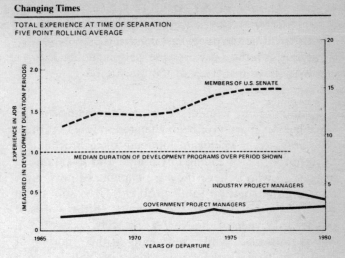

Figure 40. The turnover period for program management is very short in relation to the period of time required for development of new products.

In Figure 40 the longevity of project managers is compared with a metric based on the average longevity of the projects they manage—or, as will be determined in Figure 50, about 8.1 years. This latter period is thus equal to 1.0 on the vertical scale in Figure 40. As also shown in the figure in the case of the federal management process, the people at the top of the structure (the legislators) experience relatively *little* turnover. This is a consequence of the well-known fact that the best platform from which to run for elective office is the platform of the incumbent. It is just this dichotomy, aggravated by the very length of the government's procurement process, which in fact leads to Augustine's Law of Limited Liability:

LAW NUMBER XXX

By the time the people asking the questions are ready for the answers, the people doing the work have lost track of the questions.

Sometimes one wonders if perhaps the names on the organization chart have been changed simply to protect the *guilty*. As a Michigan politician once proclaimed, "I'm not afraid of hiding anything!" But even among executives who believe they are capable of personally dictating the solution to all problems, it is still useful to know the questions to the answers. In the words of pitcher Ed Lynch of the New York Mets, as quoted in *Sports Illustrated*, while "marveling at the erudition of teammate Ron Darling, a graduate of Yale," Lynch extolled, "I don't understand the *questions* of things he can *answer*."

31

Anonymity by Committee

"There go the people. I am their leader. I must follow them."

—A former mayor of Boston

"Something drastic must be done." So spoke the new factory manager, the fourth in three months, after but a few days on the job. This wasn't going to be as easy as it had looked. The project was unmistakably in-extremis. Quarterly reviews were being held on a weekly basis. Management, recognizing the criticality of improving communications with the work force, began a new series of meetings during which it spoke at the employees. From the viewpoint of the workers, the situation had degenerated into one of man exploiting man instead of the other way around as it had been under the previous leadership. The bright year-end profit picture painted by the public relations department was unfortunately diminished when it was found that of the $2 million reported earnings, $3 million had been derived

*from the sale of the research laboratory. It seemed
that insufficient talent was available to attack the
myriad of problems created by the earlier group
of managers. These problems were by now appearing at a frequency surpassing anything that
had even been hoped by the legal department—
which itself was rendered almost helpless by the
computerized legal research system it had been
trying to bring on-line. The solution was to form
everyone into committees. There were committees of Bear Catchers (salesmen), Bear Skinners
(factory-hands), Bean Counters (accountants),
and even of the corporate staff—the latter known
in some quarters as "Sea Gulls" for reasons not
altogether dignified but relating to their propensity to fly around the country leaving their
mark wherever they have alighted. This establishment of a profusion of committees would permit the focus of more talent on each problem as
it arose. Surprisingly, unlike most of the other
actions taken by the project's senior management, this one received widespread acclaim among
the entire work force. There were, as always, a
few skeptics—who in this case suggested that the
widespread support was merely a reflection of
the fact that under the old system too many problems were once again becoming embarrassingly
easy to associate with the responsibilities of specific individuals.*

It has long been recognized that the formation of a
committee is a powerful technique for avoiding responsibility, deferring difficult decisions, and averting
blame while at the same time maintaining a semblance

of action. It has also long been suspected that committees dealing with difficult and controversial issues generally accomplish little more in terms of resolving the issues than to agree to disagree and, of course, establish a follow-up committee. Will Rogers concluded, "Outside of traffic, there is nothing that has held this country back as much as committees."

Richard Harkness, as reported in the *New York Herald Tribune,* was even less charitable. He defines a committee as a group of the unwilling, picked from the unfit, to do the unnecessary.

Again borrowing the words of Kelly Johnson, the former head of Lockheed's Skunk Works, speaking on CBS Television's *Sixty Minutes,* "We're into the era where a committee designs the airplanes. You never do anything totally stupid, you never do anything totally bright. You get an average wrong answer. . . ."

But these minor albeit widely recognized shortcomings have in no way hampered the creation of committees, much to the joy of punsters who take pleasure in pointing out such pedantic observations as a camel is a horse designed by a committee. And, as might be suspected, the U.S. Congress is once again exerting its rightful role of leadership in the committee-proliferation arena, with the existence not only of a plethora of the customary congressional committees, but with the formation of, yes, a *Committee on Committees.* It is the duty of the Committee on Committees to assign members to other committees, which in turn assign members to the subcommittees of those committees, which in turn . . .

During William Ruckelshaus's initial term as head of the Environmental Protection Agency he is said to have reported to fifteen congressional committees. When he returned to that same job fifteen years later, he reported to forty-four.

Under one recent administration it was found that the federal government possessed no fewer than 1175 formal external advisory committees. A review of the utility of these committees (by a committee, undoubtedly) led to the conclusion that all but sixteen committees were indispensable and should therefore be perpetuated.

One committee of the North Atlantic Treaty Organization upon which the author once served actually had the audacity, upon completing its assigned task, to recommend that it be disbanded. This apparently sent out a tremor with which the organization could not contend since, when last seen some years later, the committee was continuing apace.

There is substantial evidence that it is impossible for two or more Americans to gather without forming a committee or group of some type. Each of these groups must of course be represented in Washington. Thus, we have the American Boiler Manufacturers Association, an American Canoe Association, a Concrete Pipe Association, and an Anti-Friction Bearing Manufacturers Association. There are associations of Chocolate Manufacturers, Meat Purveyors, Independent Corrugated Converters, Feed Manufacturers, and Blood Banks. There is the Association of Old Crows, the Public Gas Association, and the National Bark Producers (which leads to intriguing speculation as to membership). There is even an Association of Associations.

It turns out to be an extraordinarily challenging undertaking to attempt to actually measure the output of committees of various sizes, or, for that matter, of any size. Perhaps it is not simply happenstance that it seems to defy human imagination to identify instances wherein committees have been formed under circumstances which lead to *quantifiable* contributions. One, admittedly marginal, instance does seem to exist, however, which is an exception to this rule. This is the case of ad hoc "committees" which are created to undertake and report upon scientific research. By making the assumption that the contribution of a given piece of scientific work performed by these committees is somehow measurable in terms of the frequency with which that work is cited by other researchers as they in turn pursue their own work, one can perhaps assess the utility of the ad hoc committees themselves. The key assumption is, of course, that the value of a piece of work is proportional to the extent which that contribution is used to assist others in subsequent research. Presumably a work of no value will be relegated forever to the archives; a valuable piece of work, on the other hand, will resurface repeatedly as a building block in reference lists cited by future researchers.

Figure 41 examines a sample of 1300 research projects reported by various-size teams of authors in one technical publication. The illustration relates the *relative* frequency with which articles having various numbers of coauthors are cited in the "references" listed in support of later pieces of work by other authors.* It is

---

*In an effort to enhance objectivity in measuring worth, instances wherein authors cite their *own* prior work have been eliminated from these data. Agreements to cite each other's work remain unexpurgated! There also remains some statistical risk that articles in the particular journal examined and references cited in that journal may not be totally consistent sets. There appears to be little doubt, however, that the per capita "useful output" as measured herein diminishes significantly as committee size increases.

The More the Badder

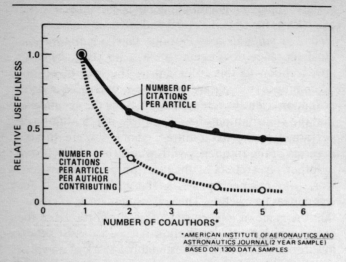

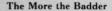

*AMERICAN INSTITUTE OF AERONAUTICS AND
ASTRONAUTICS JOURNAL (2 YEAR SAMPLE)
BASED ON 1300 DATA SAMPLES

Figure 41. Committees are a very popular management tool in government, industry, and academia. Measurements of the effectiveness of various sized committees using the number of coauthors of technical articles as a surrogate for committee size and the number of references to their work as a metric of usefulness do not produce encouraging findings for committee advocates.

found, interestingly, that as the number of coauthors increases, the number of citations *per article* clearly decreases. Further, if the number of citations is evaluated *per author* whose time is occupied (asserting, in effect, that each author might, alternatively, have been doing individual research), the above-mentioned trend is even more striking. * For some reason, articles written by committees of people are of less interest (and value?)

---

*It should be noted that there appears to be no evidence that projects involving multiple authors take less time than those involving single authors. In fact, one suspects that the opposite may be true.

to others than articles prepared by a single individual—
at least in the sizable randomly selected sample considered herein.

Thus, as shown in the figure, the least productive
committees have several members while the most productive "committee" evaluated has but one member.
Generalizing, if a committee of thirty is less good than
a committee of ten, which is in turn less good than a
committee of one, the Law of Rampant Committee-
manship can be derived by extrapolating toward the left
in the figure the data shown therein, with the following
result:

LAW NUMBER XXXI

The optimum committee has no members.

In this case, less is more. Or, as stated by Hesiod as
long ago as 700 B.C., "Fools, they do not even know
how much more is the half than the whole." Hendrik
Van Loon summarizes: "Nothing is ever accomplished
by committee unless it consists of three members, one
of whom happens to be sick and the other absent."

Committees have many other phenomena associated
with them. For example, the amount of time devoted
to the debate of a subject is *inversely* proportional to
the importance of the outcome. This is partly because
the items with major consequence often have obvious
answers ("Should we attempt a hostile takeover of
Company X which is fifty times our size?") whereas
issues offering little basis for choosing between them
naturally provoke disagreement ("Should the new caf-
eteria be carpeted or not?"). Furthermore, everyone is

an expert on carpets—very few on hostile takeovers of
industrial behemoths. Similarly, most negotiations that
collapse—for example, to purchase a new home—usually do so over the last few dollars. One committee
which included the senior leadership of the Pentagon
had the assigned purpose of overseeing the construction
of a new multibillion dollar command and control system (itself an arcane subject) and invariably devoted
the majority of its meetings to debating whether the
implementing contractor's award fee for the month should
be $220,000 or $240,000.

Correspondingly, a budget for a new magnetohydro-
dynamics test facility will be approved in minutes whereas
a new entrance to the plant will consume hours.

Another mystery commonly observed by committee
pathologists is that the time consumed in debate is dom-
inated by those with the least to offer (and to do). How
often, whether at a board of directors meeting or a
neighborhood association meeting, has one been subjected to interminable discussion only to have the resolution under consideration pass unanimously?

Committees have thus been dismissed, in the words
of Harry Chapman, with the following epitaph, in the
form of a series of rules: "Never arrive on time; this
stamps you as a beginner. Don't say anything until the
meeting is half over; this stamps you as wise. Be as
vague as possible; this avoids irritating the others. When
in doubt, suggest a subcommittee be appointed. Be the
first to move for adjournment; this will make you popular—it's what everyone is waiting for."

Although there is regrettably little evidence to support any projected demise of the committee as a social
institution, hope nonetheless springs eternal that the
committee problem may be self-healing. L. M. Boyd,

the writer, reports for example that the Ultrasaurus, a large dinosaur, had two brains. Boyd concluded that what led to its extinction may in fact have been no less than *committee* decisions. In any event, the notion seems sufficiently promising that it might be worth forming a committee or two to look into the prospect.

32

Caveat Emptor

"You know, I think you and I have some of
the same people working for each other."
—Nikita Khrushchev to Allen Dulles,
Director of CIA

*Having failed to alleviate the ever-increasing signs
of incipient financial collapse, and with disaster
lurking in the southeast corner of the profit and
loss statement, top management at last decided
to take truly decisive action. Thus a consultant
was hired. That this was a brilliant stroke became
evident when after only ten months' study, including two extensions to the consultant's re-
tainer, this advisor cut right to the heart of the
matter. "The problem," he said, when the managers had all been gathered to hear his findings,
"is that you are running out of money." Responding to questions, he continued in his incisive fashion, "Who has the most money in the
world? The U.S. government, of course. What
you must do is obtain a government contract.*

You then will become indispensable to the nation's well-being and the government just won't permit you to go broke." It must in candor be reported that the consultant's next suggestion was at first met with some guffaws—he proposed that Daedalus Aircraft, Inc., bid against several giant aerospace firms for a contract to build a real airplane. He pointed to all Daedalus's experience gained on Project X in attacking problems spanning from electronics failures and software bomb-outs to structural collapses and missed schedules. Further, he noted that the federal government actually prefers to do business with small firms and has a whole organization set up to help them win, including the use of subsidies, mostly paid for out of the taxes collected from big firms. But what clinched the deal was when he pointed out that the government would soon conduct a competition to select a company to manufacture the new, highly secret, "stealth" airplane—an airplane which had just been developed by another contractor and which had as its principal attribute that it was invisible. Now who could be better qualified than Daedalus to build an airplane one can't see? In fact, who would even be able to tell when one was built?

A consultant is an individual handsomely paid for telling senior management of problems, about which senior management's own employees have told the consultant. The consultant thus offers the advantage of generally having had no first-hand experience in the matters of interest, thereby assuring a clear mind uncluttered by any of the facts. "Make three correct guesses consecutively," says Laurence Peter, author of *The Peter Principle*, "and you will establish a reputation as an expert." Having done so and been elevated into management, there seems to be a large group of those who believe the secret of longevity is never again to make another decision. These are called Ready-Aim-Aim managers.

In the words of Sears World Trade Chairman and Chief Executive Officer Frank Carlucci, "Task forces are usually led by, if not composed of, people from outside the organization, so they will not be tainted by existing biases. It frequently happens that they are not tainted by any relevant experience, either." But with the day-to-day demands of managing and working on a project being what they are, it is usually concluded that only an external professional advisor would have readily available the ample free time necessary to undertake a study. Individuals slightly more astute than executives who hire advisors might conceivably be distracted by this paradox.

But the conduct of studies by consultants must nonetheless be concluded to be an extremely effective management technique, at least as attested to by its widespread use. Certainly, only a very powerful tool could enjoy such universal acclaim. The success enjoyed by such studies is shown in Figure 42, at least in the case of studies of the defense equipment procurement process. This figure depicts the actual number of investigations which have been conducted into that much suffering enterprise each year for the past two decades. An ever-increasing propensity to study is observed, punctuated by the *major* assessments that invariably

Major Studies of Defense Procurement

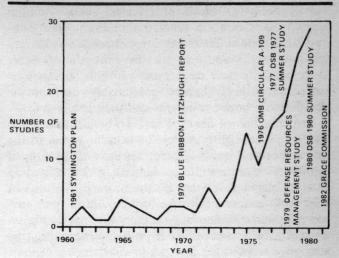

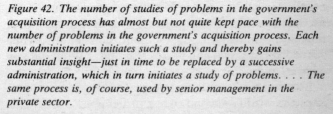

Figure 42. The number of studies of problems in the government's acquisition process has almost but not quite kept pace with the number of problems in the government's acquisition process. Each new administration initiates such a study and thereby gains substantial insight—just in time to be replaced by a successive administration, which in turn initiates a study of problems. . . . The same process is, of course, used by senior management in the private sector.

mark the beginning of each new administration or, in the case of industry, change in corporate leadership.*

Unfortunately, as has been noted, identifying *symptoms* of the maladies that torment business is relatively easy; this in fact forms the body of the canonical study for that very reason. The task of isolating the problems

---

*The author is indebted for the assistance of Richard Harris who, in the course of a review of the above-mentioned studies, provided the statistical data presented in the figure.

themselves is more complex and is thus afforded accordingly less attention. Offering *legitimate* solutions proves really difficult—and is, therefore, largely disregarded. But by far the greatest challenge of all, *implementing* solutions, is not the province of either consultants or their studies and can thus be safely ignored altogether. Thereby, presumably, deriveth the durability of both consultants *and* their studies.

Selecting the members of advisory boards to perform studies is a weighty matter, at least in terms of the amount of gold it can involve. Virtually all advisors of course offer impeccable credentials, which can easily lead to misinterpretation by the unwary. An advisor may well profess a "diverse background in both government and commercial endeavors with a long history of successful projects." That probably means that he was once responsible for coordinating the air support at the Bay of Pigs and in his salad days performed the market research leading to the Edsel. But he never missed a commission. All too many consultants, when asked "What is two and two?" respond, "What did you have in mind?"

It is thus not surprising that performing studies, perhaps the world's second oldest profession, is traditionally demeaned as being susceptible to practice by any individual possessing a briefcase and remaining at least fifty miles from where people know him. There are, fortunately, glaring exceptions to this piece of folklore; but, sadly, these exceptions are exceptions.

Consider the pathology of the canonical study. The first chapter invariably comprises a review of prior studies of the same topic and exhaustive discussion of the reasons why their findings were never implemented.

The growing body of studies in the archives makes this an avenue of ever-increasing promise. The second chapter typically recommends improved management accompanied by a better-motivated work force all bound together under a new organizational structure. The third and final chapter dutifully notes that the problem at hand has, unexpectedly, proven to be even more intractable than originally anticipated—and thus the initiation of three new studies is recommended. As La Rochefoucauld noted years ago, "Nothing is given so profusely as advice." It is noteworthy that La Rochefoucauld used the word "profusely" and not the word "freely."

From the perspective of a program's beleaguered participants who are the victims of a study, this new episode does promise a welcome respite from the day-to-day tribulations of pursuing the project—since further work must now await the consultants' report. Still better, an additional several months of diversion will generally ensue while the program's participants dutifully rebuff, one by one, all of the consultants' recommendations and demonstrate why each in turn should not be implemented because it either is impracticable or already has been implemented or both. The more prestigious the group of consultants, the longer the dismissal process necessarily consumes.

Publius Syrus observed, "Many receive advice, few profit by it." Some consultants will of course assert that their recommendations do have a chance. But then so did Custer.

Not just anyone can offer bad advice. The more impressive one's credentials, the better able one is to create chaos since those with less impeccable histories of accomplishment will usually be disregarded anyway. Consider the following potpourri from history, which serves as a warning to all would-be prognosticators:

- "We must not be misled to our own detriment to assume that the untried machine can displace the proved and tried horse."
    —Maj. Gen. John K. Herr, 1938
    U.S. Army

- "As far as sinking a ship with a bomb is concerned, it just can't be done."
    —RADM Clark Woodward, 1939
    U.S. Navy

- "The [flying] machines will eventually be fast; they will be used in sport but they should not be thought of as commercial carriers."
    —Octave Chanute, 1910
    Aviation Pioneer

- "I have not the smallest molecule of faith in aerial navigation other than ballooning."
    —Lord Kelvin, ca. 1870
    Physicist

- "While theoretically and technically television may be feasible, commercially and financially I consider it an impossibility, a development of which we need waste little time dreaming."
    —Lee DeForest, 1926
    Physicist

- "The energy produced by the breaking down of the atom is a very poor kind of thing. Anyone

who expects a source of power from the trans-
formation of these atoms is talking moonshine."
—Ernest Rutherford, ca. 1930
Physicist

• "We hope the professor from Clark College
[Robert H. Goddard] is only professing to be
ignorant of elementary physics if he thinks that
a rocket can work in a vacuum."
—Editorial, *The New York Times*, 1920

• (On the occasion of the dedication of a physics
laboratory in Chicago, noting that the more important physical laws had all been discovered):
"Our future discoveries must be looked for in
the sixth decimal place."
—A. A. Michelson, 1894
Physicist

• "Fooling around with alternating currents is just
a waste of time. Nobody will use it, ever. It's
too dangerous . . . it could kill a man as quick
as a bolt of lightning. Direct current is safe."
—Thomas Edison, ca. 1880
Inventor

• "Rail travel at high speeds is not possible because passengers, unable to breathe, would die
of asphyxia."
—Dionysius Lardner (1793–1859)

• "What, sir, would you make a ship sail against
the wind and currents by lighting a bonfire under
her deck? I pray you excuse me. I have no time

to listen to such nonsense."
—Napoleon to Robert Fulton, ca. 1800

- "That is the biggest fool thing we have ever done. . . . The [atomic] bomb will never go off, and I speak as an expert in explosives."
—Adm. William Leahy, U.S. Navy, to President Truman, 1945

- "Space travel is utter bilge."
—Sir Richard van der Riet Wooley, The Astronomer Royal, 1956

- "X rays are a hoax." —Lord Kelvin, ca. 1880

In the words of the eminent scientist Niels Bohr, "Prediction is very difficult, especially about the future."

Augustine's Law of Analytical Alchemy, germane to the proliferation of studies and advisors, can be stated in its least charitable form as follows:

LAW NUMBER XXXII

Hiring consultants to conduct studies can be an excellent means of turning problems into gold—your problems into their gold.

But a lifetime of providing advice and performing studies does exact its price. The very insulation of their profession from both the hazards and the excitement of hands-on involvement implies that its practitioners must be satisfied with the more vicarious pleasures of the workplace. Illustrative of this necessity, a recent Army recruiting poster portrayed a grizzled soldier in an airborne division proudly proclaiming, "I hate to jump; I just like to be around the kind of people who do." Lucius Aemilius Paulus, the Roman consul who was to lead the war against the Macedonians some twenty centuries ago, summarized the situation with a bit more learned verbiage but comparable perceptiveness:

> I am not one of those who think that commanders ought at no time to receive advice; on the contrary, I should deem that man more proud than wise who regulated every proceeding by the standard of his own single judgment. What then is my opinion?
>
> That commanders should be counseled, chiefly, by persons of known talent; by those who have made the art of war their particular study, and whose knowledge is derived from experience; from those who are present at the scene of action, who see the country, who see the enemy; who see the advantages that occasions offer, and who, like people embarked in the same ship, are sharers of the danger. If, therefore, anyone thinks himself qualified to give advice respecting the war which I am to conduct, which may prove advantageous to the public, let him not refuse his assistance to the state, *but let him come with me into Macedonia.*

Occasionally an advisor with a distaste for Macedonia will still contribute exactly the piece of information or perform precisely the study needed to resolve an otherwise seemingly unsolvable problem. Such cases can

generally be characterized as involving advisors or groups
of advisors who, first, have hands-on experience in the
field of concern; second, are constructive "doers" rather
than mere "viewers" (or worse yet, "viewers with
alarm"); third, offer a truly independent perspective;
and, fourth, are willing to devote the not inconsiderable
personal effort demanded to understand the intricacies
of the management and technical problems at hand—
in short, to beome engaged. *These* individuals *are* worth
their weight in gold. But absent such individuals, together with a sponsor who is truly interested in doing
something about the problem at hand (other, that is,
than studying it), it is advisable to give further study to
the idea of initiating a study.

"The headquarters review team arrived."

PART V

IMPENDING
DISASTER

33

Profiting from One's Inexperience

"Another such victory over the Romans and we
are undone."

—Plutarch

Although it was unbeknown to Daedalus's management at the time, the government's preparatory work on the invisible airplane project had much in common with Project X. The government also had stretched the schedule, reorganized, increased the number of layers of management, and hired a consultant—all to no avail. On the other hand, the government, having a great deal more experience than Daedalus at such expedients, moved to the next step almost automatically, a step which is based on the premise that if there is not enough production to support one contractor efficiently, it is then necessary to simultaneously place a second contractor into production so as to enhance competition and thereby increase efficiency. This is much akin to trying to leap deep chasms in two bounds. Nonetheless, this is exactly what the government's manager of this grim fairy tale elected to do. Somehow when the government sets out to put an end to problems, it usually does so by forming the firing squad by standing everyone in a circle. And industry's managers also decided to go for broke. As the saying among development contractors faced with second-source production competitions such as was being proposed here states, "If someone shows you a gun and asks for money, he is not necessarily trying to sell you the gun." Under such circumstances the underdog quickly becomes the overdog— which was just exactly what Daedalus needed.

Certainly there is nothing more sacred to most industrialists than that competition is the foundation of the free enterprise system—except, of course, the opportunity for an uncontended sole source contract. Almost all managers strongly endorse competition—for the other person's business.

Among the most effective means available to a purchaser for controlling cost while achieving superior product performance is to exploit competition among several potential suppliers. But even competition must be applied carefully, or unwanted results occur. Consider, for example, the practice occasionally used by industry as well as government of awarding the *production* contract for a *newly* developed item to whatever firm is the low bidder. This has the unquestioned advantage of driving down bid prices—and the disadvantage of sometimes creating a producer which has a convenient degree of optimism in pricing, coupled with a total lack of familiarity with the hard-earned lessons of how one actually goes about producing the product in question, lessons which were at least partially learned over years of agonizing effort by the developer. This lack of knowledge and experience is certainly no handicap to the uninitiated manufacturer insofar as submitting a low bid is concerned. Watching such a competition cannot help but remind one of the novice parachutist who, upon failing to successfully open his chute on his initial jump, saw to his amazement as he descended toward the ground, another individual flying *upward* past him. Calling out to the passer-by, "Do you know anything about parachutes?" he was chagrined to receive the answer, "No . . . do you know anything about gas stoves?"

Such pairings of unsuspecting purchasers and providers often become a case of competition at any cost, and upon the award of such competitive, often fixed-price contracts, the ecstasy of the marketing department is generally exceeded only by the foreboding of the finance department, which, in turn, is surpassed only by the eager anticipation of the legal department. Worse yet, the winner is often the type of company that, given a contract to teach a frog to swim, would probably end up drowning the frog.

"This is the time," according to Bert Fowler, senior vice-president of The MITRE Corporation, "when grown men gather in a room in each company and spend their time not trying to decide what the cost [of the job] would really be, but trying to guess what the grown men in the other rooms are going to guess." It's like trying to read the mind of people who haven't yet made up their mind. An executive of the Lockheed Corporation once referred to this practice as "You bet your company."

Will Rogers could have been alluding to the use of

competitive breakout procurements soon after development is completed when he remarked, "Claremore, Oklahoma, is just waiting for a high-tension line so they can go ahead with locating an airport."

In the words of John Ruskin a century ago,

> It's unwise to pay too much but it is worse to pay too little. When you pay too much, you lose a little money—that is all. When you pay too little, you sometimes lose everything, because the thing you bought was incapable of doing the thing it was bought to do. The common law of business balance prohibits paying a little and getting a lot—it can't be done. If you deal with the lowest bidder, it is well to add something for the risk you run. And if you do that, you will have enough to pay for something better.

The data in Figure 43 verify that major bid-price reductions are indeed obtainable by placing a number of potential producers in competition for an item developed by one specific contractor. In eleven different studies of competitive procurement the median savings in *bid* prices produced was about 28 percent. These data do not, however, examine whether the winning bidder was ever actually able to manufacture a useful and reliable end product—at the bid price or, for that matter, any other price. This is not to suggest that when problems do occur there is insufficient blame to be shared by all the program's participants: winners, losers, even innocent bystanders. The original developer, which in all likelihood itself underestimated the cost at the outset of the development, generally takes the viewpoint expressed by semanticist and ex-senator S. I. Hayakawa:

Effect of Competition on Price

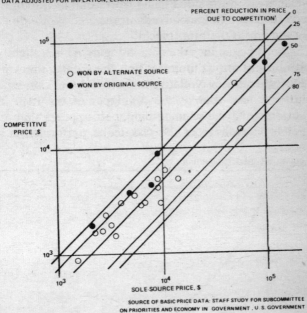

DATA ADJUSTED FOR INFLATION, LEARNING-CURVE AND QUANTITY

PERCENT REDUCTION IN PRICE
DUE TO COMPETITION

○ WON BY ALTERNATE SOURCE
● WON BY ORIGINAL SOURCE

COMPETITIVE
PRICE ,$

SOLE-SOURCE PRICE, $

SOURCE OF BASIC PRICE DATA: STAFF STUDY FOR SUBCOMMITTEE
ON PRIORITIES AND ECONOMY IN GOVERNMENT , U. S. GOVERNMENT

Figure 43. Competitive procurements have, in general, resulted in price reductions on the order of 28 percent—but there are other prices to be considered as well.

"We should keep it. We stole it fair and square." Or, as Johnny Rutherford was quoted as saying after winning the 1980 Indianapolis 500, "I honestly didn't cheat any more than anyone else." This same concept has led an occasional development contractor to graciously offer to reduce the cost of a financially beleaguered development program by altogether eliminating the data package, which is the document that would enable some other contractor to build the product in place of the developer! This is, of course, the corporate equivalent of two birds in the hand being worth one in the bush. Stated in Br'er Rabbit's words, it means "*Please* don't throw me into the briar patch!"

Figure 44 examines the data in Figure 43 in a slightly different fashion. It indicates that the greater the winner's price reduction relative to the developer's original price, the less likely is the developer of the item in question to be the winning bidder. It appears that an intimate knowledge of the task to be performed is a

Counterproductive Production

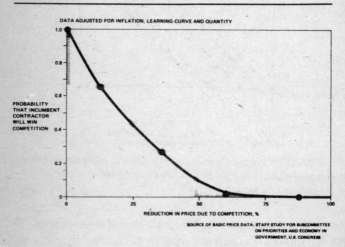

Figure 44. In cases where the incumbent is performing superbly, tooling costs are relatively high, production volume low, or the "data package" telling how to build an item is incomplete, competition for production is usually counterproductive. The attempt to force competition in such instances increases the tendency for the least qualified producers to win programs which they are incapable of executing. It is known as competition at any price.

nearly insurmountable handicap under such conditions. But it must be noted in fairness that some companies do in fact manage to win intensely competed breakout or second-source contracts—whereas others merely go on to be successful. Winning a second-source competition and actually making money is the economic equivalent of finding land on the unseen property one has bought in Florida. According to Oscar Wilde, "There are two kinds of tragedy. One is not getting what you want. The other is getting it."

As one midwestern farmer, suffering the plight of agriculture in the 1980s, remarked upon winning a million dollar lottery and being asked what he planned to do with the money, "I guess I'll just go back to farming until it's all gone."

There *must* be a message in here somewhere. Perhaps the prior participants in the program simply suffer from being grossly experienced. Several interpretations are possible of this phenomenon of the loose cannon, in the form of a marginally qualified, low-balling bidder, on the deck of a breakout procurement. One of these is expressed, with apologies to Alexander Pope, in the Law of Incipient Disaster, which is also known as the Law of Conservation of Misery:

LAW NUMBER XXXIII

Fools rush in where incumbents fear to bid.

Shakespeare in *Richard III* alludes to this problem in summary fashion:

> . . . the world is grown so bad
> That wrens make prey where eagles dare not perch.

The net impact of unknowledgeable bidders in major fixed-price competitions is thus, to borrow from another context an expression of Irving Bluestone, vice-president of the United Auto Workers, "somewhat analogous to the cross-eyed discus thrower: he seldom comes out ahead, but he sure does keep the crowd alert."

And the knowledgeable bidders, confronted with such an untenable predicament, in turn often do the only honorable thing left: They insert some fine print into the contract.

Thus, in such competitions there is a customer, a loser, and the other contractor—who is going broke, too.

It was the above law that a military aviator, in whose helicopter the author occasionally had the privilege of flying, apparently had in mind when he added to the "caution and warning" stickers that traditionally abound in the cockpits of modern rotary-wing aircraft, the following hand-lettered admonition: "Caution. This helicopter built by the lowest bidder."

Sometimes it is best simply to leave bad enough alone.

34

Justice Deserts

"Fool me once, shame on you.
Fool me twice, shame on me."
—American Indian expression

But how could a tiny, unknown firm like Dae-
dalus Aircraft, Inc.—particularly when most of
its "Inc." was red—possibly hope to defeat two
giant corporations for the production of the
world's first invisible airplane? The choice seemed
to be between the clearly disastrous and the merely
unpalatable. Little did Daedalus's management
realize at the time that being unknown might
prove to be their greatest asset. But just as the
saying goes, anybody can win—unless there is
another entrant. Or, in this case, two of them.
Each of the other competitors was in fact an
established industrial mammoth with a long rec-
ord of doing business with the government. Dae-
dalus's secret weapon lay in the government's
procurement policy, wherein everyone is treated
equally—absolutely equally—independent of

*demonstrated competence or anything else. In
addition, Daedalus found several other strong
arguments it could use in its favor. First, the
government was in the midst of a campaign to
force its contractors to adopt the metric system—
so, by the stroke of the pen, changing "inches"
to "meters" on the drawings of all its past model
airplane products, Daedalus could show a great
deal of growth potential. Second, Daedalus would
propose that upon winning it would go hire at a
reduced salary all the then-unneeded employees
away from the two big losing contractors and
thereby somehow save a lot of money. The government historically believes this logic while simultaneously believing that no employees should
have a reduction in benefits as a result of competition. Third, and most convincing of all, Daedalus once again took upon itself a new name as
it moved to meet this greatest challenge in its
history. Daedalus Aerospace, Ltd., specializing
in the manufacture of invisible aircraft, was thus
born. It was a case of do unto others before they
do unto you.*

"To err is human, but it is against company policy," or
so the saying goes. But it is certainly not against government procurement policy or even against the purchasing policy of many companies. When it comes to
selecting suppliers for future work, cold logic sometimes
falls victim to the "But we've always dealt with Acme"
syndrome. In this matter, the individual consumer probably represents the most effective procurement force.

Would any private consumer, for example, continue
to patronize a seller which had just charged more for

an item than had been indicated in the original estimate, delivered the article later than promised, and capped this off by changing the management being dealt with three times during the course of the purchase? Not likely. Yet this has been relatively common in the sophisticated process used in making major purchases, leading to what can be referred to as the "Lemming Approach to Procurement." That is not to suggest that there are no extenuating circumstances from the perspective of both the seller and the buyer. There are. But to perpetuate a procurement policy founded, perhaps even floundered, on the virtues of amnesia would seem to be contrary to the very foundation of the free enterprise system.

Many contractors, explaining away customer disappointment with their past efforts, subscribe to Frank Lloyd Wright's viewpoint. "When I was ninety," said Wright, "I was asked to single out my finest work. My answer was 'My next one.' "

Figure 45 presents evidence that whatever other problems may be attributable to the contract award process, it is at least free from discrimination. Free from discrimination, that is, in the sense that it treats good performers and poor performers with equanimity. The figure displays for a number of major governmental source selections the relative ranking of the winning and losing bidders in terms of one important measure of past performance: the degree of cost control exhibited on their in-being major programs with the same customer making the new purchase, assessed at the time of the prospective award. Were all the data points to cluster in the lower-right-hand corner of the figure, one might conclude that contractors which performed well in the past were more likely to win new business in the

Do Unto Others As They Have Done Unto You

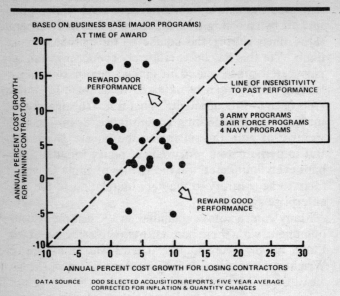

Figure 45. The process of selecting a contractor to undertake a project generally gives little formal consideration to the past records of the contending firms. Only slight correlation is found between cost control on previous contracts and the likelihood of winning future awards.

future and, likewise, that poor performers were less likely to be future winners. But, as seen from the lack of any such correlation in the data, the extant version of turning the other cheek seems merely to be to turn the other check. In essence, then, in the source selection process accumulation of, say, twenty years' experience with a poor performing supplier more accurately corresponds to accumulating one year's experience twenty times.

These results generally agree with the findings of a companion qualitative investigation which rated competing contractors on all aspects of their past record (cost, schedule, performance, etc.) rather than on cost alone. The correlation coefficient between winning in source selection evaluations and past performance ranking among the competitors was a mere 0.1 on a scale where zero once again indicates total randomness and unity indicates perfect correlation. Some encouragement may, perhaps, be taken from a trend in the more recent data points to recognize and reward good performance . . . only time will tell.

As Carl Ajello, Attorney General of Connecticut, puts it, "History is important. If you don't know where you have been, you damn sure don't know where you are going." H. L. Mencken even coined a phrase which can be applied to those who repeatedly fall victim to such oversight; borrowing from the better-known bourgeoisie, he refers to this new class as the "booboisie."

As mentioned above, the private citizen seems to have hit upon a solution to this source selection problem, not only in day-to-day purchases but also in the important matter of electing a president. The criterion in use for the latter is simply to select the taller of the two principal candidates—a criterion which has applied in twenty of the last twenty-one presidential elections. The single departure from this rule was in 1976, when Jimmy Carter pulled a three-inch upset. Those who would dismiss this occurrence as a probabilistic quirk should be forewarned that on a statistical basis the odds against having so few exceptions are about 100,000 to 1.

None of the above is to suggest that the assessment of past performance of politicians or even of contractors is particularly easy—only that at least the latter is some-how done millions of times every day by homeowners shopping, children buying candy, and, interestingly, many prime contractors dealing with *their* vendors. Real prob-lems certainly do exist: How should a new firm with no track record whatsoever, either good or bad, be rated? How should a satisfactorily performing firm acquired by a poor performer be ranked? How should a sister division of a notoriously poor performer within the same firm be treated? Or how, as actually happened in one major competition run by the federal government, should past performance be allocated when the president of one of the competing firms suddenly leaves and be-comes president of the other? Who then gets charged with or credited for his track record? Further, changes in management or even management emphasis may more than offset past problems; thus, the objective must al-ways be to maximize the chances of success in the future and not merely to assure vengeance for the past. But the practice of engaging in a source selection process which embraces no apparent memory of either past successes or past transgressions would seem to perpet-uate the belief that each time at bat is the beginning of a new season—and thereby reap all the liabilities of the widespread suspicion that Augustine's Law of the Phoe-nix must indeed be operating:

LAW NUMBER XXXIV

The process of competitively selecting contrac-tors to perform work is based on a system of rewards and penalties, all distributed ran-domly.

Under such circumstances, there will inevitably be individuals and firms who adopt the policy that "It is a pleasure to do business to you." This can, unfortunately, lead to many truly forgettable experiences.

35

A Precise Guess

"A horse that can count to ten is a remarkable horse,
not a remarkable mathematician."

—Samuel Johnson

*The new corporate name had enormously en-
hanced Daedalus's credibility and stature, both
in the stock market—where its shares were
booming—and among the government's contract award evaluators. Encouragement was also
taken from the reports coming in from field offices that as yet no one had seen any invisible
airplane built by their competitors. But those
unfortunate employees who had been assigned
the unenviable task of writing Daedalus Aerospace, Ltd.'s very first proposal to do government work were struggling mightily because of
the lack of concrete evidence that could be cited
where the pen meets the paper. The solution
almost certainly resided somewhere in citing voluminous facts, figures, and statistics—the red
meat of proposal writing. As Benjamin Disraeli*

pointed out long ago, there are individuals who use statistics as a drunkard uses a lamppost: for support rather than for illumination. This observation actually proved to be a valuable piece of insight to the Literary Engineers (almost a non sequitur—most American-born engineers speak two foreign languages: Fortran and English) who were writing Daedalus's proposal and who needed to justify their very existence armed with only the most tenuous of facts. The search thus not unexpectedly turned to methods of making the unknown, indeed even the unknowable, appear plausible to those who insist upon knowing. A powerful technique was soon discovered—thanks to Mr. Disraeli.

In the late 1950s a well-known Princeton geology professor answered a question about the age of a fossil that a student had just found by stating, with considerable authority, that it was two million and two years old. Responding to still another inquiry by students incredulous over his ability so precisely to date such an old object, he explained that another group had visited the same site two years earlier and had been told by a local farmer that the fossil was then two million years old.

In much the same vein, it is said to be commonplace for speechwriters for politicians, when encountering a morsel of soft logic, to annotate the margin with the advice, "Speak loudly—weak point."

Consider the following evidence: As reported to the Congress at the time development was to be initiated, the total program cost for the Navy's Harpoon missile program was stated to be $1,031.8 million. For the Air Force A-10 aircraft program, the corresponding cost was defined as $2,489.7 million. Not $2,400 million; not even $2,489 million. Rather, the cost would be two thousand four hundred eighty-nine *point seven* million dollars.

In the case of the Navy's F-18 aircraft program it was originally stated to the Congress that the cost would be twelve billion eight hundred seventy-five point three million dollars. A few years later an updated version of the same report listed the probable cost as twenty-four billion twenty-three million—and (still!) point three million dollars. Perhaps encouragement should be derived simply from the fact that, although the first significant figure did double, it was possible to maintain the last one unchanged.

This great degree of accuracy may perhaps be somewhat surprising to the uninitiated in view of the fact that, as already noted, history shows the first digit of past program cost estimates to have been in error, on the average, by about 100 percent.

Detailed analyses by the author show that although the initial digit in program cost estimates is virtually never correct, the last digit does prove to be correct about 10 percent of the time. This is sometimes called Augustine's principle of the last digit.

George Will, writing about a recent tax bill, describes the application of this technique of quoting great precision in conjunction with imprecise numbers in the following words: "[The President] pretended the tax bill wasn't really a tax increase—odd, considering it is supposed to siphon in $98.3 billion. (Note the precision—'.3'—from people who have been unable to guess the deficit within forty billion dollars.)" George Will had thus broken the code.

Other examples of the preservation of the last-digit principle of cost estimating? The Sydney Opera House (to have been built in six years, but which took sixteen) was to have cost 7.2 million Australian dollars but actually cost 102 million dollars. As already noted, English taxpayers were to have paid 160 million pounds for the development of the Concorde supersonic transport but eventually were billed 1,065.0 million. (Note that an initial estimate ending in "zero" assures the success of this methodology.) To prove that agony knows no international boundaries, the Bay Area Rapid Transit ("BART") in San Francisco grew from an estimated $0.6 billion to $1.6 billion in the matter of a few short years.

The whole process is something akin to "getting the last word"—in this case, "getting the last digit." But, then, one must start somewhere.

Nonetheless, by examining the data in Figure 46, it is possible to derive the logic [sic] which underlies the practice of quoting fundamentally dubious numbers with a very great degree of apparent accuracy. It is seen from the figure that there is indeed a relationship between the number of "significant figures" quoted and the true precision of the data at hand, but this relationship is just the opposite of what one might suspect if one didn't suspect so much. When quoting, for example, something so exact as the number of days in the week, the recognized sources merely indicate "7." But when stating the time at which the last flight from Atlanta to Washington, D.C., occurs on a Friday evening, an event which is almost *always* delayed by at least an hour, the official source book records the time with great exactness—10:43 p.m., to be specific.

Augustine's Law of Definitive Imprecision, which is based on a substantive collection of data such as that presented in Figure 46, therefore states:

LAW NUMBER XXXV

The weaker the data available upon which to base one's conclusion, the greater the precision which should be quoted in order to give the data authenticity.

The use of the above law is actually fairly widespread, with one example being the Army's official estimate included in a long-term contract of the inflation index which will prevail for procurement in the sixteenth year from the time of the estimate (i.e., in 1995). This index was stated to be 2.6719—five-figure accuracy—an amazing feat of prescience, particularly in view of the White House Office of Management and Budget's near-simultaneous adjustment of the inflation rate for the next twelve months by about three percentage points!

Similar confidence in projecting future international political situations is reflected in a document published by the government during 1980 with the marking prominently displayed on its cover, "Declassified on 10 January 2000." Not 1 January, *10* January. At the top of Vail Mountain in Colorado where the ski gondola culminates its rise to an elevation of over 11,000 feet, is a sign that warns, "Maximum number of passengers: 6; Maximum Weight: 2177 pounds." Now for anyone versed in structural mechanics and wondering whether someone might have sneaked an extra sandwich on board,

such a four-figure calculation would border on the su-
pernatural—however, who would allow themselves to
hang precariously from a gondola that bore a sign merely
warning, "Maximum weight: about 1 ton"? In the words
of Will Rogers, it is quite literally true that in business
as in riding gondolas, "Numbers don't mean nothin'.
It's people that count."

Exactly Wrong

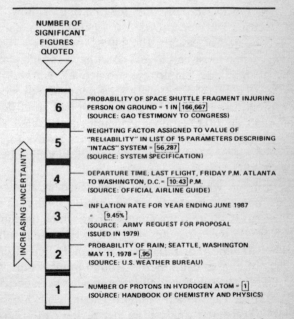

*Figure 46. The precision with which any given numerical factor is
known should presumably be reflected in the number of significant
figures with which it is quoted. This is in practice seldom the case,
thereby leading to misinterpretation of the confidence which is
assignable to data.*

Borrowing an example from the business sector to assure that there is no favoritism, there is the U.S. Trust Company's announcement that there are 574,342 people in the United States with assets worth $1 million or more. One cannot help but wonder how such an assessment could be made; or how the marginal qualifiers fared in the hour-by-hour vagaries of the stock market; or if one of them might not have dropped a few grand at the race track and failed to have promptly informed the U.S. Trust Company. Or, for that matter, how the U.S. Census Bureau knows "In 1980 the U.S. labor force consisted of exactly 104,449,817 workers"—particularly when most employers don't have any idea how many of their own employees are actually workers. It may be that this is all simply a consequence of more widespread use in financial circles than had heretofore been realized of O'Brien's Principle, also called the $357.73 theory, which states, "Auditors always reject any expense account with a bottom line divisible by 5 or 10."

A problem which has long been faced in applying Augustine's Law Number XXXV has been what to do in those cases wherein the analysis from which the numbers were derived provides only rather discrete results, such as $10 billion, or 100 miles, or 1 ton. Samuel Johnson has of course cautioned, "Round numbers are always fake." The solution to this dilemma has been derived by Air Force Lieutenant General Glenn Kent, himself a highly respected analyst, in his reviews of a large number of quantitative investigations. His solution is quite simple: It consists of simply converting all data from the English system of measures into the metric system!

A derivative of this English-to-metric technique,

wherein 39.4 inches of course equates to 1 meter, accounts for such phenomenal accuracies as are identified in a bulletin recently carried in the United States from a European wire service source concerning a citizen whose private airplane was reported to have missed crashing into the control tower at an airport in Europe "by less than 39.4 inches."

That such undeserved precision can be hazardous, particularly when combined with Law XVIII (which was already promulgated on page 158 to show the unreliability of electronics), is made abundantly clear in the following excerpt from a news article carried by the Associated Press regarding "a fuel shortage which caused a Boeing 767 to make an emergency landing. . . . The plane, with 61 passengers and a crew of eight, went into a powerless glide from 39,930 feet to a bumpy landing on a Gimli, Manitoba airstrip. . . . Airline workers had resorted to a manual fueling procedure when an electronic system on the aircraft . . . failed. The fuel in the craft is measured in centimeters and converted to liters before departure. That figure is converted to pounds and then to kilograms so that the pilot can calculate the flight plan. It was during this procedure that the error was made, the airline spokesman said." What is apparently needed is a universal approach to business—and American managers are doing their best to attain it as they follow their customary practice that as soon as another bad management procedure is discovered, they promptly seek to export it.

A related concept for seeking confidence through dubious accuracy appears to have been used in testimony provided to the Congress by the General Accounting Office in which it was stated that the chances of a person on the ground being injured by a falling piece of a Space

Shuttle launched from Kennedy Space Center "are 1 in 166,667." It may or may not be coincidence that 1 chance in 166,667 equates almost precisely to 6 divided into 1,000,000. But one would not be nearly as safe knowing that the chances of being hit on the head by a falling piece of the Space Shuttle are about "half a dozen in a million" as when the probability of that happening is a single chance in *one hundred sixty-six thousand six hundred sixty-seven*. Exactly.

In the same vein of reporting the uncertain with great certainty, the Associated Press released the following story rife with precision concerning the impending crash to earth of the Soviet Cosmos 1902 satellite: ". . . tracking experts said later in the day that the satellite . . . would re-enter the atmosphere between 4:45 a.m. MST Sunday and 6:17 a.m. MST Monday. . . ." Then in a burst of candor the AP continued, ". . . with Sunday evening the most likely time."

A story in *USA Today* about Storer Communications similarly noted, with three-digit precision, "Analysts say the shares would be worth between $85 to $117 in a takeover." Such advice must be terribly helpful to investors teetering on the brink of a major investment decision.

NASA itself embraces the use of such precision, reporting to the press after the first Shuttle launch that the fuel consumed cost "approximately $72,936.90." Not to be outdone, the National Football League tells us that the average weight of its players is exactly 221.84 pounds, and the Federal Education Data Acquisition Council estimates "9,495,967 man-hours will be spent filling out forms" in a given year. Clearly, that sort of intolerable situation is much more likely to stir beleaguered citizens into action than if only about ten million hours were going to be spent.

Still another approach for the creation of exactness underlies the fiscal year 1979 appropriation of $25.418 million for one element of the Navy's Aegis fleet air defense system. Certainly, a great deal of detailed study must have been required to define the program's funding needs with such specificity. But, alas, when scrutinized more closely, it is found that the figure is merely the result of a compromise brought about by a dispute between the House and Senate whereby a lump sum of $11 million was for some reason simply patched on top of the original request by the President, which was for $14.418 million! Similar results are commonplace where the two Houses of Congress compromise by dividing *precisely* in two the difference between the rough estimates embraced by one or the other bodies.

But there are times that it pays to be very, very precise in one's calculations, as the Rohm & Haas Co. discovered in its dealings with the Internal Revenue Service as reported by the Knight-Ridder Newspapers: "The Internal Revenue Service contended that Rohm & Haas Co. owed it $4,488,112.98 in payroll taxes for the period that ended June 30, 1983. The giant chemical manufacturer had deposited $4,488,112.88—exactly 10 cents less. One month later, Rohm & Haas received a notice from the IRS's Philadelphia service center. The agency sought a penalty for the 10-cent late payment. The penalty: $46,806.37."

For sheer audacity in applying Law XXXV, however, not even the GAO, the IRS, and the Congress *combined* can rival Sir Arthur Eddington. Eddington begins his scholarly book *The Philosophy of Physical*

Science with the observation: "I believe there are 15,747,724,136,275,002,577,605,653,961,181,555,468,-044,717,914,527,116,709,366,231,425,076,185,631,031,-296 protons in the universe and the same number of electrons." One can only marvel at the contribution which has been made to scientific knowledge by the digital computer; such a high-confidence analysis would never have been possible with a slide rule.

George Gamow, in his book *One, Two, Three . . . Infinity*, provided useful advice to those who are infatuated with large numbers:

> There was a young fellow from Trinity
> Who took $\sqrt{\infty}$
> But the number of digits
> Gave him the fidgets;
> He dropped math and took up Divinity.*

Actually, Sir Josiah Stamp, Her Majesty's Collector of Inland Revenue, was well on the track of Law Number XXXV nearly a century ago, except that he applied it only to the government and neglected its frequent use by industry, academia, and others. Sir Josiah pointed out, "The Government are [sic] extremely fond of amassing great quantities of statistics. These are raised to the nth degree, the cube roots are extracted, and the results are arranged into elaborate and impressive displays. What must be kept ever in mind, however, is that in every case, the figures are first put down by a

---

* $\sqrt{\infty}$ is the mathematical symbol for "the square root of infinity."

village watchman, and he puts down anything he damn well pleases!"

In the vernacular of the modern computer age, this is simply and widely known as "GIGO": Garbage in . . . Garbage out. Or even more devastatingly, Garbage in . . . Gospel out.

36

Paper Airplanes

"I read part of it all the way through."
— Samuel Goldwyn

It was the twenty-fourth day of December and the government, after a mere ten months' administrative delay, had finally released the Request for Proposal* to industry soliciting bids for what many said would be a program the likes of which had never before been seen. The veteran proposal writers at each of Daedalus's huge competitors of course already knew that the government always releases Requests for Proposals on the twenty-fourth of December. That is why "RFP" is a four-letter word. For over three years

---

*A Request for Proposal, or "RFP" (pronounced "R-fuh-P"), is a document issued by a customer seeking goods or services which prescribes the properties of the item being sought, the schedule on which it is needed, etc., and forms the basis of the would-be supplier's proposal: The RFP document can often be very long, laborious, and tedious, depending upon the complexity of the item or service sought—and upon the number of lawyers on the customer's staff.

*the two giant firms had been hard at work pre-
paring themselves for this day. Operating divisions within their mammoth organizations had
been forming teams with divisions from other
immense corporations who on other days would
have been their fierce rivals. An alternative would
of course have been to form teams with sister-
divisions from their own companies; however,
this is rarely done because of the prohibitive difficulty of cooperating with one's own corporate
colleagues. Giant teams had sprung into action
preparing the proposal documents which would
be submitted to the government, with the engineering departments struggling to grind out
market-oriented sales documents, the finance
departments wrestling with the problems of estimating the engineering man-hours that would
be needed to develop a microprocessor, and the
marketing departments determining the actual
cost of the program which would be bid. This
would be a particularly challenging project because of the urgent need to recover during the
production effort the two years which had been
lost while the government tried to decide whether
it was really worth undertaking this now absolutely crucial program to develop the essential
new airplane. Thus were the makings of what
would prove to be, truly, a crash project.*

Modern alchemists of the aerospace industry, having
presumably despaired of turning lead into gold, have
progressed into taking what used to be aluminum and
turning it into paper. That they have done so with con-

siderable alacrity is indicated by the fact that the most
critical aerospace material is no longer cobalt, titanium,
or chromium, but is now widely considered to be wood
pulp. This situation has not prevailed since the halcyon
days of Howard Hughes's famed plywood aircraft known
as the Spruce Goose. In fact, the only material playing
a more pivotal role than paper in aerospace today is
celluloid, commonly used in the thousands of viewgraphs which are required to subdue would-be opponents of proposed projects by briefing them into
submission.

Figure 47 relates the number of pages in typical proposals for new projects to the dollar value of the programs they potentially produce, the latter based on the
plan at the time the proposal was submitted. The points
above the trend line often correspond to projects deemed
by the contractor to have significant "growth" potential
(of one kind or another) while those below the line may
have been page-limited by fiat or discounted in value
by the competitors due to the likelihood of premature
project cancellation. An important underlying measure
of merit for proposals is derivable from the data shown
and is called the "Load Factor" (often misused to represent acceleration levels or passenger occupancy in
commercial aircraft), and is found by dividing the height
of the pile of paper required to compete for a project
by the dollar-value of the project.

The empirically determined value of the single-copy
Load Factor for programs in the multimillion-dollar range
is seen to be approximately one millimeter per million.
It is believed to be significant that this factor implies
that the pile of paper required to compete for a billion-
dollar program, assuming the traditional fifty copies are
submitted, must equal the "worth" of that program as

The Grossest National Product

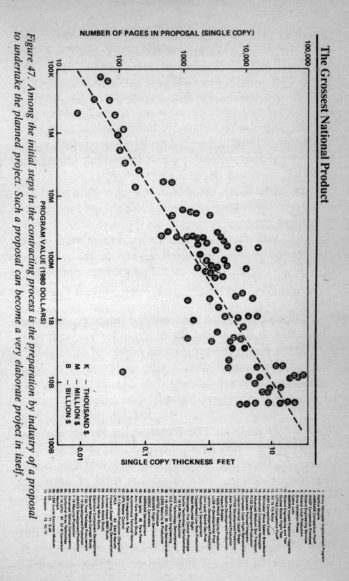

Figure 47. Among the initial steps in the contracting process is the preparation by industry of a proposal to undertake the planned project. Such a proposal can become a very elaborate project in itself.

represented by a stack of 2000-dollar bills. The fact that there are no such bills should not be viewed as any particular deterrent, at least not in comparison with much of the other material that finds its way into proposals. Contractors are firm adherents to the views of Horace, "*Brevis esse laboro, obscurus fio,*" which, when liberally translated, means "When I struggle to be brief, I become unintelligible." The problem is that in the case of most contractors, when they don't struggle to be brief, they also become unintelligible.

One enthusiastic proposal manager described the process in the following terms: "We shipped more than thirty-two cases of proposals to the customer. Stacked up, the content of these cases would have made a pile at least seventy-five feet high. Everyone really pitched in to meet our deadline—word processors worked day and night, and 'Reproduction' printed more than 284,000 pages."

The truly classic cases include the relatively infamous TFX aircraft developed during the Johnson administration for which the total set of copies of one bidder's proposals submitted during the four rounds of competition reached a final height of 211 feet. In the case of the C-5A transport aircraft, just one of the three bidders submitted a total of 1,466,346 pages weighing in at 24,927 pounds. The Request for Proposal issued to industry by the government itself occupied 1200 pages—and was later supplemented by a "Clarification Document" of over 1600 pages. A total of some 500 evaluators occupied months wading through the material provided by the three bidders.

This procreation of verbosity is abetted by the common industrial practice of "join 'em if you can't beat 'em"—leading to entire *teams* of companies to disgorge words. For example, *Aerospace Daily,* speaking of the forthcoming Space Station competition, duly reported that "The key subcontractor on the team led by Boeing is Teledyne Brown and other subcontractors include Aerojet, Camus, Inc., Eaton, Fairchild Republic, Fairchild Weston, Garrett, General Electric, Hamilton Standard, Hughes, Lite Systems, Lockheed, OAO, Perkin Elmer, Rocketdyne, Rockwell Autonetics, Sundstrand, Telephonics, Thermacore, TRW, Umqua, Vought, and Westinghouse."

So all-encompassing is paperwork that it can even ground the most modern aircraft. According to an Associated Press bulletin, "The next space shuttle flight, which had been set to lift off February 20 with Senator Jake Garn aboard, will be delayed at least a week because of troublesome thermal tiles and a backlog of paperwork. . . ." Wernher von Braun, the rocket pioneer, remarked decades earlier that "We can overcome gravity, but sometimes the paperwork is overwhelming."

A more recent trend is to require that contractors provide much of this data on computer tapes, very few of which are probably ever actually examined. This leads to the suspicion among disgruntled contractors that most of their work goes to "Bit Heaven" . . . raising a question rivaling the age-old puzzle facing office-supply managers, "What becomes of the paper clips?"

"Why use one word," as the saying goes, "when ten will do?"

The degree of improvement in the end products being sought wrought by the growing length of proposals and contracts as they have evolved over the years is suggested in the following tale of two airplanes. When the Army Signal Corps purchased the development of an aircraft from the Wright Brothers, the Request for Proposal document issued by the government consumed fully one page; the entire contract (a relatively imaginative fixed-price incentive type) comprised two pages. The latter was the result of a forty-day competition among forty-one bidders which culminated in a nine-day evaluation period by the government. An award was made (without protest) and the aircraft flew successfully some six months later.

The primitiveness of this early management system contrasts sharply with the more sophisticated approach used today which, in the case of the giant C-5A transport, generated contractor proposals the paper for which would have more than filled even the C-5A itself—the Free World's largest airplane. In this latter case there were only three competitors and the contractor selection period occupied some nine months (allowing for one recycling and one abortive selection of a source). The Advanced Helicopter Improvement Program competition exceeded even this relative standard of achievement, with one contractor's proposals (all required copies) exceeding the takeoff weight of the helicopter.

Many systems, it seems, are now quite literally worth their weight in paper. In fact, the president of Vought Aeronautics once estimated in *The Dallas Times Herald* that each time a new military airplane flew over the fence at their plant, 27 percent of its cost was attributed to paper. A single copy of a winning proposal for a modern aircraft requires a document embodying a preparation cost per pound (including the contractor-sponsored effort to develop the information) about 400 times the cost per pound of the aircraft itself.

But the above data include only the initial proposal and not all the resubmittals which often double or triple the pile which must be provided. Nor do the data include supporting documentation which must eventually be generated—such as the MX Environmental Impact Statement, which ran a full 8000 pages even in its draft form and was eventually discarded in one of the periodic changes in deployment concept suffered through four administrations, all of which *supported* the missile. A recent government publication on the marketing of cabbage contains, according to one report, 26,941 words. It is noteworthy in this regard that the Gettysburg Address contains a mere 279 words while the Lord's Prayer comprises but 67.

Fortunately, the United Nations recognized the existence of this situation on an international scale and established a Committee on the Reduction of Paperwork. The Committee eventually released a 219-page report summarily concluding that paperwork should be reduced. Similarly, the U.S. Commission on Federal Paperwork produced a widely distributed 74-page report, which was unfortunately soon surpassed by a 113-page report on the same topic generated by the succeeding administration. A five-page form recently issued to participants in Keogh plans had a sixth page added which was dedicated in its entirety to an explanation of how the form complied with the Paperwork Reduction Act. In fact, in 1982 the Internal Revenue Service handled some 600 million documents. With the help of the Paperwork Reduction Act and something called TEFRA (an innocuous sounding Tax Equity and Fiscal Responsibility Act), the number had grown to 950 million two years later.

Not to be outdone, the Defense Department has commendably taken steps to page-limit proposals submitted by its would-be contractors. One of the first efforts to accomplish this involved limiting proposals for one particular project to 1000 pages, a laudable concept had not the government's own Request for Proposal bulged to 1114 pages. The initial response of the industrial bidders, who for years had been complaining about the length of proposals, was not particularly commendable either; they produced documents with margins seemingly one millimeter wide and print size which rivaled the best products of their microelectronics production facilities and invented something called "foldouts."

The blame for this verbosity is not, however, entirely assignable to the contractors. They, too, are often faced with a veritable flood of vagaries to which a specific and detailed response is demanded. Reluctance by the government to state specific scoring criteria, for example, results in bidder confusion and statements such as the following taken from one recent Request for Proposal: "The weighting of technical factors exceeds that of all other individual factors but is less in value than the sum of cost and schedule. Technical excellence is weighted more heavily than cost which in turn receives more value than schedule which is equal in value to the combination of management and past performance. No one factor represents half of the total weighted value to be used in the contractor selection."

A story in *Government Executive* magazine tells of one federal official pointing out to his contracts manager that the length of one recent Request for Proposal, taken in concert with the allotted thirty-day response time, would pose problems to industry. Specifically, he noted, if one were to work twenty-four hours a day, seven days a week, for the entire month, only ten minutes would be available to read, digest, and prepare a response to each page of the government's request!

Recent efforts to select contractors for new items of hardware by conducting "flyoffs" of actual prototype hardware instead of conducting paper engagements have produced some astonishing results. In those cases where the selection has been based upon a conventional evaluation of paper proposals, the incumbents, defined as the builder of the previous generation of the item of equipment to be replaced, and thus the group best equipped for "wordsmithing," won about two-thirds of the competitions. In contrast, when flyoffs of actual hardware were involved, the dark-horse (newcomer) exactly reversed the above odds, winning two times out of three. Mother Nature is a very dispassionate judge.

The explanation of this happenstance has its origins in biblical times: "He multiplieth words without knowledge" (Psalm 35:16). Or, in more contemporary parlance, "I should have asked the question you answered." Thus, the age-old maxim, "If you can't convince 'em, confuse 'em."

The law resulting from these considerations appropriately has its title derived from computer parlance and is known as Augustine's Law of the Core Dump:

LAW NUMBER XXXVI

The thickness of the proposal required to win a multimillion dollar contract is about one millimeter per million dollars. If all the proposals conforming to this standard were piled on top of each other at the bottom of the Grand Canyon, it would probably be a good idea.

To paraphrase the old vaudeville doublet, "What do you call 100 voluminous proposals at the bottom of the Grand Canyon?"

Answer: "A good start."

37

Hope Springs Infernal

"I was shipwrecked before I got aboard."
—Epistles 87:1

Each of the three competing contractors had evolved its own intricate strategy for winning. For example, one of the two Fortunate 500 industrial giants was seeking special consideration as a "Disadvantaged Small Business Firm" on the grounds that if it did not win it might in fact someday become a disadvantaged small business firm. The second was encouraging the government to adopt contract terms and conditions that were so incredibly onerous and risky that, according to its strategy, the rest of the competitors would have management prudent enough to withdraw from the competition altogether so that they themselves could win by default. Daedalus was proposing a "low risk, minor upgrade" to an already existing item it had been producing (the upgrade consisting of a factor of 10,000 in-

crease in weight, a factor of 4000 in thrust, and a factor of 2000 in range), a practice known as "jacking up the nameplate" in recognition of the fact that the name of the original product would indeed be preserved as an evidence of minimal risk. The advertising brochure stated that the new hardware was fundamentally the same as the old based on such facts as, for example, the new electronics used the same type of electrons as did its ancestor. Daedalus sales staff even put out a release claiming that together with IBM they now controlled over 70 percent of the world's computer market. As with most such competitions, a dispute had actually boiled within both of Daedalus's competitors over whether to participate in so intensely competed an effort in the first place. The marketing departments had argued against bidding because of a concern that their company might lose. The finance departments, on the other hand, had argued with equal intensity for a "no bid" because of a concern that they might win. The legal department, in this instance, was indifferent; it would of course win in either event, preparing contract claims in one case or a protest over the loss in the other. However, the engineering departments in both companies had prevailed with their argument about the exciting technological challenge the bid would engender. But certainly no one could argue that this was anything other than a vicious competition from the very outset. There had been allegations of buy-ins and bail-outs, with the allegators in turn being accused of benefiting from leveling and leaks. Such accusations became so

*flagrant that for a considerable period it ap-
peared that the contract might be the very first
ever to be awarded posthumously.*

When it comes to accuracy of cost estimating and pricing
(two fundamentally different arts) for many activities
of the recent past, customers were, as the saying goes,
apparently expecting very little, and therefore certainly
were not disappointed. They might even have settled
for mediocrity, if their suppliers could have achieved
it. In fact, the overruns in many large-scale product
development projects, due largely to unforeseen—as
opposed to unforeseeable—tasks, were so large that,
if it weren't for the bad luck embodied in those projects,
they might have had no luck at all.

The eccentricities of cost estimating reach their zenith
in undertakings where the uncertainties are sufficiently
great that no specific "fixed price" can be ascertained
a priori. In such cases, ranging from building custom
houses to performing exploratory surgery and from developing airplanes to repairing plumbing, a "cost reim-
bursable" contract is generally used whereby the
purchaser agrees to pay all reasonable costs plus some
form of fee. Most such contracts are preceded by an
estimate which both the buyer and seller, ironically, are
subliminally desirous of believing to be a low number.
Therein lies the rub.

The habit of unjustifiably concluding, early in an undertaking, that one is in a better position than the facts
warrant has been found to have spread beyond the matter of estimating the cost of industrial projects. For
example, a press release by an underdog Army football
team just before a recent Army-Navy game, noted:
"The season began well enough, with Army taking a

10-10 lead into the fourth quarter [of its first game]."
Actually, though, this proved to be quite prescient as,
in the game that ensued, the Army gained what almost
all agreed was a 3-3 victory over Navy. Thus, numbers
do not tell all—*especially* numbers pertaining to the cost
status of newly initiated technological programs or other
activities having a similarly high emotional content.

Law VIII (page 71) indicated how to adjust typical
(i.e., wrong) cost estimates at any *perceived* point in a
development program so that the correct estimate could,
on the average, be determined. But what if one were
not satisfied with merely being correct on the *average*?
Supposing one wanted to be, say, 90 percent certain
that the cost estimate for a given undertaking would
not be exceeded? What then?

Figure 48 presents historical data, corrected for inflation, concerning a substantial number of large and
complex development projects conducted on behalf of
the government by U.S. industry, from which one can
determine the chances of an overrun of any given magnitude occurring. It will be seen immediately that only
10 percent of the time were programs completed within
the original cost estimate. Stated differently, contractors and their government overseers were undertaking
development projects (involving presumably cost-reimbursable contracts) at about a 10-percent confidence
level—although they probably didn't know it at the
time. How can this be? Why don't such improbable
estimates stand out like fur coats on a grocery list?
Particularly when programs which were terminally ill
(i.e., ultimately canceled prior to completion) have not
even been included in these statistics. Viewing overruns
from this perspective, it should certainly be no surprise
that we are frequently surprised. With this type of op-

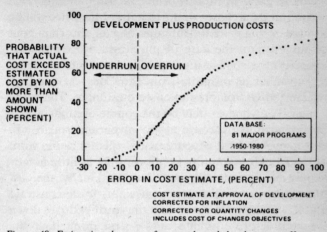

Figure 48. Estimating the cost of research and development efforts inherently involves uncertainty. This is a significant ingredient in the probabilistic character of cost growth.

timistic mathematics it can readily be seen that it would indeed be odd to come out even.

The reason for the problem, simply stated, is that the cost-estimation process as it exists in most cost-reimbursable contracting environments is fundamentally unstable. Further, when dealing with tasks involving substantial technical risks or uncertainty about the details of the end product, the only type of contract which is in fact equitable is one where the buyer bears actual costs. But, as already noted, under this type of contracting structure the prevailing forces can all act in concert to drive *estimated* costs downward to unreasonable levels—with seemingly no effective counterbalancing influence in existence. First, the prospective seller quite naturally wants to submit a lower bid than any of its competitors in order to win ("half of nothin' is nothin', and two-thirds of nothin' isn't a lot more"); second, the purchaser wants to believe the price will be low (as, say, a patient contemplating an uncertain bout of surgery). In the case of purchases by government agencies, the sponsoring organization wants to obtain approval for its program from the Congress and thus inadvertently promotes an austere estimate. Third, the "bank," or whoever may be the source of funds, wants to minimize its exposure in any given undertaking. In the case of federal procurements, this takes the form of the Congress wanting to appropriate as little money as possible prior to the next election. Finally, the customer's contracting department wants to demonstrate that it is a tough negotiator and thus further drives down the contractor's estimate; and so on throughout the entire process. It is like sending lettuce by rabbit.

It is soon learned by those on both sides of the negotiating table that if you will just go 60 percent of the way, the other side will go the other 60 percent. It could be called, once again, the "PLEEEASE, don't throw me into the briar patch" school of negotiating. The participants in the process may have attended different schools, but they seem somehow to have attended them together. It all adds up—or, more accurately, subtracts down—to a cost estimate for the "winning" contractor which is far too low, even when arrived at through what the participants believe to be a highly logical process. The cost *estimate* has in effect become a cost *desirement*. In Euripides' words, this would be categorized as a bad beginning making a bad ending. But in modern industrial parlance, it would be described as "giving each other the business." The old story of the lost tourist asking the farmer how to get to Chicago summarizes the situation very succinctly. After pondering the question for an extended period, the farmer finally advised with considerable authority, "If I were going to Chicago, I wouldn't start from here."

Or, as Sebastian Brant, a writer who understood this overall problem as early as 1494, put it, "The world wants to be deceived"—and according to C. N. Bover, "The worst deluded are the self-deluded." There are allegedly sixty-two ways to underestimate costs and it has been said by some optimists that bidders have not resorted to one of them. If that is the case, what needs to be done is to find out what that one is, so some semblance of safeguard can at least be established against it.

When Alice, in *Through the Looking Glass*, told the head bureaucrat of the time, the Queen, that it is impossible to believe impossible things, the Queen—in keeping with her position—replied, "Fiddlesticks, I've believed as many as six impossible things before breakfast." The Queen would fit right into today's contracting management.

It is thus discovered that, in mathematical terms, cost estimating deals with truly complex numbers—each having a real and an imaginary part. This is stated in a more erudite fashion in what is known merely as Baldy's Law: "Some of it, plus the rest of it, equals all of it."

The whole process ultimately degenerates into one of "Do unto others before they do unto you." An old-fashioned auction results. Although such procurement practices are usually avoided, some of their properties have a subtle manner of creeping into far too many purchases. Conservatism is scarce in intense competitions, with contractors making claims such as "There is only one approach to this objective and we have patents on both of them."

If either the buyer *or* the seller seeks to break free of this self-defeating manner of conducting one's affairs, the other party in effect forces the malcontent back into the pattern. The problem is much like the one encountered by the businessman who discovered a card in his hotel room stating, "If you have a problem with alcoholism and need help, call 344-2920." Calling the number, he discovered that it belonged to a liquor store.

Upon the completion of such a competition the winning contractor, safe in the knowledge that superior ability had once again prevailed, and the losing contractor, reassured that political influence had once again snatched defeat from the jaws of victory, can turn their undivided attention to the tasks at hand: seeking changes to the contract and preparing a protest, respectively.

For most projects which employ the above techniques of cost estimating, matters generally deteriorate steadily after the initial disastrous start. But this has not dissuaded a long line of managers from believing that they, unlike all their predecessors, will be able to manage their programs in such a way that they encounter no unforeseen events—and complete the job for the specified cost. Shakespeare wrote about this kind of manager in *Henry IV*:

> GLENDOWER: I can call spirits from the vasty deep.
> HOTSPUR: Why, so can I, or so can any man; but will they come when you do call for them?

One partial solution to this dilemma, that of incentive contracting, has on occasion been traced to the Wright

Brothers' original agreement with the U.S. Army, which was, as has already been noted, an incentive-type contract. But this solution—and the problem it addresses—were extant long before the Wright Brothers were even considering diversifying their bicycle business. It turns out, according to Marcus Vitruvius Pollio, the architect and engineer, that the ancient ancestral law in the Greek city of Ephesus demanded engineers to file a formal cost estimate with the magistrate prior to initiating work on a public project. If the work was completed for the specified amount, the engineer was rewarded with decrees and marks of honor. An overrun of up to one-fourth was financed by the treasury without the imposition of penalty. But excesses over one-fourth were drawn from the engineer's personal property, which had to be pledged as security at the time of response to the Request for Proposal. As seen from Figure 48, were such a practice to be reinstated some twenty-five centuries later, approximately 55 percent of the engineers would be spending their nights sleeping on the steps of the Parthenon.

It is of the utmost importance to note that in matters entailing enormous inherent uncertainty, such as research and development of sophisticated systems, no one need actually be guilty of equivocation; everyone needs simply to be wildly optimistic—a disease that is highly contagious in the absence of any effective vaccine or antidote. In terms that Jimmy the Greek (if, not sadly, many cost estimators) would most assuredly understand, to obtain a fifty-fifty chance of completing a prescribed undertaking within the estimated cost for the types of projects addressed in Figure 48, the bid costs, determined through traditional practices of the past two decades, would have to be increased by 31 percent. To have obtained a 90 percent confidence of not exceeding the estimate, one would have needed to increase the estimates by fully 148 percent. The disparity between these two figures, incidentally, lies at the very core of the reason why fixed-price contracts are simply not suitable instruments for most research and development tasks involving prescribed end-items. The reason is that *no one* really knows precisely what they will cost because research and development of a given item has, by its very definition, never been done before. The same is true of estimating the impact of economic inflation or making certain types of difficult-to-diagnose repairs, whether they be of automobiles, washing machines, or the dog's broken leg. Who would like to have a heart surgeon working under a fixed-price contract?

The solution to this dilemma is to account for uncertainty when making cost estimates—to provide for the unexpected on an actuarial basis just as is done by insurance companies. This, of course, results in higher initial cost estimates than would otherwise be the case, which some argue will make it more difficult to obtain approval to start new projects. To a degree one *can* assert that this has the same shortcoming as the principle that if one eats a live toad first thing each morning then the day will show continued improvement. The objective in business, however, is to measure how many undertakings are *completed*—not how many can be *started*. There are simply no other alternatives. One can either face reality at the outset or one can disseminate the bad news on the installment plan. Proponents of the "don't produce high (read, 'realistic') estimates—the project won't be approved" school have probably best been answered by none other than Winston Churchill. In the book *The Last Lion* a story is told of a woman Member of Parliament who, after an extensive tirade at a social function, scornfully told the Prime Minister, "Mr. Churchill, you are drunk," to which Churchill replied, "And you, Madam, are ugly. But I shall be sober tomorrow."

All this is not to say that realism is necessarily pleasant. Frank Cahouet, chairman of Crocker National Corporation, promised upon taking over the helm, to restore "realism to the balance sheet." But according to *Newsweek*, "Reality has turned out to be pretty grim. Last week Cahouet announced a projected fourth-quarter loss of $215 million. . . ."

Unlike fine wine and quality pearls, bad news seldom improves with age. Those involved in research and development activities rank among the all-time great proponents of what, in some less sophisticated circles, is referred to as the "slow reveal." "I'll think on it tomorrow . . . I can stand it then. Tomorrow I'll think of some way," said Scarlett O'Hara.

Although projects conducted by the Department of Defense, which comprise the data base for Figure 48, are generally characterized by significant technological challenge on the basis of seeking to gain a potentially life-saving edge over potential adversaries, cost-estimation problems are by no means the exclusive province of defense programs. Dulles Airport suffered an overrun of a factor of 1.49 when it was constructed, and the Tennessee Tombigbee Waterway exceeded the initial estimate by a multiple of 1.76. The corresponding figure for the Appalachian Development Highway is 2.65; for the New Orleans Superdome, 3.22; and for the Trans-Alaska Pipeline, 4.25. Estimates for the De-

troit Rapid Transit system began at $89.5 million but
have now passed the $210 million mark even though
only the concrete columns are in place—hence its de-
risive moniker, "Detroit's Stonehenge." Chicago's sev-
enteen-story building, the State of Illinois Center, began
at about the same price as Detroit's edifice ($89.8 mil-
lion), but even though showing an unrespectable cost
increase to $172 million, has been unable to match De-
troit's pace. On the other hand, New York's Westway
highway doubled in cost to $2 billion before construc-
tion was even begun and Los Angeles's Century Freeway, not to be outdone, rose from $0.9 billion to $1.6
billion even though eight years of work are *estimated*
to remain. Even the Canadian Olympics, scheduled to
cost a reported $400 million, wound up costing nearly
$2 billion.

The Dearbrook nuclear power generating facility is
a good example (of bad estimating). Originally bud-
geted at $970 million, the estimate was passing through
the $9 billion barrier when work was halted in 1984.
When last seen, construction had been restarted at a
cost of $4 million per week; however, the prognosis was
cloudy due to intense political fallout.

Some of the *all-time* world-class overrun leaders have
been identified in data collected by Myron Kayton, a
consulting engineer, in his studies of new-technology
projects in the nineteenth century. He reports the suf-
fer-factor for the Erie Canal as 12,000 percent; for the
Cincinnati-Covington bridge as 730 percent; the Hoosac
Tunnel in western Massachusetts as 2500 percent; and
the Brooklyn Bridge as a mere 85 percent—at least on
the occasion of its *initial* sale: It would seem that even
during the 1800s to have a dismal record would require

considerable improvement. No question but that misery loves company.

These data, of course, all relate only to the past. But in spite of these limitations, there seems once again to be little reason to doubt George Santayana's admonition that "those who cannot remember the past are condemned to repeat it." And, in this respect, there would seem to be many alive and well today, particularly in the product development trenches, who are suffering through at least their third reincarnation—all the while fully confident that the future will not include unhappy surprises and oblivious to the fact that the past *always* included unhappy surprises. And in this case, the past goes all the way back to the building of the Suez Canal (200 percent overrun), the Panama Canal (70 percent), and even the Roman Aqueduct (100 percent). Mercifully, the pharaohs kept only sparse records on the pyramids.

The above assessment indicated what cost estimate should be used in order to ensure that, say, half the programs undertaken are completed for less than their projected cost (and the other half for more). It may be of greater significance to assure that the *money* saved on the programs which do in fact underrun is sufficient to compensate for the losses on those which suffer overruns. The above two statements are obviously not equivalent since the probability distribution is *skewed*. A plethora of programs endure overruns of 100 percent—but there is a noticeable paucity of programs which offset this growth with *underruns* of 100 percent. It is thus seen that, as might have been expected, the odds are indeed odd. This is, of course, indirectly related to the principle that causes people to drown in streams having an average depth of six inches. Or to the principle which governs the airport pick-up buses run by car rental firms, said buses arriving, as advertised, an *average* of every five minutes—always in bunches of four.

The factor which, if applied in recent years, would have guaranteed that the house breaks even for the overall set of projects considered in Figure 48 can be determined approximately from the data used to prepare the figure. This factor equals at least 1.52 and is known as the "Las Vegas Factor of Development Program Planning." Normally it is quoted to at least seven significant figures; however, this neglects the fact that even this metric is subject to change depending upon the amount of risk that is entailed in a specific program. Graphically, this degree of hazard is represented by how flat (risky) or steep (certain) is the slope of the curve in Figure 48 for the particular project addressed.

One might expect, in keeping with the fundamental laws of economics, that contracts which entail the greatest risks would be those which would return the greatest profits. Quite the contrary, at least in the case of government purchases, where such highly volatile endeavors as research and development carry the smallest *realized* profit margins, routine matters such as the provision of spare parts carry the largest, and intermediate risk-bearers such as serial production, reside, in terms of profit rate, somewhere in between. This finding is thus seen to match the illogic of investment risk versus return, discussed in Chapter 21.

All the above mathematical meandering can be distilled into Augustine's Law of Apocalyptic Costing:

LAW NUMBER XXXVII

Ninety percent of the time things will turn out worse than you expect. The other 10 percent of the time you had no right to expect so much.

Those who consider such findings implausible must explain, say, why 90 percent of the world's air traffic arrives and departs from the 10 percent of the gates farthest from the terminal building.* As the saying goes, you have to kiss a lot of frogs to find a prince.

In the words of Peter Hall, in the concluding sentence of his work *Great Planning Disasters*, "There may be some excuses for great planning disasters, but there are not nearly so many as we think."

Figure 48, of course, deals only with the matter of estimating *costs*. If one makes a similar plot showing schedule outcomes or performance outcomes (speed, range, accuracy, payload, etc.) for defense projects, it is found that while there is only a 10 percent chance of meeting *cost* goals, there is a 15 percent chance of meeting *schedule* goals and a 70 percent chance of satisfying *performance* goals. The long-suspected priority hierarchy is thereby mathematically derived: Performance reigns supreme. For many years it had appeared that nothing could ever make the record of schedule-control look good. That was before the cost-control record came along.

Some 2400 years ago, Thucydides got to the very root

---

*Art Buchwald has suggested that the outlying arrival and departure gates at airports in neighboring cities be joined so that passengers could then merely walk from airport to airport—thereby altogether avoiding the hassle of air traffic delays, lost suitcases, and the likes. An alternative might be to establish commuter air service to the outlying gates.

of the cost-overrun problem: "Their judgment was based more on wishful thinking than on sound calculation of probabilities; for the usual thing among men is that when they want something they will, without any reflection, leave that to hope, while they will employ the full force of reason in rejecting what they find unpalatable." It is not that contractors do not know how to estimate costs realistically. Nor is it that they do not know how to win competitions. The problem resides in the fact that most do not know how to do both simultaneously.

With all participants in the cost-estimating process motivated more by the law of survival than the law of probability, what other outcomes could we have expected? How could we possibly be surprised? To quote astronaut Pete Conrad, speaking from space aboard Gemini XI, "We're on top of the world. You can't believe it . . . utterly fantastic. The world is round."

The fact that many purchasers, including the government's managers, *know* they have incentivized contractors to be optimistic in estimating costs and yet express surprise at the outcome suggests that the following conversation from Peter Ustinov's *Romanoff and Juliet* involving a general and two ambassadors might just as well have taken place among a general and two contractors:

GENERAL: . . . Incidentally, they know your code.

AMERICAN AMBASSADOR: We know they know our code. . . . We only give them things we want them to know.

GENERAL: Incidentally, they know you know they know your code.

SOVIET AMBASSADOR: . . . We have known for some

time that they knew we knew their code. We have acted accordingly—by pretending to be duped.

GENERAL: . . . Incidentally, you know—they know you know they know you know . . .

AMERICAN AMBASSADOR: What? Are you sure?

More recently, the following passage, in a related vein, appeared in *The Washington Post*:

U.S. Navy ships escorting the aircraft carrier *Kitty Hawk* lost sonar contact with a Soviet submarine before the sub hit the flattop in the Sea of Japan, the Defense Department's chief spokesman said Thursday. But a Navy spokesman disagreed, saying the escort vessel had broken sonar contact deliberately with the sub about two hours before the collision Wednesday night. . . . Lt. Cmdr. John Woodhouse said . . . We know they are there and they know we know they are there. Other Navy officers agreed.

Thus, knowing what one's counterpart is up to does not in itself assure that a collision can be avoided . . . either at sea or in the hazardous passages of business.

38

Shark Propellant

"If I'd wanted a trophy I'd 'a bought me one."
—Minnesota Fats*

The waiting was by far the hardest part of all. The proposals assembled by the three contractors had long ago been submitted and the government, symbolically, was conducting a nine-month evaluation of each. The quiet had been deafening, although rumors did abound—frequently circling back to those who had started them in so credible a form that they too believed them and passed them along for another cycle of embellishment. This only added to the shock when the front page of The Wall Street Journal carried the story right alongside the three columns that everyone actually reads, saying that one of the two giant competitors for the invisible

---

*Speaking at award ceremony . . . after losing an exhibition match offering trophy, not money, as prize.

*airplane contract had unexpectedly bought con-
trol of the other in what was termed "an unfriendly takeover." This latter description proved
to be an understatement, like referring to a cannibal as a humanistic gourmet. But the other
shoe was yet to drop. Two days later, the Board
of Directors of the company which had just been
acquired retaliated by abruptly buying a controlling interest in its antagonist. The acquirer
thus became the acquiree—and vice versa—with
each firm now owning a controlling share of the
other. The intense dislike which had flamed between these two huge corporations for many years
was further stoked when each, to prevent its antagonist's Board from gaining control of the anticipated stealth airplane contract, submitted a
formal protest to the government stipulating that
the invisible airplane contract could not now be
awarded to itself. This action was altogether
without precedence in the annals of jurispru-
dence and sent shock waves throughout the entire industry. Daedalus Aerospace, Ltd., for its
part, decided to adopt the old Napoleonic maxim
that one should never interfere when the enemy
is in the process of destroying itself. In contrast,
the government, as lawyers, bankers, and arbitrageurs swarmed everywhere, found itself with
both feet planted firmly in midair. It had clearly
stated in the Request for Proposal that a contract
would be awarded, but if it awarded the contract
to either of the two major aerospace firms who
had bid, it would in essence be giving the contract
to the loser since the loser now owned the winner—whoever that might be. Worse yet, the*

"winner" had already placed a formal protest on record against its becoming the winner. It was at this point that the proposal evaluators decided perhaps they should read Daedalus Aerospace, Ltd.'s proposal one more time.*

"The fox knows many things. The hedgehog knows one *big* thing."

That, according to Aesop, is the key to survival in the forest. The same may be said to be true of corporate survival in the thickets of a business jungle abounding with takeover artists. There have been literally hundreds of takeover attempts in the last few years alone, actions wherein one company seeks to buy control of another. These efforts come in two flavors: (1) friendly, (2) not-so-friendly. The latter usually turn into street brawls that reverberate throughout the financial and legal communities for months or even years and eventually wind up aground in the court system. Various forms of legislation, such as the antitrust laws, have been introduced from time to time to enforce a modicum of dignity upon these proceedings; however, the Marquess of Queensberry would no doubt still be appalled by the deportment of the participants. As Stanislaw Lem once wrote, "Is it progress if a cannibal uses a knife and fork?"

By and large, such free-for-alls stir little empathy from the man on the street. The one exception was

---

*The author acknowledges that this escape from so convoluted a plot is almost as implausible as, say, a novel about a President of the United States who secretly tape-records his own private conversations which in turn lead to his expulsion from office. Nonetheless, the following excerpt from the book *Three Plus One Equals Billions—The Bendix–Martin Marietta War*, by Allan Sloan, is offered as token defense: "In December 1982, when the exchange of stock took place, Marietta owned 11,900,100 shares of Bendix (a majority). Bendix . . . owned 25,852,500 shares of Marietta (a majority)." (Parenthetical notes added.)

when an assault was made on the corporate body of Mickey Mouse, Donald Duck, and Dumbo. *That* proved to be too much, as the correspondence secretaries of numerous Congressmen quickly learned. Nonetheless, the financial value of mergers and acquisitions consummated in 1984 alone approached an unhealthy $122 billion. The first billion-dollar acquisition took place in 1969. Since then there have been forty-seven more—forty of which took place in the last four years. In the most recent year alone there have been six separate billion-dollar takeover attempts where the victim company escaped—only to be swallowed by still another corporation. According to business writer Allan Sloan, "Who is safe? Only those companies in such wretched shape that no one wants them. . . ."

A whole arsenal of imaginative defensive strategies has been devised in recent years to ward off such attacks when a company has been, as they say in the trade, "put into play." After all, necessity *is* the mother of invention . . . and survival. One of these strategies is known as the "scorched earth" approach, wherein the intended victim company takes actions to assure that there is nothing left of itself worth devouring in the event the takeover attempt succeeds. Closely related is the "crown jewel" strategy, wherein specific parts of the company under duress which are particularly attractive to the raider are summarily obligated to be sold off. As one corporate officer observed following the implementation of such a strategy, "We realized we had to do something really drastic to get the thing over with . . . so we sold off our crown jewels."

There is also the Pac-Man defense, named after the video game wherein little pill-like creatures dash around the display screen eating one another. In the corporate version of this children's game the victim company suddenly seeks to swallow the attacker by buying *its* shares in retaliation. In a moment of sheer frustration a judge once quoted from the bench during an infamous takeover case involving a Pac-Man defense, the Shakespearian line, "A pox upon *both* your houses." "Shark repellents" are another form of defense which have been introduced by over 400 companies in 1983 and 1984 alone, most often in the form of a "supermajority amendment" to the corporate character, whereby a very high approval ratio is required for any change in corporate control. Friendly "White Knights" are sometimes called upon to buy a company that is under attack and thereby rescue it from the unwanted suitor. "Poison Pills" are actions taken to assure that a company would not be digestible by any firm considering an unfriendly takeover, and "greenmail" is a form of ransom payment which is made by a victim company to induce its antagonist to go elsewhere to satisfy its hunger. "Doomsday machines" are legal devices set into motion that can potentially be catastrophic to both companies if the unwelcome advances continue beyond a specified trigger-point, sort of a corporate deterrent akin to mutual assured destruction (better known as "MAD") in the strategic nuclear warfare arena. "Trap-doors" are legal devices set up for the unwary to fall through and "Trojan Horses" are equally enticing entrapments. "Golden Parachutes" are financial agreements which spring into effect in the event a takeover succeeds and are intended to keep a victim's key management from bailing out during the takeover attempt (takeover attempts usually draw not only hordes of arbitrageurs but also swarms of "head hunters" seeking to entice key executives to jump to other companies and escape the uncertainty the future holds) as well as to insure a reasonably safe landing in case all else fails. Then there are bounty hunters, lash-back warrants, self-destruct devices, and so on . . . and on . . . and on. The effect of all this is that sometimes even takeovers which fail succeed. As investor Carl Icahn tells it, "I go in and tell the company I'd like to be on the board. I'll stand still for fifteen years—I won't buy any more stock beyond the 15 percent I already have. And they tell me, 'Look, we're gonna sue you, or do "poison pills" on you—or on the other hand, we'll give you ten million bucks if you go away.' What am I supposed to do? I'm not Robin Hood."

There are frequently *no* winners in these encounters—except perhaps the lawyers and bankers to whom is left the job of burying the survivors. Thus the expression "the agony of victory." In the forty-five hostile takeover attempts examined in the present investigation, 24 percent were successful and the target was devoured. But that's only the appetizer. A recent study by Goldman Sachs & Co. found that only one in five target companies remain independent within five years after a hostile bid. A related study by Kidder Peabody & Co. reveals that the ultimate survival probability may actually be more like one in ten. All this, needless to say, can get very complicated. An article in *Forbes* dutifully reported, "CIT Financial and Utah International have both changed hands twice. Esmark bought Norton Simon and sold businesses to help pay for it, then sold itself to Beatrice Corp., which is selling businesses to help pay for buying Esmark."

In 1984 alone there were 2,543 mergers and acquisitions involving $122 billion. But according to management consultant McKinsey & Co., a study of fifty-eight major acquisitions revealed that twenty-eight failed both major tests of success used in the study and thirty-four failed at least one. These tests related to return on capital (as compared with cost of capital) and performance in the stock market (as compared with competitor's performance). This is presumably the reason the number of cases in the corporate divorce courts has jumped by 35 percent in the last five years alone.

Figure 49, derived from data made available through the courtesy of First Boston, presents a statistical glimpse

Size of Combatants (Book Value, $B)

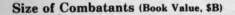

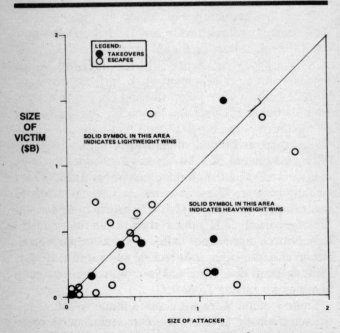

Figure 49. The statistics governing the outcome of corporate takeovers favor being large and striking first.

of three years' worth of the more significant recent take-over attempts. The lesson to be derived is "Strike First and Be Big." As one Ivy League quarterback remarked to his freshman understudy, "Just remember, the bigger they are, the harder they hit." Again quoting Allan Sloan, "If your business is a troubled one, don't break your back dealing with the problems, just trade it in for a different model." Or, as one takeover artist has observed, "The poor widows of this world aren't my responsibility."

Law Number XXXVIII, known as the Law of the Jungle, tells it like it is in the world of Corporate Raiders:

LAW NUMBER XXXVIII

The early bird gets the worm.
The early worm . . . gets eaten.

The reprehensible lack of decorum evidenced by some of the combatants in past corporate donnybrooks has, unfortunately, given warfare a bad name. Actually, not all takeovers are necessarily bad. In fact, takeovers of the so-called "friendly" type are frequently to the benefit of all involved. Under certain very select circumstances even unwelcome takeovers can be beneficial. However, Carl Icahn, a veteran of many raids, advises, "You learn in this business: If you want a friend, get a dog."

There is nothing tender about a tender offer.

Even the labor movement has been (reluctantly) forced into the mergers and acquisitions business due to plummeting membership and concomitant declines in in-

come. The Bureau of Labor statistics reports that since
the original AFL-CIO merger took place in 1955, there
have been an additional eighty-six union mergers—
twenty-nine of which took place in one recent six-year
period.

It is not altogether evident that Damon Runyon had
corporate takeovers in mind when he gave his famous
advice on gambling, but his words certainly seem to
apply: "The race is not always to the swift or the battle
to the strong," he said, "but *that* is the way to bet."

39

So Old for Its Age

"The first Indian hospital was built in the U.S. last year. It took 400 years from the time the white man arrived here. Just think what the Indian must have to look forward to in the next 400 years."

—Will Rogers

It was right there on the front page of The Wall Street Journal: *Daedalus had won! David had slain Goliath! Daedalus Aerospace, Ltd., was now in the big time, with two of America's industrial giants working as its subcontractors. In business, some things are done for profit, others for revenge! It was awesome. In fact, Daedalus's top management looked a bit like the dog that caught the car. It has to be recorded, in fairness, that by this point neither of the two major bidders were any longer seeking the contract—they had given up on getting any cheese and just wanted out of the trap. Daedalus's employees all gathered for the victory party, except, of course, for the engineers, who once again disappeared into their laboratories to start changing their winning design. It was a new experience, dealing with so gigantic a customer as the federal government. But one thing for sure, when you wrestle with a 500-pound gorilla, you rest when the gorilla wants to rest—and DAL, as it was now widely referred to in the media, (the Stock Exchange, exhibiting its usual clarity, had dubbed it QXFTZ) was eager to go to work manufacturing the world's very first invisible airplane. The problem was, the gorilla wanted to rest. In fact, this strange gorilla seemed to want to hibernate.*

Speaking of his academic career at the University of Iowa, Alex Karras of Detroit Lions fame confided, "I never graduated. I was there for only two terms—Truman's and Eisenhower's."

World War II was won in about half the time it takes today to develop a new military system. In fact, one can characterize the current development process as having two speeds: slow and stop.

Figure 50 shows that the average major system development for national defense now takes slightly over eight years to complete. Even commercial developments, although much faster than those conducted by the government, still seem to take an inordinately long time. The question arises why this glacial pace should prevail. Figure 51 sheds some enlightenment on current management practices in government and industry by indicating conclusively as well as surprisingly, at least for aerospace projects, that the "doing time" (for example, the time from the beginning of the design effort on a new airplane until its first flight) has not changed significantly during the last quarter of a century. But if

Time Marches On—and On—and

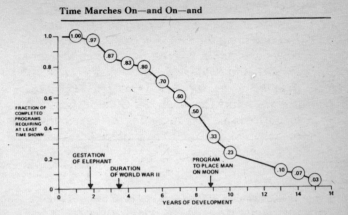

Figure 50. The median development program for a major military system in the last two decades has encompassed eight years from start of full development to initial operational use. Seventeen percent of the programs have, however, managed to be completed in less than four years, providing at least an existence theorem for more rapid transition from laboratory to the customer.

the "doing" or execution time for *both* government and commercially funded projects has not been changing, yet overall time consumed is increasing, where is the missing time going? Could it really be that nostalgia just isn't what it used to be?

The solution to the mystery of program geriatrics is to be found in Figure 52.

What *has* changed is the decision and approval time it takes to get a new project started, together with the time it takes to get the end product fielded once the development has been completed. The historical ratio of *planning* time to *doing* time for a number of major aerospace system developments is shown in Figure 52 and, on the average, the total time it takes to develop

Getting off the Ground

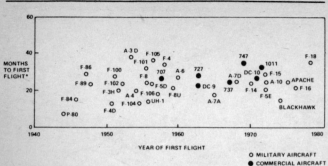

Figure 51. The duration of the design and build phase of aircraft development programs has remained virtually unchanged for forty years. This period is approximately the same for government projects, commercial projects, and, for that matter, projects undertaken in the Soviet Union.

a new system, including decision and approval time, increased at a rate of three months per year, for fifteen years. This has culminated in the belief in some quarters that progress should no longer be measured in terms of milestones. Inchstones are said to be more appropriate.

Dr. Gene Fubini, a former chairman of the Defense Science Board and one-time Assistant Secretary of Defense, describes an incident during World War II wherein he proposed a new electronic countermeasures technique to the Navy. Asked how quickly he could produce the item, he promised, "Just as quickly as you can make up your mind that you want it." The captain responsible for electronic warfare devices, apparently a pragmatist, responded knowingly, "If it takes that long, I don't want it."

Relationship of "Decision" Time to "Doing Time"

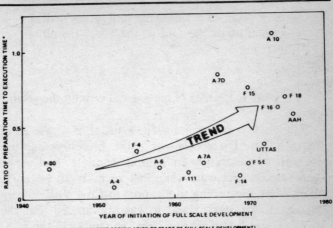

Figure 52. The time that elapses from agreement upon a need for a new item to the start of a program to fulfill that need has steadily increased, as has the time from first flight of a development article to deployment of a significant operational capability. These are the principal contributors to growth in schedule duration.

The captain, if he could see the management system as it exists four decades later, would probably apply for preventive sick leave.

Based in part on the fact that the half-life of most technologies has been determined, as previously noted, to be on the order of three to ten years, it appears that if current glacial developmental trends persist, most new systems will be obsolete only slightly before they are born. This leads to Augustine's Law of Extended Gestation (also known as the Law of Deferred Gratification):

LAW NUMBER XXXIX

Never promise to complete any project within six months of the end of the year—in either direction.

A bureaucracy's idea of moving out is to hit the ground sitting.

The nuclear power industry, as usual, is a case all of its own. The Diablo Canyon plant, fifteen years after its start and eleven years behind schedule, had yet to generate its first watt when last seen. It all began in 1968 when, according to a report in *USA Today*, construction was started and it was announced that the plant would be on line in 1973. But in 1973 the U.S. Geological Survey found a seismic fault three miles from the plant. In 1981 the Nuclear Regulatory Commission nonetheless issued a low-power operating license to the plant. But fifty-nine days later the NRC suspended the license. In 1984 the NRC restored the license and later in the year approved full-power operation. But fifteen days later a court suspended the license. Two months later an appeals court restored the license. And so it goes. But one thing is ahead of schedule at Diablo Canyon and that is its cost—including, not incidentally, the cost, for better or for worse, of complying with burgeoning regulations. The original $320 million estimate for the plant is now reported to have eclipsed $5 billion.

The average nuclear plant has suffered delays that lengthened its completion period from an original estimate of six years to a final twelve years (some to infinity). Perhaps the most realistic aspect of the U.S.

nuclear power effort is the selection of a name for the Millstone plant. In the meantime, the Japanese, French, and Germans have been hard at work. In France alone, thirty reactors have been built and twenty-seven more are underway. But in the United States, the entire industry has gone critical.

Even in the commercial world, a study conducted by the National Science Foundation found that the time typically required to develop an idea from the laboratory into a salable product was thirteen to eighteen years.

The aerospace record for prolonged gestation is probably held jointly by the Patriot and Aegis air defense radar systems, either of which eclipses the proverbial elephant by some fifteen years. Each was one of those instant successes that took eighteen years. The advice offered by George Bernard Shaw seems appropriate: "Do not try to live forever," he suggests. "You will not succeed."

It is readily understandable that there is not inconsiderable concern that those planning and budgeting for the above-mentioned two programs may learn of studies by biologists that attribute the incredible success of a bat's "radar" (including chirp pulse compression) to over 50 million years of continuing perfection. All that is needed is a little more time.

40

Off Again, Off Again

"What's the use? Yesterday an egg, tomorrow
a feather duster."
—Mark Fenderson, ca. 1900

*Operating under government funding was prov-
ing to be a learning experience. The negotiators
had finally resolved the impasse by agreeing to
use the contractor's promised statement of work
and the government's proposed price. The contract was thus finally signed a full eighteen months
after Daedalus Aerospace, Ltd., had first been
announced as the winner of the competition. As
luck would have it, this original announcement
had taken place on what happened to be the very
first day of a new fiscal year for the government.
In keeping with tradition, Congress had not yet
gotten around to appropriating funds for that
year—it seemed that it was still busy with the
previous year. The government's contracting officer, implausible as it may appear, at this point
asked Daedalus, in view of the importance of*

the project to the nation, to float the government for a few weeks—"at DAL's risk, of course." It seemed that the government had too much year left over at the end of the money. DAL's management greeted this news with genuine dismay, and moved to establish a government liaison department as part of the only recently formed government affairs section. This new group soon reported that the government's budget preparation process was proceeding apace. Each governmental management layer was at work using the technique already perfected in the commercial sector of deleting the favorite projects of the people in the layer immediately above it in the hope of forcing add-on's of funds as the senior managers scrambled to restore their own sacred cows. This practice is commonly referred to as "gold-watching," a reference to the desire of each organizational strata to save the "gold watches" it had so long coveted and therefore implanted into the budget. The fundamental viability of the tactic is, of course, dependent upon unsuspecting compliance by the next-higher management layer, a condition somewhat complicated by the fact that the next-higher management layer is itself simultaneously identifying the gold watches it will be using to circumvent its next-higher layer. Simultaneously, the staff in the Senate had been making preparations to double the requested funds for the invisible aircraft program, whatever they might be, so as to posture itself for a suitable compromise with the House of Representatives, which in turn was halving the budget request on the program as they had done each year since *the project first appeared in the budget. Thus were the machinations of the bureaucracy—a bureaucracy which seemed to have the innate ability to reduce a good contract to rubble in a matter of a few short weeks.*

The common belief that the funding for major projects can be turned on and off much like a water faucet while the projects themselves meander through their various phases has resulted in senior managers in both government and industry spending more time seeking to keep government funded projects alive than in seeing to their proper execution. This is an area of sharp distinction between government and commercially supported programs. In the commercial world, once approved, it borders on the ludicrous that members of the firm in question would continue to seek to undermine the decision that had been made. In contrast, this is not only the norm for government programs but it is practiced quite openly and with great vigor. It sometimes appears in the latter case that program participants and fund-providers may have rather different things in mind when they embrace the seemingly mutual objective of overseeing a project's execution.

The image of managers striving to accomplish difficult and challenging tasks only to see funds reduced and goals changed at each step along the way, sadly reminds one of a peripatetic Charlie Brown repeatedly seeking to kick a football only to have some Lucy snatch it away at each critical moment. The only apparent advantage to having the world changing so fast is that it's not then possible to be wrong *all* the time.

The roller-coaster lifestyle of many a program is exemplified by the experience of the Air Force Satellite

Communications System, AFSATCOM. Figure 53 traces the funding level for the program as it ricocheted through the Congress. During the year examined—just one year out of many in the program's lifetime—the program manager was faced with a projected budget swing ranging from $72 million to $19 million, and did not know the correct figure until three months *into* the year. Furthermore, these data do not even reflect the puts and takes which occurred in the process leading to obtaining

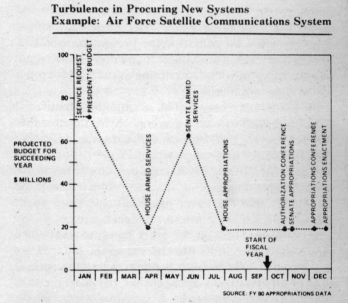

Turbulence in Procuring New Systems
Example: Air Force Satellite Communications System

SOURCE: FY 80 APPROPRIATIONS DATA

Figure 53. Sudden changes in a program's projected funding can be extremely disruptive, expensive, and demotivating. Unfortunately, such changes are commonplace. The data shown reflect only those potential changes occurring during the final phase of the funding process; similar turbulence is often experienced over the preceding several years.

the President's approval prior to congressional action's ever being initiated. One might believe that approval by the President of the United States and by the Secretary of the Whole Defense might have some meaning, but alas, that is an overly optimistic conclusion. It thus becomes apparent why most contractors have routinely added vice-presidents of marketing, why many are now installing vice-presidents of congressional relations, and why a few are actively recruiting vice-presidents of clairvoyance. One firm actually, although presumably inadvertently, released a notice informing the world that it was appointing a new "vice-prescient." But it must be stated on behalf of the present process that there is one residual advantage: If you don't know where you are going, any road, according to the Turkish proverb, will get you there.

As has already been noted, a situation often faced by management in such a perilous environment is that it must begin the working year with a dispute still raging as to the budget level which will ultimately be approved for that year. This necessitates a decision either to reduce the spending rate in order to protect against the eventuality that the lower figure in contention might prevail (which makes the lower budget figure essentially a *fait accompli*), or, on the other hand, to *not* reduce the spending rate. If, in this latter case, the lower figure does subsequently become a reality when the issue is finally settled well into the fiscal year, the program manager falls in violation of what is known as the antideficiency law, a serious matter indeed. The choice is thus, on the one hand, to undermine one's position or, on the other, to engage in a game of fiscal chicken. The chances of a favorable outcome are somewhere between zero and none. As the saying goes, it is the kind of decision that could affect you the rest of your life—if you lived that long.

As but one example, in one recent year the House Armed Services Committee added money to the funding requested by the President for the Precision Location and Strike System, and the Senate Armed Services Committee zeroed the budget. The following year, the Senate Armed Services Committee doubled the funding request and the House recommended zero. Thus is derived the expression, "a firm maybe."

But the prize for the quick-switch goes to the House Appropriations Committee as reported in the following item from *Aerospace Daily:* "(Congressman) Addabbo's proposal first carried on a 19-17 show of hands, but opponents quickly mustered sufficient support for a roll-call vote in which they turned it around!" This is known as interrupting the interruptions.

The process reached its ultimate stage in the 97th Congress, late one Monday morning, when the U.S. Senate, as described by *Newsweek,* "in effect, voted to decide whether to vote to decide whether to reconsider a decision not to vote." In the words of a Colorado State Senator, "There's something in here to offend everybody." Or, in the words of the Ambassador to the Court of Saint James's, "Compromise makes a good umbrella, but a poor roof. . . ."

During the Senate debate on the Fiscal Year 1984 budget for the much-suffering but on-going MX missile program, over 500 amendments were offered for consideration. This is known as the "Ready . . . Fire . . . Aim" school of management. Turning to 1985, a logjam of more than 1200 disputes between the House and the Senate on the defense authorization bill alone stacked up when differences on the MX could not be reconciled.

These changes often originate at the highest levels in government, sometimes beginning with the President and working upward through the congressional staffs.

An even more innovative process has recently been gaining widespread acceptance in budgeting circles: that of cutting budgets for the development of a piece of hardware as a punishment for having encountered technical problems. As implausible as this practice may seem, examples abound, such as *Aerospace Daily*'s routine report of one congressional action affecting an Army project: "The committee cut the $30 million request in half because it felt the Army was taking too long to develop the system." This seems to fit the category of one of those fundamentally poor ideas that never worked out.

That the phenomenon of "involvement" is on the upswing is suggested by the following data, which examine the fraction of major programs suffering budget changes by congressional action in recent years.

"Involvement" in this context differs from "commitment" in the same sense as the pig's and the chicken's roles in one's breakfast of ham and eggs. As stated in

**Percent of Programs Having
Budget Changed by Congress
(Relative to President's Request)**

Year	%
1977	28
1978	42
1979	47
1980	55
1981	63

the old adage: "The chicken was involved—the pig was committed."

In more recent years the above percentages have continued to increase with individual committees now making changes of the magnitude that had heretofore taken the best efforts of the entire Congress. Studies have shown that there are only two kinds of programs which suffer incessant budget tampering: those which are behind schedule and those which soon will be.

In a remarkable display of evenhandedness, the Congress can't even resist the temptation to change its own work. The *Congressional Record*, for example, offers the following recent passage: "Mr. Chairman, I offer an amendment to the amendment offered as an amendment to the amendment offered as a substitute for the amendment."

Returning to the nuclear power arena once again, Florida Power and Light began construction of its St. Lucie 2 plant with a design 70 percent complete. Seventy percent complete, that is, until the Nuclear Regulatory Commission issued a few changes—such that the design suddenly receded to the 30 percent complete point. Bob Dick, Duke Power's construction vice-president, has been quoted as saying, "You design, you attempt to erect, you change, you analyze, and it may recycle two or three times." Also quoted in *Forbes*, Stone and Webster senior vice-president John Landis observes, "You lose workers, usually the very best workers, and when you restart, the workers that remain make mistakes. The delays are, in my opinion, the most costly factor in the nuclear power economic picture."

A report attributed to a Spanish Civil War communiqué pretty well sums up the situation: "Our troops advanced today without losing a meter of ground."

And the above omits altogether the omnipresent changes in the overall business climate to which businesses must adjust. One example is the prime rate which determines the cost of borrowings, a rate which changed once every six months in the 1960s, once a month in the 1970s, and once a week early in the 1980s.

The law that relates to the above-mentioned lack of program stability is known as Augustine's Law of Universal Agitation:

LAW NUMBER XL

Most projects start out slowly—and then sort of taper off.

Truly, the seventh month of a pregnancy is not the most opportune time to begin discussions of family planning.

Unfortunately, most managers seeking to manage in such an environment of incessant externally-imposed change all too soon develop a disturbingly detached perspective of responsibility for budget control. It is much as was the case with Ilie Nastase, the tennis pro, who explained his failure to report the year-old theft of his wife's credit card by noting, "Whoever had it was spending less than she was."

41

The Law of Diminished Returns

"The mountains will be in labor, and a ridiculous mouse will be brought forth."
—Horace, 8 B.C.

Shortly after beginning work in earnest on the invisible aircraft contract, albeit using money Daedalus had borrowed from the personal assets of the consultant who had advised them to go into this business (he was now quite wealthy), a contract change notice arrived from Washington reducing the planned production rate by a factor of four due to new budgetary restraints. DAL's management was chagrined to say the least and was reminded of Will Rogers' prophetic words, "Everyone says something must be done—but this time it looks like it might be us." And it was just at this moment that the headquarters review team arrived at the plant. Nonetheless, every effort was made to reduce costs. The entire productivity department (except of course for the administrator) was eliminated; testing was re-

> *duced drastically; the quality assurance effort
> halved; the data package eliminated; even the
> planned increase in the marketing budget was
> slightly reduced; and the head of engineering was
> transferred from the operating division to the
> corporate headquarters, an action which, it was
> widely rumored, had increased the average IQ
> of both organizations. The reduction in the ad-
> vertising budget created such a furor that the
> head of marketing actually returned from the
> Bahamas where he had been on a six-week trip
> scouting foreign sales prospects. But he as well
> as everyone else eventually got behind the cost
> reductions since it was now realized that they
> were in the world of Big Government.*

The path of least resistance in allocating scarce production funds among an abundance of competing projects within a company seems to be to build at least some
of everything, an approach which can be thought of as
the minimum noise solution. The same methodology is
used by governments at all levels to allocate their always
limited funds among too large a population of undertakings. The problem, of course, is that the greater the
variety of projects pursued, the fewer, for a fixed budget,
that can be adequately funded. In the case of manufacturing projects, the quantity produced of each type
must then be curtailed. It follows then that everything
is produced at its least efficient rate because of the small
quantities involved. The managers of starved factories
attempting to produce on such a basis will find special
meaning in the words of former San Francisco Giants
manager Dave Bristol, who, paraphrasing Gene Kirby
of the Montreal Expos, advised his sagging team,

"There'll be two buses leaving the hotel for the ballpark tomorrow. The two o'clock bus will be for those of you who need a little extra work. The empty bus will be leaving at five o'clock."

The tendency for production to stabilize at its least efficient rate is verified in Figure 54. This figure happens to apply to a number of projects pursued by the Defense

Marginally Inefficient

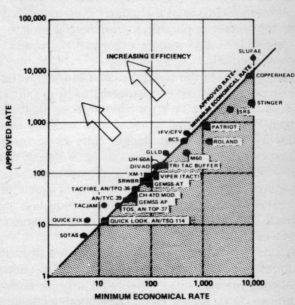

DATA SOURCE: HOUSE ARMED SERVICES COMMITTEE

Figure 54. For every production line there is a minimum efficient output rate below which the rhythm of the line is lost and excess capacity and concomitant inefficiency prevail. Most production programs in recent years have been operating on the threshold of this throughput precipice.

Department and illustrates the actual production rate
for a variety of hardware items as compared with their
minimum economical rate (generally defined as the output on a minimal one-shift, five-day-per-week basis).
The further a program moves away from the shaded
region in the figure, the more efficient becomes factory
operation. Operation *within* the shaded region is generally uneconomical. Yet, as is seen, nearly all programs
hover menacingly along the cliff of the shaded region.
Sadly, this tendency to pursue too broad a spectrum of
projects is not unique to the federal government but is
probably equally applicable to commercial firms such
as publishers, social welfare organizations, churches,
and a host of other organizations.

The problem in the case of manufacturing projects
working in a fixed market is exacerbated by the already
discussed commonplace error whereby costs are underestimated—which, when compounded with the inevitable externally imposed budget cuts, cause further
reductions in output and factory usage; which, in turn,
causes production to "move further up the learning
curve" due to the smaller quantities built; which then
generates an attendant increase in unit production cost;
which thereby requires a further decrease in production
rate; which . . .

Where does all this end? It seems to end when the
available funds are stretched to their utmost limit in
supporting the maximum number of projects, each at
its marginally inefficient rate. Thus, another unnatural
law seems to have been discovered which has all along
been at the root of the well-recognized dilemma whereby
each factory invariably seems to be struggling to stay
afloat, from an efficiency standpoint, independent of
substantial increases or decreases in the *overall* avail-

ability of funds for production. Augustine's Law of Marginal Survival explains the loss in total real output due to inefficiency when an ever-greater *variety* of under-funded programs is pursued:

LAW NUMBER XLI

The more one produces, the less one gets.

Test range photo, U.S. Army

"It is 'better than it sounds.' "

PART VI

DISASTER

42

Going Out of Business—For Fun and Profit

"If rats are experimented on, they will develop cancer."

—Morton's Law

April 1, the day of reckoning, literally crashed upon the scene. They were in the sixth day of a four-hour test. Suddenly It occurred—with a note of finality that astonished even the most confirmed pessimists, the headquarters independent cost analysts. The event was the dreaded appearance of test results, in this case the worst form of that malaise—flight test results. It had been a truly forgettable experience. Thinking back to the time the decision had been made, it had seemed like a profoundly good idea to save schedule time by proceeding with high-rate production and then conducting the flight tests whenever it became convenient. Now, as Daedalus's management surveyed their factory (which was bulging over onto the employees' golf course with unflyable airplanes) that was not so certain.

Mother Nature, it seemed, does not respond well to many of the modern management and marketing techniques which had proved so successful back in the proposal-writing days. Even such tried and true methods as declaring the flight—which was prematurely terminated by the crash on takeoff—as being 80 percent successful (successful checkout, successful start-up, successful taxi, and successful ground run—all before the disastrous lift-off phase) no longer seemed to wash. Such events had always been termed in the press releases as "successful destructive tests," but a consensus now began to emerge that something even more substantive might have to be done to extricate the program from the jaws of the testers while at the same time recovering some much-needed funding. The solution was to further reduce the amount of testing and fire the testers.

The Law to be promulgated in this chapter concerns the testing of new products and reflects a view expounded by Casey Stengel, late of the New York Yankees and Mets, and apparently shared by baseball managers and program managers alike: "I've had no experience with that sort of thing," he said, "and all of it has been bad."

Product testing, it will be seen, has much in common with discussions at high level meetings—namely, most of the time consumed is devoted to the least significant part of the problem. Were one to examine the relationship between the amount of testing that is required of a newly developed product and the complexity of that product, it might not be unreasonable to expect that the less complex the item the less testing it requires. That is, an anvil might be expected to require less testing than a new automobile. If, for example, a chart were made showing the number of flight tests of various missile systems against some measure of their complexity, the two parameters would presumably be directly related, and the trend thereby observed would show a direct correlation, i.e., a line sloping upward to the right. That is, the more complex the missile, the greater the number of flight tests. Such a plot is actually presented in Figure 55, based on the assumption that unit cost is a not unreasonable surrogate measure of "complexity." It is seen that, in keeping with the now well-established implausibility principle of business, the correlation is not direct but rather is inverse, with the line sloping *downward* to the right exactly as should have been unexpected in the first place. Thus, one finds that the amount of testing needed actually *decreases* as an item becomes more complex, providing still another motivation for designers to avoid simplicity and at the same time reduce the likelihood of having the failings of their equipment exposed during the test program.

The amount of testing required seems to be more nearly explainable in terms of tradition than in terms of any technical rationale. One suspects that the testers may have taken quite broadly the instruction to "test the system." Relatively simple, unguided artillery projectiles somehow demand literally thousands of test rounds, whereas a new 6000-mile intercontinental ballistic missile needs only a few handfuls of test flights to demonstrate its adequacy. Thus, the less complex the system, the more testing it requires, a consequence of which forms the basis of the Augustine-McKinley* Law of Complicational Simplicity :

LAW NUMBER XLII

Simple systems are not feasible because they require infinite testing.

The data in the figure can be extrapolated to determine that it will be impossible to test hardware which itself costs *more* than one trillion dollars since that cost corresponds to the limiting point on the graph at which only a single test is possible. The Space Shuttle lies perilously close to this point based on its four-flight development program and one-billion-dollar-plus price tag.

A very useful "inverse" corollary exists to the above law. It will be noted that when the number of flight tests which are planned in a missile development program is *known,* one may use the curve in Figure 55 to predict the unit cost of the item in question! This, in contrast with the more conventional and more comprehensive manner of projecting unit costs, requires only a few man-seconds of unskilled labor. Furthermore, it produces results that compare quite favorably in terms of accuracy with the official cost estimates supplied for programs during the past two decades. In the sample examined during this investigation, the above-mentioned fast-track costing technique produces an estimate of unit cost which in 40 percent of the cases is within plus or minus one-third of the correct value. The

*Charles H. McKinley, vice-president, Vought Aeronautics.

Relationship of Complexity (Cost) and Number of Tests Required

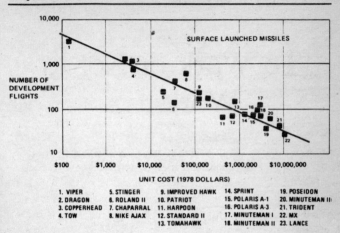

Figure 55. Very simple products often require literally thousands of test articles. Very complex items apparently require very little system test hardware.

official cost estimation record in recent years is 50 percent within one-third of the true value—a not altogether dissimilar result. Furthermore, the present method not only overestimates the cost about half the time—a phenomenon foreign to the official computation techniques—but also reduces the danger of one's becoming lost inside a computer while pursuing the more conventional techniques of analysis.

43

To Work or Not to Work . . .

"Stand by to crash."
—H. V. Wiley, April 4, 1933
Last command to crew of dirigible *Akron*

What a time for the roof to leak. Just when it was raining. Not only was the flight hardware not working, but it was actually getting worse with each passing day. And this was on the heels of the chief engineer having just assured top management that the new design would fix the problem forever again. The project seemed to have much in common with the gentleman about whom Winston Churchill once said, "He is a sheep in sheep's clothing." It is widely recognized that hardware is unable to withstand the pressures of functioning in the world of reality— working well on the practice field but failing miserably when the chips are down. In this case even the great American cure-all of throwing money at the problem seemed merely to purchase high reliability that the product would not be reliable

382

at all. Not unexpectedly, perhaps, the PR department was still clinging to the philosophy of Mark Twain who, commenting on the music of Richard Wagner, asserted that it is "better than it sounds." The only good news was that the efforts to strengthen the department which oversees quality had been so successful that waivers to accept errors in workmanship were now being processed in less than three hours. On that note of encouragement, and in recognition of the latest market environment study conducted jointly by the strategic planning department and the newly established Paris office, Daedalus took on still another name—one which would properly recognize its changing stature. Hereafter, it would be known as Daedalus Industries, International. And the new committee on the urgency of increasing profitability had now been meeting every other Friday for two consecutive weeks. But somehow it seemed that the words of one well-known college football coach might apply to Daedalus: "The light at the end of the tunnel," he said, "may be a freight train."

There is still another annoying property exhibited by hardware even after its cost has been established and after its design has been finalized. This is the propensity of hardware to sense when a malfunction would be the *most* harmful—and then invariably to fail precisely at that moment. The failure will thus most often occur in the midst of a customer demonstration, at a trade show, or when the customer is using the product for some critical purpose far away from any customer service support. This is why stoves fail on Thanksgiving Day and air conditioners fail in July. The subconscious and widespread acceptance of this concept among those engaged in the design of hardware is suggested by the offhand remark of a senior engineer making a report several years ago at the flight failure investigation of a major space mission. With noticeable satisfaction and no small amount of pride he announced, "We have never had a solder joint fail except for the one during the flight." Such remarks would lead one to believe that this type of hardware must be originating from factories such as the legendary one which was said to be so disorganized that when it was struck by a tornado over three million dollars of improvement was done.

Figure 56 quantifies this intransigent behavior of hardware based on a sampling of reliability outcomes actually exhibited by a number of items. The data are spaced along the abscissa of the plot in a manner which preserves the same sequential order of the programs examined for each phase shown. It will be noted that for each step a given item of hardware moves closer to its intended use, its reliability decreases by a factor of two. In moving from analytical predictions to laboratory tests, for example, the mean time between failure deteriorates by a factor of two. In moving from laboratory test to actual customer use, the mean time between failure erodes by another factor of two.

It has, of course, often been pointed out with respect to such results (usually by the builders of the hardware in question) that laboratory tests frequently do not involve so severe an environment as is encountered in the real world, or that human-induced failures in actual operation should not be counted at all. General Jack Deane, once commander of the Army's 100,000-person development command, has said that the definition of

Hardware Can't Stand Real World Pressures

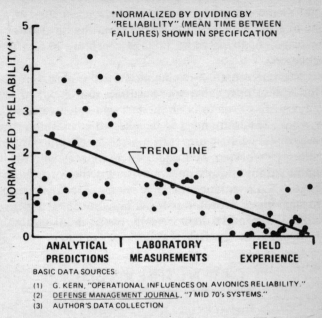

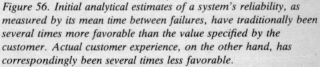

BASIC DATA SOURCES:

(1) G. KERN, "OPERATIONAL INFLUENCES ON AVIONICS RELIABILITY."
(2) DEFENSE MANAGEMENT JOURNAL, "7 MID 70's SYSTEMS."
(3) AUTHOR'S DATA COLLECTION

Figure 56. Initial analytical estimates of a system's reliability, as measured by its mean time between failures, have traditionally been several times more favorable than the value specified by the customer. Actual customer experience, on the other hand, has correspondingly been several times less favorable.

an American GI is a person who, if left alone overnight on a barren desert with absolutely nothing in his possession but an anvil, will have broken the anvil by dawn! These explanations, however, leave unexplained insofar as reliability testing is concerned what then might be the purpose of conducting tests or performing analyses that do *not* relate to the actual circumstances which the beleaguered user of the items in question will have to face—or, for that matter, why laboratory tests are not then conducted in a *truly* benign environment so as to free the developer *altogether* from the burdensome nuisance of fixing those failures which are in fact uncovered.

The only possible explanation for the observed deterioration in reliability as hardware moves out of the laboratory seems to lie in the fact that either reliability figures are not intended to be assessed in a fashion that relates to what a user can expect or else hardware, although working well under circumstances when it is unimportant, simply does not possess the fortitude to work when it experiences the pressures of the real world. Dismissing the former as being unreasonable, the true explanation must then logically reside in Augustine's Law of Hardware Belligerency:

LAW NUMBER XLIII

Hardware works best when it matters the least.

If nature is *not* belligerent, one then must explain why the *last* side of the windshield to defrost is always the driver's side. Or why virtually all diets can be summarized in five words: "If it's good, it's bad."

Dr. John Allen, president of General Research Corporation, maintained for a number of years a graph of the trend in reliability of certain types of airborne radars as a function of the year of their development. Reliability, that is, as reflected in the design *specifications* for new systems—or, in other words, the goals which had been established for them. The improvement in the *specified* average time between failures of the most advanced systems was truly spectacular, improving at a rate of a factor of ten each decade.

Unfortunately, the same analysis revealed that the average time between failures actually being realized in *operational* units was always simply a fixed number, far below the specified values. Thus, there was no real relationship between what was expected and what was occurring. Apparently some new universal reliability constant, like pi, was at work throughout this period which was undermining the great advancements which were being made in the state-of-the-art of writing specifications. Fortunately, recent trends are much more encouraging, but it was nonetheless necessary to arrive at the conclusion that "airborne electronics are not responsive to enthusiasm." The same, it might be added, is true of radar ovens, automobiles, electric trains, and water heaters—to cite but a few more down-to-earth items.

The consequences of the above law of enduring recalcitrance are exacerbated by the tendency of human managers, when faced with the prospect of a funding shortfall, to eliminate that part of a program which has the least near-term impact, is quite costly, and is not mandatory in terms of demonstrating the so-called fundamental capability of the product at hand—i.e., they cut reliability improvement and testing efforts. This is the very area wherein the Japanese, by properly emphasizing quality, have excelled—and to the amazement of many American managers have demonstrated, as already noted herein, that it absolutely costs less, not more, to manufacture a quality product. To oversimplify, this is because it costs less to do something once than it does to do it twice. An accurate assessment of the impact of sloppy quality practices is given by Dallas Green, manager of the world-champion Phillies, on the heels of his team's fourth straight defeat the following year, as to how they had fallen into their last-place status: "We've earned it," he declared.

44

A Long Day's Night

". . . a knife without a blade, for which the handle is missing."
—Lichtenberg, 18th century

It had been demoralizing to learn that all the money which was being poured into the invisible airplane was merely guaranteeing that it wouldn't work. Some of the employees were even beginning to believe Michael Flanders' comment, quoted in his obituary: "If God had intended us to fly he would never have given us railways." Even the excitement generated by the first nonstop takeoff in the flight test program could not long overcome the depression of the work force. The corporate auditor dismissed the event with the words, "We fell forward this time." Rumors among the factory hands were rampant: one noted that there was good news and there was bad news. The good news was that management was buying everyone on the assembly line a turkey for Christmas. The bad news was that they had only ordered ten turkeys. But the really bad news was yet to come. This had to do with some questions about the eventual maintenance of broken aircraft. Fortunately, however, this particular problem could be deferred because of management's foresight in previously eliminating all the maintenance planning activity from the budget. This step had been taken during the funding reductions which were needed to finance the animated movie which would show potential customers how well the invisible airplane was going to look. Unfortunately, not inconsiderable embarrassment and controversy surrounded even this seemingly innocuous venture when the corporate PR department carelessly registered the movie with the Library of Congress under the category reserved for Science Fiction—a particularly grievous error in that the fuss which followed diverted attention from the fine job the chairman had done in narrating the now widely distributed film. But the legal department once again saved the day, plowing altogether new forensic ground in the field of warranties, proffering an iron-clad guarantee to each customer which in its most fundamental form promised that if anything broke, the customer would get to keep both pieces.

For many years a great deal of discussion has been devoted to the matter of building equipment which can be easily maintained, and in particular maintained by individuals with only limited time in which to master their sometimes demanding calling. For example, a decade ago attentive visitors to one of the major control centers for the defense of North America against attack by Soviet airplanes would have observed, hanging inconspicuously from the door knob of a giant room literally packed with the most advanced electronics, a small tag noting reassuringly, "All equipment in this room has been checked and OK'd by Private First Class Smith."

Actually, considerable time and effort have been devoted by the manufacturers of new products to the preparation of maintenance plans, spares plans, fault isolation plans, and training plans, all of which are essential to good customer support. The problem is that, in the bureaucratic stampede to give this area greater and earlier attention in the process of creating new products, most of the plans have suffered from a minor oversight: They were constructed long before anyone knew what the actual hardware was going to comprise. Similarly, dozens of reliability analysts were placed diligently to work multiplying long strings of nines (reliability analysts need only learn to multiply nines, as in 99.99 percent reliable), but their usually encouraging mathematical results seldom bore any resemblance to the failures which ultimately produced the disasters. These latter events were instead the consequences of a bracket rubbing on a wire until it broke, a seal installed upside down, a leaky valve, an overheated resistor, a cold solder joint, a flake of dust, an improperly torqued nut, or a fuse holder which melted without blowing the fuse.

Worse yet, so powerful became the cult of the "ilities" (reliability, maintainability, availability, etc.) in the 1960s and early 1970s and their incessant awareness campaigns that attention was actually diverted away from the real task of designing and building high-quality hardware. The ultimate consequence was that in more than one company, large but carefully isolated groups were established off-line simply to make posters and fill in the ponderous forms demanded by their compatriots in the "ilities" departments of their corporate customer or in the government—but to do so in a manner which would minimize the interference to those charged with actually designing the hardware. Thus, the critically important matter of assuring maintainability became, in the real world, even more peripheral. The fact is that reliability, as already noted, must be designed into the product by the designer and built into it by the manufacturer—it cannot be inculcated by the quality department.

It should not be surprising then that the average American fighter aircraft uses 300 different *kinds* of fasteners (rivets, bolts, etc.) and the removable panels alone on one aircraft required nine different *kinds* of fasteners to be released before full access could be gained. In a large variety of consumer products the parts which break most often are the ones buried the deepest inside the machine, always carefully located adjacent to the sharpest and hottest component to be found. Or that, as often happens, nonstandard, peculiar wrenches, bolt threads, washers, and wire gauges are specified in maintenance manuals, which themselves always relate to the previously phased-out model.

One Army maintenance manual advised the mechanic in effect that all he had to do to repair an automotive item was "remove the center nut and accompanying washer affixing the left anchor bracket

(when viewed from the right side of the platform looking toward the forward panel) by turning the nut in a
counter-clockwise direction with a standard socket
wrench, using extreme caution not to interfere with the
high voltage electrical power supply immediately to the
left and below the adjacent connector and harness."

So much for the volunteer Army. It may be safer to
be an infantryman than a mechanic.

Worse yet, it has all too often been found that when
a trained mechanic is in fact available who possesses
the mind of an Einstein, the dexterity of a surgeon, and
the agility of a chimney sweep, the needed replacement
parts are not available. Even a systems analyst would
be able to understand that it makes little sense to buy
twice as many airplanes or automobiles only to have
three-fourths of the total grounded for the lack of spare
parts. Subway cars are an interesting case in point—in
New York City the demands for maintenance are so
great that it is difficult in the extreme to keep a fleet
rolling under the streets.

But this is not a case of bad news and good news.
This is a case of bad news and worse news. It may in
fact be true that, as has already been noted in Chapter
18, as more and more money is spent on an item of
hardware, the more often it breaks; but it is also true
that the more one spends for an item of hardware the
more maintenance hours will likely be required to try
to fix it. This is illustrated in Figure 57, wherein it is
observed that, at least in the instance of military airplanes, as investment cost goes up the average time
between failures may get shorter—but at least the maintenance man-hours increase! This is, presumably, good
news only from the standpoint of someday assuring zero

The Price of High Cost

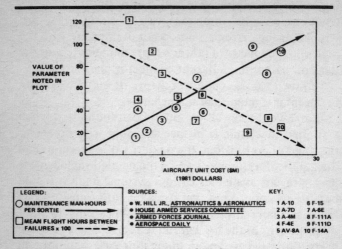

Figure 57. When hardware becomes relatively more costly, and therefore usually more complex, it is often characterized by increasing maintenance demands. This of course need not be the case—it merely is.

unemployment. Some of the new aircraft now entering the inventory will, it is to be hoped, reverse this trend—only time will tell.

The real difficulty, however, stems from the fact that the parts which break are, as discussed earlier, always the ones located in the most inaccessible places. Therefore, only a few mechanics are able to crowd around them simultaneously—an observation which may seem elementary but which in fact will be seen to have dire consequences.

Consider the matter of maintaining a modern high-performance military airplane, an airplane which in most instances will have been designed to fly at least one mission each day. The difficulty which arises is that, as suggested in Figure 57, when more and more money is spent on an aircraft, eventually the sum of the required maintenance crew-hours plus flight hours will exceed twenty-four hours each day! What then?

In view of the well-established impossibility of reducing maintenance demands by virtue of reducing the cost of high-tech products, some other more realistic solution must be sought to negate this dilemma. Such expediencies as developing a breed of miniature mechanics who can cluster around the broken part in large numbers, or adopting in-flight maintenance (similar to in-flight refueling, but using accompanying airborne garages instead of just filling stations) might be considered.

The space program, it should be noted, has already adopted the concept of spaceborne garages—as for example the use of the Shuttle to rendezvous with the ailing Solar Max spacecraft so that an astronaut could replace a blown fuse in the attitude control system. Thus, for the price of a fuse (plus a little bit of overhead cost to fly the fuse and astronaut into space) essentially a brand-new working spacecraft was obtained.

The most promising solution to the problem of ever-increasing maintenance demands, however, seems to reside in the Augustine-Morrison* Law of Unidirectional Flight, which is based on the very real possibility of a day longer than twenty-four hours:

*James B. Morrison, vice-president and general manager, Huntsville Division, Coleman Research Corporation.

LAW NUMBER XLIV

Aircraft flight in the 21st century will always be in a westerly direction, preferably supersonic, crossing time zones to provide the additional hours needed each day to fix the broken electronics.

Horace Greeley was insightful.

45

For the Want
of a Nail

"It was a turkey."
—Charles Dickens

Looking back, the end had begun in an unan-
ticipated manner, with the failure of a solder
joint. This in turn had created what is referred
to among experts as a "flight anomaly." Sub-
sequent to collecting the parts which survived
the anomaly (this took considerable time since
they were scattered over several square miles of
countryside), it was found that the design had
been in error, the parts that had been built did
not match the design, and the quality control was
defective and had failed to discover the mis-
match. Everyone was working alone together.
Aside from this, however, the new project man-
ager who had taken command the previous day
did appear to be regaining control. Disappoint-
ment over the rash of hardware and software
problems was nonetheless intense, particularly

in view of the record in the aircraft's flight test program which had only recently achieved three successful strings of one-in-a-row. An argument broke out between the faction which believed that if the aircraft had been designed with more engines the consequences of an engine failure would have been reduced and those who argued that increasing the number of engines would merely have increased the chances of a failure. The company's head statistician was a bit suspect anyway, largely because of his calculations at the annual company ball where he disclosed the extremely remote likelihood that any employee would ever be on an airliner on which two totally separate people were carrying bombs—and his subsequent suggestion that all employees should therefore carry a bomb for safety purposes whenever flying. To make matters worse, the government's project officer on the invisible airplane program was now being investigated by the OSI, FBI, GAO, IRS, and KGB for having accepted a souvenir necktie from a contractor some twelve years earlier. Morale was further battered by renewed criticism from those who some months before had pointed out that if the test program had been still further curtailed, this sort of failure might not have occurred at all. It was becoming increasingly apparent that the happiest time on this project had been the period between the announcement of the contract's winner and the end of the victory party.

For some inexplicable reason, when dealing with a multimillion dollar piece of equipment the part that fails is always a seven dollar seal, a seventy cent bolt, or even more likely, a seven cent solder joint.

The truthfulness of this suspected behavior of hardware is verified by the evidence presented in Figure 58, which examines flight failures occurring in the space program. Each data point represents the loss of an entire space mission due to a booster hardware anomaly

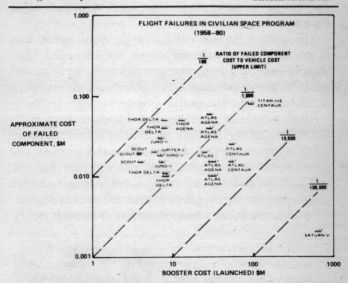

Figure 58. Most test failures of major systems are due to seemingly innocuous faults in components which themselves represent but a small fraction of the cost of the overall system. Extraordinary discipline and attentiveness to detail are thereby demanded in major technical undertakings since hardware is very unforgiving of human failings, no matter how well intended.

(read, "explosion") and relates the cost of the hardware launched, *excluding* payload, to the approximate cost of the item causing the mission to fail. The cost shown is that of the lowest replaceable unit with which the cause of failure can be associated based on available data, and thus represents a maximum cost. In nearly all cases the cause of failure is probably traceable to a far lesser component costing at least a factor of ten less than shown in the figure. As pointed out in Klipstein's Law, an expensive "transistor protected by a fast-acting fuse will always protect the fuse by blowing first." See Figure 59 for verification.

The reason for such behavior is, once again, that potential major problems which are identified (and feared) early in a program receive intense scrutiny and are thereby most often averted. Rarely are the problems which actually plague major programs even to be found on the list of concerns at the project's outset. It is usually left to one of the literally millions of routine tasks or small components that comprise a major product and which demand such great personal vigilance and discipline from all levels of workers and managers, to fall prey to the unforgiving laws of probability or of neglect. This diligence is the reason commercial airliners can be

Figure 59. Fuse and holder from author's son's automobile. Prompt melting of costly wiring harness and fuse holder successfully saved inexpensive fuse from damage.

built with such reliability that they fly an equivalent of 40,000 times around the Earth for every fatal accident they suffer—yet it is a testimonial to our managerial genius that those same airlines manage to delay, lose, or destroy suitcases entrusted to them with remarkable consistency. As the saying goes, breakfast in New York, lunch in Los Angeles, and baggage in Baghdad. Seldom are we plagued by lions. More often we suffer the ignominy of being eaten by ducks. A poster displayed prominently in many flight operations centers of airports catering to private pilots aptly points out, "Aviation in itself is not inherently dangerous. But to an even greater degree than the sea, it is terribly unforgiving of any carelessness, incapacity, or neglect." This could, perhaps to a lesser degree, be generalized to encompass many other areas of business.

This unforgivingness would be attested to by, among others, the designer of the tie-down bolts for the original Viking rocket—a rocket which to this day holds the world altitude record for static firings—when the bolts failed and to everyone's consternation the rocket took off. Or the guidance system for the early and errant rocket which came to be known as the world's first ICBM: "Into Cuba by Mistake."

Sometimes a single hardware malfunction can even bring down an entire industry. Probably of greater consequence to the U.S. nuclear power industry than all the other challenges which beset it was the political fallout from a stuck valve at the Three Mile Island facility.

Based upon extensive evidence of the type cited above, Augustine's Law of Amplification of Agony can be derived:

LAW NUMBER XLV

One should expect that the expected can be prevented, but the unexpected should have been expected.

The history of aerospace is just one industrial example rife with instances of this phenomenon, many rich with irony as well as agony. The developer of one particular aircraft engine, after suffering a series of highly destructive failures on a test stand due to foreign objects (bolts, washers, small tools) being inadvertently left inside test engines, dictated a procedure whereby prior to each run an inspector would physically enter the inlet of the engine and personally inspect for extraneous objects using a flashlight and thence certify *in writing* that no such objects were to be found. Only then would a test be initiated. As one should expect, it was only a short time until still another destructive failure occurred—this time due to the inspector's flashlight having been left inside the engine.

A somewhat more exotic failure was narrowly averted during a critical series of flight tests conducted at the personal direction of the Secretary of Defense to determine whether or not the Army's new air defense missile should be canceled. Just moments prior to launch of the very first flight, a bobcat climbed a power pole at Holloman Air Force Base, some miles from the missile test center at White Sands, suffering an electrifying experience and in so doing shutting down all power at the missile site. Had this occurred just seconds later, the missile would have automatically self-destructed for safety reasons due to the loss of ground tracking. Fortunately, in this instance due to a breakdown of the Law of Natural Belligerence, a result of the bobcat's having climbed the pole four seconds too soon, the only effect was a delayed launch and a number of sets of jangled nerves.

On another project, this one in the 1960s, two missile electrical boxes manufactured by different contractors were joined together by a pair of wires which connected into each of the boxes. Thanks to a particularly thorough preflight check, it was discovered that the wires had been reversed, and instructions were thence sent out for the contractors to correct the problem. It was left to the ensuing postflight failure analysis to reveal that the contractors had indeed corrected the reversed wires as instructed. In fact, *both* of them had made the correction—proving once again that *two* wrongs do *not* make a right.

Nor, for that matter, do *three*. A harrowing in-flight shut-down of *all three* engines on a wide-body commercial passenger jet was recently traced to the failure of mechanics to properly install inexpensive "O-rings" in the fuel system. It is a fundamental axiom of mathematics that redundancy protects only against *independent* errors—hence it is not acceptable merely to be consistent if one is consistently wrong.

Some would attribute these events to luck, or the lack thereof. Unarguably, something called luck does affect many events, but the fact is that much of what passes for bad luck is nothing other than human neglect—the lack of the discipline to "do it thoroughly and do it right." One needs to take the viewpoint that there is no such thing as the widely heralded "random failure" of hardware. All failures occur for a reason. Don Shula, coach of the Miami Dolphins, dismisses luck in the following terms: "Sure, luck means a lot in football. Not having a good quarterback is bad luck."

But the plethora of stories of hardware failures attributable to so-called minor components notwithstanding, the solution apparently being pursued to the problem of low-cost components causing malfunctions warrants questioning. That solution? As previously implied in Law Number XVI (page 143), simply eliminate all low-cost components by making every component a high-cost component. As any reasonable sales manager could then point out, such parts are absolutely failure-proof and, furthermore, are easily repaired.

46

The Big Bang

"It is so soon that I am done for.
I wonder what I was begun for."
—Tombstone, Cheltenham churchyard

It had been a first in the annals of program management: three consecutive months as the recipient of Senator Proxmire's Golden Fleece award for exceptional incompetence. It had been particularly embarrassing when the news media discovered that the company's chief test pilot, prior to moving into that position, had been working as a baggage smasher for one of the local airlines. Still, it was a total surprise when on December 7th the telegram arrived. It was like finding a "see agent" entry listed after one's flight on the departures board at the airport. Ironically, most of the program staff was away at the afternoon happy-hour which had followed the awards luncheon at the new club which had just opened across the street from the plant. It turned out to be the very day that the marketing and legal departments were being honored, in what was later to be known as The Last Supper, for their significant contributions to the project. As the management noted during the presentation of the bonus checks, things were actually progressing pretty well, at least on average: Costs were running ahead of plan while schedule was running behind. That things were serious after the telegram to the company's president arrived became rapidly apparent when the announcement was made for the entire legal department to return to the plant without even stopping to pick up their golf clubs. No mention was made of the engineers or factory employees, since all the factory workers had been back at the plant all day wandering around looking for the parts they needed to do their jobs, and no one had seen the engineers in the six weeks since the personal computers had been distributed. Up to this point there had actually grown to be a common bond between the government's and contractor's legal departments, based on a shared concern that peace might break out between the two respective organizations' contracting groups.

The quintessential question is posed, as one should expect, by Yogi Berra. Inquired Berra while observing his roommate, Dr. Bobby Brown, as Brown was studying *Gray's Anatomy,* "Let me know how it ends."

One consequence of the myriad of problems examined herein is the relatively high mortality rate previously noted among development projects, whether they be aimed at the commercial market or the government market. This is a likelihood which, incidentally, is rarely reflected in a firm's long-range sales plan, but which nonetheless is itself highly predictable in the aggregate. Ill-conceived programs simply have highly foreseeable outcomes; much as was suggested by Sammy Baugh, the quarterback, who answered a question as to whether the outcome of his team's 73-0 defeat in the 1940 professional football championship game might have been different had his team scored first. His judgment: "Sure. It would have been 73 to 6."

In order to survive to completion, every program must maintain an extremely high single-skirmish-survival probability in its encounters with the various steps in the budget cycle. This is particularly true of programs conducted for the federal government, because in the congressional approval process alone, a research and development program's budget will be voted upon at least eighteen times a year, or a total of 144 times in the average program's lifetime—thus the need to keep a program moving rapidly so as to reduce its exposure. Managing programs in this environment is much like raising cattle in some of the more barren areas in Texas, where a cow is said to have to graze at sixty miles per hour just to keep from starving.

The mortality data presented in Figure 60 are derived from over 300 significant projects conducted by the government in the past two decades and verify the precariousness of such undertakings. The data reveal the probability that any given project will fail to survive the threats to its existence which arise prior to any given year in its lifetime. It is seen that there is about a 4 percent probability of cancellation of a program each and every year except for the first year, sometimes referred to as the honeymoon. After that brief respite, defeat can be snatched from the jaws of victory at al-

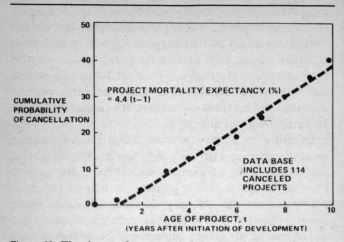

Figure 60. The chance of a program's being canceled is more or less proportional to its exposure duration. Within limits, both cost and likelihood of cancellation are minimized by fully funding a program so that it can be conducted on a relatively aggressive schedule.

most any time. This appears to be relatively independent of program maturity, presumably even for such aged endeavors as the two programs mentioned in Chapter 39 (see page 353) which have successfully defied the laws of probability and soon will have been in development for eighteen years. In fact, the only reason for optimism with respect to such geriatric programs is offered by George Burns, who notes, "Once you get to be 100 you have it made. You almost never hear of anyone dying who is over 100."

Many projects are thus seen to share the malady once attributed by the above-mentioned Mr. Berra to an altogether different arena. "In Yankee Stadium," he explained, "it gets late early."

This is of course a particularly disappointing conclusion in that nearly all new projects begin with such great promise and fanfare. But then, as retired Lieutenant General and former astronaut Tom Stafford reminds us, "Yesterday's headlines are today's fish wrappers."

When asked if it did not thrill him to know that every time he spoke the hall was packed to overflowing, Winston Churchill once responded, "It is quite flattering, but whenever I feel this way I always remember that if instead of making a political speech I was being hanged, the crowd would be twice as big."

Indeed, many business projects seem to have had a brilliant future behind them. The problem is, of course, that managers must spend inordinate amounts of time trying to keep their projects fed—rather than overseeing their proper execution. But it is just human nature to seek to save one's undertakings when they are in danger of cancellation, as is recognized in Augustine's Law of Incomplete:

LAW NUMBER XLVI

A billion saved is a billion earned.

Managers of challenging development projects can understand the chagrin of Iowa citizens who one day read in the weather forecast column of their local newspaper that "there is a 90% chance of tomorrow." The French poet and philosopher Paul Valéry once noted, "The trouble with our times is that the future is not what it used to be."

The existence of this law does provide encouragement, on the other hand, that not *all* managers are successful in working their programs into that position, apparently ultimately sought, wherein termination costs exceed the cost-to-completion. *That,* it is said, is the essence of job security.

It has also been said that there are only two things one needs to know about business: How to get into it; and how to get out of it. Perhaps the more difficult of the two is the latter—knowing when to crater a long-pursued undertaking.

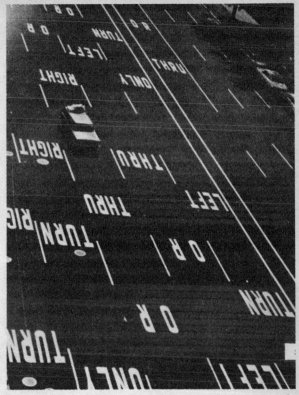

"Regulations . . . would preclude any difficulties ever again."

PART VII

DISASTER REVISITED

47

Help Strikes Again

"You may fire when you are ready, Gridley."
—Admiral George Dewey
May 1, 1898

"This undertaking will without doubt be the most significant contribution of your entire project," the newcomer announced at the staff meeting the morning following the cancellation of the world's first invisible airplane project. It was soon learned that this individual had been assigned to exhume the remains of the effort and to determine what had gone wrong so that it could absolutely never, ever, happen again. The speaker was obviously well qualified, having never had his own professional reputation besmirched with the types of problem that had plagued the project whose entrails he was now to examine. There were, of course, those few malcontents in the back of the room who in this case mumbled something about the speaker having never been involved in any project, but even they were soon

silenced by the enthusiasm which built up for the undertaking when the buses from headquarters arrived. The two least credible sentences in the English language have been said to be "The check is in the mail" and "I'm from headquarters and I'm here to help you." Soon, the headquarters staff was careening throughout the organization, spreading death and destruction wherever it alighted. The effort to pin blame began to gain such momentum, expedited enormously by the fact that several formerly key members of the project were now off selling real estate, that virtually everyone eagerly joined the fray. Hindsight is the world's most exact science. All in all, judging by the number of auditors and representatives of the media who were present—and the "distance" being built by the workers—the art of management was fast in danger of becoming America's favorite spectator sport.

The base newspaper of a military installation in Texas which had been beleaguered by a streak of bad luck once headlined, "Inspector General and other problems arrive."

Joe Sherick, the Defense Department's very dedicated and able Inspector General, speaking of his boss Caspar Weinberger, once said: "My good news is his bad news." At very best, in the world of audits the good news is that there is no bad news. That's as good as it gets.

Auditors, reviewers, inspectors, and other forms of overseers perform a truly important role, but that role can be beneficial only when applied *constructively* and with considerable moderation. The prevailing trend would suggest the existence of an explosion in the over-seer business, with an ominous threat approaching that there will soon be no one left for the auditors to audit. When this day of an infinite watcher-to-worker ratio arrives, it will presumably be necessary to focus audits on the mistakes which would have been made had in fact there been anyone doing anything. As Figure 61 indicates, the increase in magnitude of the oversight effort by the federal government alone is on the order of 200 percent per decade, possibly making it America's fastest growing industry. But perhaps this is to be expected in a world which pays a network television anchorman several times as much to *report* the news as it

The Auditing Boom

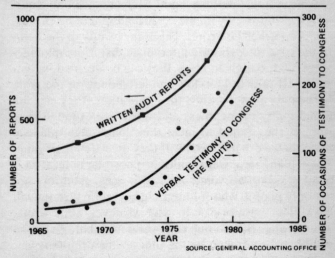

SOURCE: GENERAL ACCOUNTING OFFICE

Figure 61. The amount of activity devoted to reviews and audits has increased markedly in recent years in spite of frequent protestations to the contrary.

pays the President of the United States to *make* the news.

There are fully tens of thousands of federal auditors of one type or another at large today, of whom a disproportionately large 20,000 are assigned to ferret out the Department of Defense's transgressions—via both internal and external audits. No matter whether the production rate in the factory is one per month or 1000 per month, the grandstand is always full. Chuck Mills, a former football coach at Wake Forest, reminds us that a spectator is a person "who sits forty rows up in the stands and wonders why a seventeen-year-old kid can't hit another seventeen-year-old kid with a ball from forty yards away . . . and then he goes out to the parking lot and can't find his car."

An auditor, like any good Monday-morning quarterback, endowed with the 20-20 hindsight of his profession, can never be wrong. This is the beauty of the field. In the case of corporate internal audits, if the management bid too high and lost, they can be deemed incompetent. If they bid too low and left money on the table by heavily undercutting the opposition, they can be found guilty of ineptness and waste even though they won. If they failed to meet their long-range financial plan, they were ineffective. If they exceeded their long-range plan, they were guilty of poor planning at best or of padding at worst. And so it goes. Auditors are the only people who if four are gathered in a room will have eight opinions as to why whatever went wrong went wrong. But no one can ever doubt that, given the choice, it is better to be the mugger than the muggee.

As Sugar Ray Leonard, the prize fighter, told a group of students at Harvard, "I consider myself blessed. I consider you blessed. We've all been blessed with God-given talents. Mine just happens to be beatin' people up."

Major League umpire Bruce Froemming puts it this way: "We're right 99 percent of the time—make that 99.9 percent." He concludes with a smile, "I never made a call I didn't like."

Lord Barnetson, chairman of the *London Observer*, has had attributed to him the following anecdote about how a management critic would review Schubert's *Unfinished Symphony:*

It appears that for a considerable period of time the four oboe players had nothing to do. The number should be reduced, and their work spread over the whole orchestra, thus eliminating peaks of activity.

All twelve violins were playing identical notes. This seems unnecessary duplication and the staff of the section should be drastically cut. If a large volume of sound is really required, this could be obtained through an electric amplifier.

Much effort was absorbed in the playing of demisemiquavers. This seems an excessive refinement, and it is recommended that all notes be rounded up to the nearest semiquaver. If this is done, it would be possible to use trainees and lower grade operators.

No useful purpose is served by repeating with horns the passage that has already been handled by the strings. If all such redundant passages were eliminated, the concert could be reduced from two hours to twenty minutes. If Schubert had attended to these matters, he would probably have been able to finish his symphony after all.

One thing is certain: If you try to please everybody, somebody isn't going to like it.

A new branch of specialization is now emerging in order to assure that the auditors are themselves performing their assignments effectively; this new branch is called watching the watchers. The possibilities for still further expansion of this specialty are boundless: e.g., watching the watchers watch. The creation of such opportunities represents a breakthrough in that it ensures the perpetuation of the auditing and reviewing trades even in the dread event that the last individual actually doing any work gets fed up and decides to join the legions of watchers overseeing his meager output. The media will undoubtedly note this event in passing by reporting something like: "The nation's work force, wearing a yellow sports shirt, today retired from active employment amid a crescendo of criticism by the auditing community that the action was ill-conceived, mal-timed, and mandatory of investigation."

In an effort to augment its number by recruiting amateur or part-time watchers, the government's Office of Management and Budget, an arm of the administration, established a telephone hotline to receive tips on waste in government. As luck would have it, the General Accounting Office, an arm of the Congress, had been planning to do exactly the same thing but was beaten to the switchboard by two days. The ensuing squabble over turf rights led *The Washington Star* to note editorially, "That raises the question of whether there is sufficient coordination or possibly a wasteful duplication of effort in the war on waste."

But it never pays to argue with auditors any more than with the media. Presidential Press Secretary Jim

Brady is said to have advised, "Never pick a fight with anyone who buys ink by the barrel."

The process of evaluating proposals submitted by competing companies seeking government contracts serves as an example wherein truly enormous numbers of man-hours are expended not so much to assist the decision-maker in making good selections but rather to build a protest-proof audit trail. A similar problem exists but to a lesser extent in the commercial world. Were the number of man-hours involved in proposal evaluation reduced by a factor of five, it is doubtful that the sources ultimately selected would differ substantially— but the ability to fend off protests and audits might deteriorate markedly. The value of a Pearl Harbor file thereby remains unchallenged. Auditors and reviewers are no different from anyone else, only more so.

Any bureaucrat worthy of the name will soon strategize that a fail-safe way to guard against criticism is *never* to take risk, even when that risk may be very prudent and may have significant probable payoff. Extrapolating the theory that the only people who never make bad decisions are those who never make any decisions, we can logically conclude that the only people whose work cannot be criticized are those who produce no work. Managers thus quickly learn to fear bad news with even greater fervor than they covet good news. We are inevitably led to the observation by Meg Greenfield of *The Washington Post* that "there is a profound commitment in this country today to not letting anything happen."

Or, as Bum Phillips, coach of the New Orleans Saints (and, as previously noted, former coach of the Houston Oilers), stated with equal profundity but perhaps less eloquence, "You gotta have rules, but you also gotta allow for a fella to mess up once in a while." Like the time the Denver Broncos' celebrated rookie quarterback, suffering a difficult first season, inadvertently lined up for the snap, in full view of 70,000 people, not behind the center but behind a *guard*—to the enormous surprise and consternation of *at least* one person in the stadium.

As the old saying goes, "There is a difference between giving and handing people their head." In Woodrow Wilson's words, "If there is one principle clearer than any other, it is this—that in any business, whether of government or mere merchandising, somebody must be trusted."

All of which leads to Augustine's Law of Perpetual Emotion, borrowed from naval lore and based in turn upon the observation that auditors seldom acquire ulcers, although many are suspected carriers:

LAW NUMBER XLVII

Two-thirds of the Earth's surface is covered with water. The other third is covered with auditors from headquarters.

Murphy taught that if anything can go wrong it will, but it was left to Evans and Bjorn to point out in their law, "No matter what goes wrong, there will always be somebody who knew it would." The only thing most audits fix is the blame.

One contractor actually stumbled across the ultimate solution to the problem of a penetrating and intransigent plant auditor who had been assigned to oversee its activities: The local management wrote a letter to the auditor's supervisor praising the fine job he was doing!

But the statement credited to Teddy Roosevelt is perhaps the most eloquent defense of the man or woman living where the rubber meets the road that has yet been offered:

> It is not the critic who counts, not the man who points out how the strong man stumbled, or where the doer of deeds could have done them better. The credit belongs to the man who is actually in the arena; whose face is marred by dust and sweat and blood; who strives valiantly; who errs and comes short again and again; who knows the great enthusiasms, the great devotions, and spends himself in a worthy cause; who, at best, knows in the end the triumph of high achievement; and who, at the worst, if he fails, at least fails while daring greatly, so that his place shall never be with those cold and timid souls who know neither victory nor defeat.

An astute observer by the name of K. S. Booth has noted that "The best parachute folders are those who jump themselves."

48

Much Ado About Nothing

"Speak with words that are soft and sweet. You never know which ones you may eat."
—American cowboy saying

It was Friday—and not a moment too soon. At the retirement party for the chief engineer, much reminiscing took place about his early days on the invisible airplane project shortly after he had graduated from college. It was hard to believe that the six redesigns and accompanying flight test series had taken so many years. It was pointed out how his career had skyrocketed him through the organization: first as a tool designer during the initial proposal phase, then as a task leader during the production engineering phase, subsequently as a group engineer for the first redesign, as a section chief on the second, and finally as chief engineer—where he made his impact doing failure analyses during the crashes. Here, truly, was a man who proved the invalidity of the Peter Principle, rising not one but several

*levels above his level of competence. Mean-
while, having completed the task of segregating
the heroes from the villains, effort by the project's rear guard turned toward explaining to those
astute enough to have not been involved in the
project just what had happened. Daedalus's program manager had of course been resigned and
was now consulting for six small companies seeking to do business with the government. His government counterpart had, in keeping with federal
employment practices, been retired in place. The
task of explaining the events which had so regrettably transpired thus ultimately fell to the
company's newest employee, a young business
major who was assigned the task of representing
the corporation in Washington at The Hearings.*

Major James Wesley Powell, organizer and leader of
the first expedition through the rapids of the Grand
Canyon, was basically a scientist. His major focus during the trip was on gathering technical data using his
barometer, compass, sextant, and keen powers of observation. His report on the trip, not surprisingly, almost entirely comprised detailed descriptions of the
geological structure of the canyon. It must, therefore,
have been to his great dismay when a few years later
the approval of funds he was seeking in his testimony
before a congressional committee to enable further exploration was made conditional upon his writing an *adventure* story on his earlier trip through the canyon!

Happily, this congressional insistence led to one of
the truly great books on exploration. Unhappily, at least
from Major Powell's viewpoint, it interfered with his
getting on with the next phase of his research. Showing

his usual resourcefulness, he did manage to limit the distraction by merely publishing a somewhat expanded version of his diary.

More modern adventurers through the treacherous rapids of the Congress (and its commercial parallels) have encountered not altogether dissimilar expectations, with demands being made on officials for testimony with such frequency that many seemingly have little time to do anything but tell what they would have been doing if they had not been too busy testifying. In the author's own experience, due to a Machiavellian conjunction of confirmation hearings and the budget cycle, after having been on the job as a Presidential appointee for only one and one-half hours, the next three days were spent providing testimony to the Congress. This distills down to about ten minutes in which to tell of each minute's work! But then, there have been many individuals who spent a month on the witness stand in a single day.

Witnesses, incidentally, *always* begin their testimony before Congress by remarking, "Mr. Chairman and Members of the Committee, it is a pleasure to be here today to tell you about . . ." (say, "the factor of two cost growth on my program," "the crash of the test airplane into the Washington Monument," "the eleven-year slip in schedule," "the 300 square mile oil slick off Miami Beach," etc.). One would think that with such a start the speaker's veracity would be in such immediate doubt that no witness would ever need to continue further. But such symbolism is far too subtle for official Washington; which may be the reason one industrial executive, Peter Teets, affectionately refers to the Capitol building—and in fact most headquarters—as "The Cave of the Winds."

But the propensity to ask ever-more detailed questions is a birthright of each management layer, particularly the more exalted layers. For example, in October 1984 the following item appeared in the media: "The Senate Appropriations Committee has directed Defense Secretary Caspar Weinberger to submit a report by December 31, 1985, on the extent of the microelectronic chip problems . . . and the schedule and cost for resolving them"! The fallacy is not only that the members of so high-level a committee would probably not know a microchip from a buffalo chip, but rather that someone who does must spend a year preparing a report for them. Fortunately, it is highly unlikely that any additional time will be wasted by anyone actually reading the report. This is known as the "Black Hole Syndrome" of management reports—with its obvious parallel to the celestial bodies into which everything nearby is drawn inside but nothing ever comes out.

Such a syndrome is certainly not unique to Capitol Hill. To cite but one other example, former Soviet leader Leonid Brezhnev, appearing in a nationally televised address, once inadvertently read the same page twice and no one seemed to even notice, including the Premier himself.

As the old saying goes, "A closed mouth gathers no feet."

Every researcher has experienced the problem wherein so much time is spent in justifying his or her existence and in submitting periodic reports on work that was supposed to have been accomplished that little time remains to actually accomplish any work. Under the evolving system, Columbus and COMSAT would probably still be busy testifying on how they were going to get satellites to turn the corners as they passed around the edges of the earth. It is very fortunate indeed for the space program that the Earth did turn out to be round.

The problem is that philosophizing is no substitute for doing something—doing something, as someone put it, even if it is right.

But if words sometimes fall short of the mark, it certainly does not seem to have hurt the demand. Figure 62 presents information on the number of hours various Secretaries of one major federal department have devoted to delivering testimony before the Congress about what is to be done in the future or what should have been done in the past. The numbers shown on the scale at the left of the figure do not, incidentally, include preparation time—which, if assumed to equal three hours

Speaking Defensively

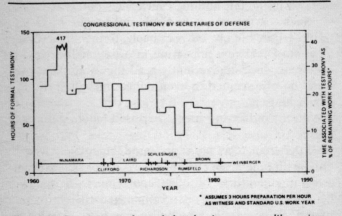

Figure 62. Requirements for verbal and written reports, like reviews and audits, place heavy demands on the time of program participants and senior executives alike.

for each hour of testimony (a number which veteran members of Congress would almost certainly dispute), brings the total time spent on testimony to about one-fourth of the time remaining in a standard 2000-work-hour year. Encouragement might be derived from what appears to be a slight downward trend in verbosity as the years have gone by, but earlier laws suggest this is merely a consequence of the increasing demands to spend time writing regulations and answering correspondence.

During 1985, according to the *Armed Forces Journal,* Defense Department representatives testified before no fewer than 91 congressional committees, with a thousand witnesses providing 1453 hours of testimony. In addition, using 1983 as a base year, there were 21,753 different pages of justification documents submitted and responses prepared to over 84,148 written congressional inquiries. And this does not include responses to questions for the record that arise at an average rate of forty per hearing if one can generalize the Chief of Naval Operations' testimony that 110 hearings produced over 4500 such requests. Nor does it include the 592,150 formal telephone inquiries received during 1983 alone.

A basic instability exists: If things go badly, then more and more time is consumed to explain what went wrong, thereby further decreasing the time available to work, with the result that more and more things go wrong. On the other hand, if things go well, such as the Apollo or Shuttle programs, it is difficult indeed for the key figures involved not to spend the next year or two responding to demands for speeches on how well things went.

The steady growth of the *Congressional Record* as a

publishing enterprise bears eloquent witness to the validity of Augustine's Law of Oratorical Engineering (known in Roman times as Nero's Law):

LAW NUMBER XLVIII

The more time you spend talking about what you have been doing, the less time you have to do what you have been talking about. Eventually, you spend more and more time talking about less and less until finally you spend all your time talking about nothing.

49

Growing Like a Regulation

"Every man's life, liberty and property are
in danger when the Legislature is in session."
—Daniel Webster

Perhaps everyone had simply taken too much
comfort from the fact that the company's balance
sheet had remained in balance right up to the
bitter end. Although a few of the workers on the
now defunct project had elected to retire, most
were solidly established in positions of greater
responsibility on the new government contract
which had just been awarded to help write regulations which would in the future prohibit failures of the type which had occurred. The
experience gained over the years in dealing with
so many cantankerous problems had actually
qualified many individuals for substantial promotions. It had, of course, become agonizingly
clear that the difficulties of the past could not be
permitted to recur, and in order to assure this,
activity was carried out with a renewed frenzy,

*particularly by those on the government side, to
write regulations which would preclude any such
difficulties ever again.*

The fallacy in using regulations to prevent problems is
that if managers could ignore the old regulation they
can ignore the new one, too. The following law provides
the mathematical foundation of Lamennais' apothegm,
which states, "Centralization breeds apoplexy at the
center and anemia at the extremities." The apparently
inherent tendency of some senior managers to draw
unto themselves authority for making even minute decisions and then to seek to govern by fiat is a proven
formula for disaster. It is equivalent to the alchemist's
turning gold into lead. Further, as learned in Chapter
26, at each point along the way to the senior manager
a pyramid of approval steps must be climbed, each of
which is inhabited by individuals too often vested only
with the authority for saying "no"—and sometimes little accountability even for that. Thomas Carlyle referred to this process as "the everlasting no."

The futility of such extreme centralization was first
recognized a number of years ago when Jethro, father-
in-law to Moses, observed that great confusion reigned
as Moses led his people out of the land of the Pharaoh.
Jethro remarked that Moses seemed to be sitting alone
"while all the people stand around you from morning
to evening" awaiting direction. Dr. Mort Feinberg, the
industrial psychologist, points out that Jethro became
the first management consultant in history when he advised Moses, as recorded in the book of Exodus, "What
you are doing is not good. You and the people with

you will wear yourselves out, for the thing is too heavy for you; you are not able to perform it alone."

Teddy Roosevelt, experiencing the same sort of problem, albeit to a different scale, protested, "I can do either one of two things. I can be president of this country, or I can control Alice. I cannot possibly do both."

Sadly, the next evolutionary step beyond "in-person" management centralization is that of ruling by decree or regulation. It is pointed out by proponents of the latter process that increased delegation increases the risk of occasional failures. The counter to this is that the present system seems to be eliminating the risk of occasional successes. It will be recalled that the Charge of the Light Brigade was ordered by an officer who was not at the scene and was not familiar with the territory.

Large organizations seem to be particularly susceptible to the notion that regulations can become a substitute for sound management judgment. Until recently, for example, the U.S. government had imposed a set of 23,000 words of specifications on those who would sell to it a simple mousetrap. The specification for chewing gum totals 15 pages and the specification for Worcestershire sauce is said to run 17 pages.

The *Armed Forces Journal* points out that in 1946 the U.S. Atlantic Fleet comprised 778 ships and sailed under regulations contained in a 72-page pamphlet. In contrast, today's Atlantic Fleet may only have 297 ships but it is well equipped with regulations—308 pages of them.

In spite of the profusion of rules, it is soon discovered that special cases and special problems still somehow occur, each requiring additional rules for its prevention.

But none of this matters anyway. Most builders of high-technology systems are so sufficiently intransigent that they would view even the Ten Commandments as no more than the Ten Suggestions.

Of course, as new rules are added, none of the old rules are ever discarded; none, that is, until the entire management-by-regulation concept disintegrates of its own weight and a new cycle begins based on an altogether new set of regulations. One veteran laborer confided to a student (later to become a national union leader) beginning a summer's employment in a large factory, "If you *really* want to mess up the company, do *exactly* what they tell you."

One particularly interesting but unfortunately not atypical example of the growth of restrictions is to be found in the procurement regulation which for many years has governed the purchase of everything used in the nation's defense, from aircraft carriers to the paper on which the regulation itself is printed. Figure 63 shows that this regulation, as is the case for most others, has a life of its own as measured by the number of pages it contains. This number of pages is seen to have grown markedly as the regulation matured. Thus, whereas the government used to attack problems with vigor, it is now seen to attack them with paper. The figure also shows the pattern of growth of certain plants found in nature as determined in botanical studies and to no one's surprise the growth patterns of regulations and weeds are virtually identical. It is recalled, in this regard, that the Ten Commandments required only ninety-nine words for their statement. To invoke the proverbial expression, there is bad news and there is good news. The bad news is that our regulations don't work. The good news is that we've got lots of them.

Growth of a Regulation

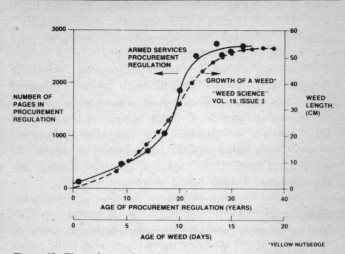

Figure 63. The volume of regulations imposed on participants in engineering and production activities has grown rapidly with time, paralleling the behavior of certain natural phenomena. The imposition of regulations can sometimes be quite subtle, for example flowing down references to subordinate regulations. In one such case, a court held a contractor liable for failure to comply with a regulation at the fifth level of an indentured tree of specifications cited only in references. The data shown in this figure apply to the Armed Services Procurement Regulations, but generally parallel most corporate purchasing manuals as well.

Not only does the length of individual regulatory and policy documents promulgated by governments, corporations, universities, neighborhood associations, social clubs, banks, and other institutions increase with time, but so also does the variety of such documents. For example, the number of policy documents listed in 1971 as the umbrella defense procurement policy state-

436 · **Augustine's Laws**

ment was 15, but by 1977 the figure had grown to 26. This, however, was hardly the beginning; by 1980, there were 114 documents listed—and the pace is still increasing. Seemingly for every action there is an equal and opposite government policy—and when it comes to preserving areas which are as yet somehow relatively free of multitudinous regulations, it must be reported that it is not nature alone which abhors a vacuum.

The endorsement of Charles Schulz on the cover of Dr. Laurence Peter's book *The Peter Principle* seems to apply with broad generalities to books of regulations as well: "Great! This book will probably change my life. At least, I think it will. Maybe it won't."

Consider, for example, the regulation governing the whistles the government buys for its military police. More rigorously, consider the regulation governing the *packaging* of the whistles the government buys for its military police. Part of a sixteen-page specification ordains in section 5.1.1.2 that:

> *Twenty-five whistles of one type only shall be packed in a folding paperboard box conforming to variety 1, style III, type G, class i, sub-class 1, of PPP-B-566, or in a setup paperboard box conforming to type I, variety 1, class A, style 4 of PPP-B-676.*
>
> *Unit pack shall be arranged five in length, five in width and one in depth within an intermediate box. Inside dimensions of each paperboard box shall approximate 12½ inches in length, 6¼ inches in width and 1 inch in depth. The box closure shall be secured with 2-inch minimum width gummed paper tape conforming to type III, grade B of PPP-T-45 applied at the center of the length opening and*

extending along the bottom and up each side at least ½ inch.

With all these safeguards against the occurrence of problems, one would expect to find a veritable flood of reports of government projects successfully completed within their original budgets. One such report is said to have poured in a few years ago. But overall, it is clear that not much has been accomplished other than to tie the hands of those who in fact happen to be able managers. The principal thing we have accomplished seems to be that we have denied our managers the latitude to manage. Over 200 initiatives were, for example, introduced in the 98th Congress alone allegedly to make the federal procurement system function in a more streamlined fashion.

Unfortunately, this abundance of guidance has not been totally successful in freeing our nation's managers from at least a residual degree of uncertainty and confusion. Consider the new "test of applicability" proposed in a recent directive on purchasing which instructs the user to "select four but no less than two acquisitions on which to apply the test." Or the Federal Communications Commission application form which instructs (original emphasis): "All fees have been suspended January 1, 1977. DO NOT SEND FEES UNTIL FURTHER NOTICE. MAILING APPLICATION: Mail your application and fee to the Federal Communications Commission." Or the draft environmental impact statement for a now-defunct government construction project in Utah which profoundly advises anxious readers that "Utah prairie dogs do not occur in Texas or New Mexico."

One recent demand originating somewhere in the

Congress requires a federal agency to provide a report, R00403-071, "Proposed Minor Construction Projects Costing More Than 50 Percent over the Maximum Amount Specified by Law by Minor Construction Projects."

When in 1981 the President issued a half-page memorandum instructing federal agencies to cut back on "superfluous publications," the Office of Management and Budget promptly released a ten-page "bulletin" explaining what the President meant. Then they followed this with a twenty-page "control plan" explaining what *they* had meant. Presumably of particular value were the eight attachments and the new form provided to implement the instruction.

In Baltimore, a city ordinance requires hospitals to keep the hot water in patients' rooms at no less than 110 degrees. A federal statute demands that water in patients' rooms must be no more than 110 degrees. A meat packing plant is reported to have been told by one federal agency to wash its floors several times a day to assure cleanliness. Another federal agency instructed the plant to keep its floors dry at all times to promote safety.

But the all-time classic is the following excerpt from an Equal Employment Opportunity Commission management directive: "REPORTING REQUIREMENTS: Federal agencies and designated major operating components (as described in MD-702) are required to submit their sexual harassment plans to the Office of Government Employment EEOC, 60 days after effective date of this directive." The next step will presumably be a request for a listing of all employees broken down by sex.

It is also a source of some consternation that for years

the government has been issuing directives to industry regarding one of its favorite topics, saving money by standardization of materials, on 8 × 10 inch sheets of paper—the use of such paper being unique in the free world to none other than the U.S. government! *Everyone* else (well, everyone, that is, except the lawyers) had been using standardized 8½ × 11 inch paper for decades. And this is no trivial matter; the federal government in 1978 alone purchased the equivalent of over sixty-six billion sheets of paper, which if unwrapped in a long roll would extend from the Earth to the Moon and back twenty times. The government's procurement regulations and laws alone occupy 1152 feet of shelf space. In fact, the nation as a whole is, as shown in Figure 64, in imminent danger of sinking under a giant mound of paper.

The management school founded on this principle appears to have adopted as its model the strategy of the squid: "If something threatens, cover it with ink."

The net impact on business of the weedlike growth of regulations was eloquently stated several years ago by S. W. Tinsley of the Union Carbide Company in response to criticism leveled by government officials at U.S. industry for its failure to create new products which would in turn provide the jobs that would eliminate unemployment and thereby generate the exports to reverse the adverse trade balance the nation was suffering. Tinsley's reply: "Government officials keep asking us where are all the golden eggs, while the other part of their apparatus is beating the hell out of our goose!"

One recent request to industry for a proposal to supply equipment to the federal government cited, *among others*, the following social and economic programs with which compliance was required: The Buy American

One Cannot Live by Bread Alone

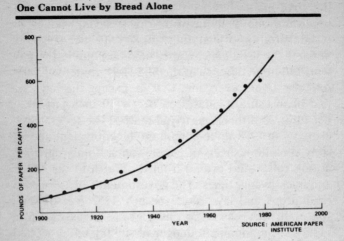

Figure 64. The per capita consumption of paper in the United States is such that many have suggested that some form of diet may be in order.

Act; Preference for United States Food, Clothing and Fibers; Clean Air Act of 1970; Equal Employment Opportunity Act; Anti-Kickback Act; Fair Labor Standards Act of 1938; Acquisition of Foreign Buses; Release of Product Information to Consumers; Prohibition of Price Differential; Required Source for Jewel Bearings; Gratuities; Prison-made Supplies; Care of Laboratory Animals; Required Source of Aluminum Ingot; Small Business Act; Labor Surplus Area Concerns; National Women's Business Enterprise Policy; Noise Control Act; Resource Conservation and Recovery Act of 1976; Federal Water Pollution Act; Officials Not to Benefit; and the Convict Labor Act.

It is to be emphasized that many of these endeavors are probably extremely meritorious. It is suggested only that their worth should be exposed to the sunshine, with the cost of complying with each provision being separately priced and not buried in the cost of achieving some other capability which is being sought. Only in this manner can cost-benefit judgments be soundly exercised.

One of the most imaginative uses of regulations is attributed to George Washington upon the introduction of a resolution by Elbridge Gerry at the Continental Congress in 1787. Gerry's resolution—to limit the size of the Continental Army, by law, to 10,000 people— was defeated only after George Washington was heard to mutter, in effect: "A very good idea. Let us also limit by law the size of any invading force to 5000 men."

We are thus led to the ubiquitous Law of Consternation of Energy:

LAW NUMBER XLIX

Regulations grow at the same rate as weeds.

No fewer than 324,000 regulators are today at large in the federal government alone, a number equal to the combined populations of thirteen of the nation's state capitals. John Heywood noted nearly five centuries ago, "Ill weed groweth fast."

Small wonder John F. Kennedy is quoted as having described Washington, D.C., as a city of southern efficiency and northern charm.

50

Regulatory Geriatrics

"How long halt ye between two opinions?"
—I Kings 18:21

The effort to generate regulations proved to be a very lucrative and satisfying one. If nothing else, at least paper never crashes. Thus, there was no longer the aggravation of the people from the test lab incessantly pointing to still another failure. Actually, the experience in writing the failure reports had proved to be excellent training for writing rules and policies, and there still remained several senior individuals who had the good fortune to have been on leave of absence during the final cataclysmic flight period and were thus still available at Daedalus to recall all the way back to the original proposal effort. Best of all, it became clear that the regulations which were now pouring forth would need to be updated periodically so that a degree of job security was guaranteed which was never enjoyed back

442

on the old invisible airplane project. But as the words flowed and good times prevailed, a few unspoken doubts began to arise, particularly among the old-timers, as to how effective the new rules would actually prove to be in legislating problems out of existence. Somehow, most had the familiar ring of the semiannual solution of the decade that they had been hearing about for years to the problems which had been bedeviling the system for centuries.

Abigail Adams once remarked, "We have too many high-sounding words, and too few actions that correspond with them." Law XLIX canonized the fact that we similarly have many high-sounding regulations, but among them precious few solutions to our problems. Each time we seek to solve a *problem,* we somehow seem to depart with a regulation and a problem, to paraphrase the earlier observation concerning meetings.

Businesses have their own answer to regulations; these are known as corporate policies. And, as with regulations, every time anything goes wrong a new policy appears in the corporate policy book. Eventually, the book becomes so thick that no one reads it (except the auditors) and then, ironically, it does not even provide the protection originally intended for those things which truly *are* important.

"I think a large number of today's procurement problems were yesterday's procurement solutions," remarks Senator Sam Nunn of Georgia.

Although it was noted that regulations tend to grow as weeds, the truth is that it would be fortunate indeed if regulations *did* grow like weeds. Weeds, it seems, are a member of the "annuals" family and, therefore, survive only for one year. Regulations, on the other hand, are seen in Figure 65 to endure an average of not one but seven years—sort of a seven-year itch—after which they are, of course, replaced by still another regulation or two . . . or three. In fact, one-fourth of the regulations which are created have a life expectancy exceeding ten years.

There is an element of cyclical behavior in regulatory and policy pronouncements which is discernible as alternating generations of regulators, in their zeal to avoid emulating the mistakes of their immediate predeces-

Regulatory Geriatrics

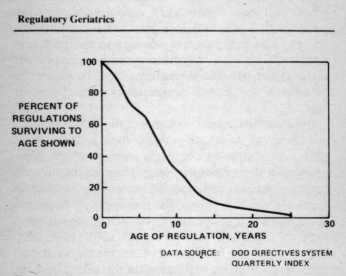

Figure 65. Once created, most regulations have proven to be extremely durable before being eliminated—or more likely, being replaced with several new regulations. The attempt to use regulations as a surrogate for management competence does not appear to rank among mankind's greater successes.

sors, repeat the errors of their forebears once-removed. This pendulum principle is the cause of the phenomenon whereby people who have lived too long will recognize each "new" initiative which is introduced as merely a reincarnation of some earlier idea long ago tried and discarded. We thus learn to commit old sins in new ways. But this does not dissuade each new generation of regulators from promulgating anew its rediscovered philosophies. It would be for the common good were the approach of Lloyd Smith, coach of the Toronto Maple Leafs, to be more widely adopted: "I have nothing to say," he said, "and I'm only going to say it once."

The average top-level government official (a Presidential appointee) has, over the past decade, demonstrated a survivability in his or her position of only 2.1 years and the lifespan of a senior corporate official has been seen to be about twice this period. Herein lies the root of the weed problem: One can achieve bureaucratic immortality by creating regulations which will endure long after their procreator has passed into oblivion. This proves to be an almost irresistible temptation, particularly in government, where life is otherwise so short.

But if the life expectancy of a regulation is so long as to inspire mortal policymakers to create them, it is much too *short* to provide the continuity needed to assure a stable lifetime for the average project. As noted previously, the average major item of defense-related hardware requires 8.3 years merely to develop, and remains in the inventory for 23 years thereafter in the case of an airplane and 33 years in the case of a ship (even excluding the lag between the end of development and the production of any individual item). Thus, viewing the development phase alone, there is in that period an average of one complete turnover of the regulations which were in being when a project was initiated, resulting in a whole superstructure of totally new regulations imposed subsequent to its birth. This is akin to changing the scoring system in a basketball game at halftime. Compound this regulatory turbulence during these formative years with the three aforementioned "streamlined" senior management decision-making council meetings, four successive sets of senior government officials, two sets of corporate leadership, eight budget cycles, and 144 votes in Congress on funding, and the miracle is not that many programs fail to survive but rather that some programs actually survive to fail.

The real hazard is that regulations sometimes endure long enough to take on altogether different meanings than were originally intended. The Prompt Payment Act offers a nontrivial example. The Congress, concerned over the siphoning from industry of the capital needed for investments in such areas as increasing productivity, discovered that a few government payment centers which issue funds to cover the government's bills were sometimes delinquent in meeting due dates by two, three, and even more months (although the great majority were paying within about two weeks). To discipline the slow disbursers, the Congress—to the applause of industry—passed legislation called the Prompt Payment Act demanding that all bills thereafter be paid within thirty days. Unfortunately, those who implemented the legislation issued instructions that all bills were to be paid *not within thirty days* but rather *on the thirtieth day*! The net result was a further major *outflow* of capital from U.S. business, since prior to that time, the government's chronic offenders notwithstanding, the *average* bill had been paid in much *less* than thirty days. The Prompt Payment Act thus actually *delayed* payment! Such is the great and mysterious working of Big Government.

The law which has been found empirically to describe this proclivity of regulations to endure beyond the life of their creator but pass away long before their dependent projects are mature is sometimes referred to as the Law of Enduring Pestilence. It states:

LAW NUMBER L

The average regulation has a life span one-fifth as long as a chimpanzee's and one-tenth as long as a human's—but four times as long as the official's who created it.

51

Employer of Only Resort

"Nobody goes there anymore because it's too crowded."
—Yogi Berra

Daedalus's top executives had arrived at the conclusion that they would have to maintain much greater personal control over future undertakings. This perspective was even more strongly embraced by the government's senior officials. Furthermore, this latter group had concluded that by bringing more tasks into the government for execution as well as direction it would be possible to streamline lines of authority. It would also be possible to eliminate unnecessary costs which had been incurred previously in such tasks as establishing competitive sources and evaluating proposals. Furthermore, there would be major savings achievable by no longer having to pour money into unproductive areas such as profits.

The percentage of civilian workers in the United States

employed by government at the federal, state, and local levels is displayed in Figure 66. A growth trend is observed which has been very predictable and monotonic throughout the history of the nation. A modest extrapolation into the future, shown by the dotted portion of the trend line, indicates that the time is not too distant when one can expect 100 percent of the working population, and perhaps even some who are not, to be employed by the government. Taking the next logical step, one can state the Law of Instinctive Herding:

LAW NUMBER LI

By the time of the United States' Tricentennial, there will be more government workers than there are workers.

Big Government

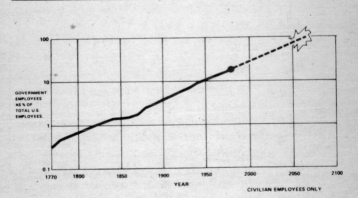

Figure 66. The fraction of the nation's work force which is employed by government at all levels is increasing on a steady course—but the end is in sight.

When this happens, the loyal civil servant will be replaced by the civil serpent. Significantly, the Civil Service Commission, which was established to exercise control over the bureaucracy, has itself far outstripped its dominion, growing at a rate five times that of the federal government as a whole.

A nonnegligible by-product of the boom in government employment is, of course, the explosion of the regulation business. When capable individuals are placed in positions with no access to factories or other means of productive output, it is instinctive to devote themselves to the regulation of those who do have such access. The suspicion that the productivity of regulators

The Nation's Most Productive Industry

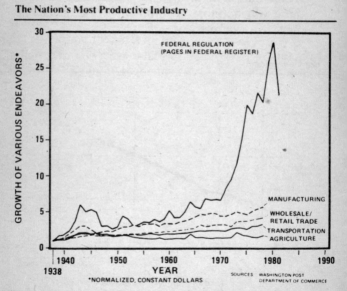

Figure 67. The growth of regulations has far outstripped the growth of other less productive segments of the economy.

has far outstripped the rate of increase of output of regulatees is verified by the data shown in Figure 67. Perhaps the foremost index of the productivity of regulators is the number of pages in the *Federal Register*— sort of the *Literary Digest* of the regulation business, but with a reading excitement level that rates it slightly ahead of the *Congressional Record* but well behind the *Commerce Business Daily*. The brief trend under President Reagan since 1980 is perhaps encouraging, but, as has been noted by others, one robin does not make a spring. The first of the Seven Wonders of the World, the great pyramid, was constructed by 100,000 men in just twenty years. If he tried to do it again today Khufu would need that many lawyers just to file the draft environmental impact statement.

One final step in the demise of productive growth, however, remains: for the government simply to take over the economy itself and establish a *new* order based totally on the production of regulations. In Chaucer's words, "It is nought good a slepyng hound to wake."

But this could never happen in a society founded on the principles of free enterprise.

52

For What It's Worth, Save Your Money

> "Nearly all men die of their remedies, not of their illnesses."
>
> —Molière

And so drew to a close the final chapter, Chapter Eleven in reality, in the tortured life of Daedalus Industries, International; AKA Daedalus Aerospace, Ltd.; AKA Daedalus Aircraft, Inc.; née Daedalus Model Airplane Company. Certainly the only thing model about its history had been its original name. They had started out with nothing, and ended wishing they could get it back. As one football coach observed, "We lost it in the last fifty-eight minutes." It proved to have been sadly correct that the motion picture telling the tale of this project should have been shown backward to permit a happy ending. But such is the nature of high-technology undertakings near the edge of the state-of-the-art—particularly when it is not altogether clear which side of the edge

*they are on. Nonetheless, optimism among Dae-
dalus's former employees continued at a high
level since all the participants in the earlier de-
bacle were now firmly entrenched in their new
positions with the federal government; ample
funds were available; the nuisance of competitors constantly yapping at their heels was gone;
and, best of all, they were now part of the fastest-
growing team anywhere in the Free World. At
least that's what the two founders told their enthusiastic class at the local business school as they
gave their final lecture before graduation. The
two students in the front row, close friends through
their interest in the model railroading club, listened attentively.*

The trend in the growth of government as measured by
the number of people it employs is, of course, paralleled
by the government's control of the economy as a whole
as measured by financial receipts; and in turn by the
government's ability to conduct its own projects on its
own behalf as it sees fit. There is now a tax collector
somewhere in the United States extracting a dollar from
someone every twenty-five milliseconds—including
roughly half of each dollar of the profits earned by
industry and perhaps half-again of the remaining portion passed along to shareholders. The average citizen
now works until May 11 of each year simply to pay his
or her taxes. By extrapolating the trend shown in Figure
68, it can be seen that the government will by the year
2120 have all the money that is generated in the U.S.
economy and, as has already been noted, will directly
employ all the people about sixty years prior to that

time. What will happen during the interim period between these dates is not yet clear, but poses the interesting question of whether the last person left in the
private sector will have to support the entire nation's
work force, or whether this last tenacious individual
instead will enjoy the full benefit of those residual funds
not yet controlled by government.

In terms of the fraction of the gross national product
absorbed in government receipts, one can also use the
extrapolation presented in Figure 68 to ascertain that
in this respect the United States lags behind England
by only seventeen years, Sweden by only fifty-six years,
and the Soviet Union and China by about 125 years.
As former Senator S. I. Hayakawa noted, regarding his
experiences in reviewing money legislation, "So in five

The Demise of Free Enterprise

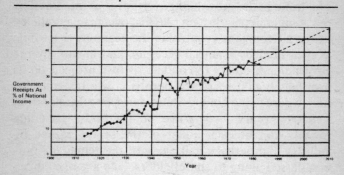

*Figure 68. Governmental dominance of the national economy
should help establish the bond which some say is lacking in the
United States between government and industry since even today
government truly is industry's partner, thoughtfully sharing the fruits
of industry's labors with industry on a roughly fifty-fifty basis (not
including, of course, the government's subsequent additional sharing
of any dividends that flow to the owners of industry).*

minutes we have disposed of *two billion bucks,* two billion, not two million; I never realized it could be so easy. It's all simple addition. *You don't even have to know subtraction!*" Bill Schneider, an associate director of the Office of Management and Budget in Washington, warns, "One thing we must particularly guard against is the danger that we might get all the government we pay for."

The challenge which this unrelenting trend will pose for future presidents is stupefying. George Washington, for example, needed to dispose of only $14,031 per day during his period in office. Abraham Lincoln, abetted by a war, needed to sign checks for but $2,228,989 each day. Even Franklin Roosevelt had to contend with only $82,679,783 per day, but by Jimmy Carter's time his responsibilities for spending had grown to $1,618,958,904 daily. Today, it takes less than a second for President Reagan to dispose of what George Washington required an entire day to discard. Think of the challenge which will be found by whoever will be president in the year 2000. Based on the established trend, this individual will awaken each morning faced with the task of unloading five trillion dollars before nightfall.

Of course, the possibility does remain that inflation may yet make this easy. Yogi Berra, for example, tells us that "a nickel ain't worth a dime anymore."

Furthermore, the expenditure stakes are accelerating: It took the federal government seventy-seven years to build up to where it could dispose of $1 billion in a single year. It reached the $10 billion level in another fifty-three years, jumped to $100 billion in just forty-three more years, and required only twenty-five years to smash through the $1 trillion ($1,000,000,000,000.00

for those who like figures) barrier. "Blessed are the young," said Herbert Hoover, "for they shall inherit the national debt."

The significance of these observations to a businessperson in the private sector is obvious. Their significance to a government manager, although perhaps less obvious, is nonetheless every bit as devastating: namely, that competition among potential sources is the essence of a buyer's leverage, and the absence of a multiplicity of strong competitors caused by the government's election to provide its own goods and services can only lessen the government manager's own chances of success.

It is thus with guarded optimism that Augustine's Final Law, the Law of Bureaucratic Absorption, is stated:

LAW NUMBER LII

People working in the private sector should try to save money.
There remains the possibility that it may someday be valuable again.

Randy Jayne, formerly of the Office of Management and Budget and now an executive with the General Dynamics Corporation, offers the encouraging observation, "There *is* life after government." But unfortunately, much of the evidence is to the contrary. As noted, it seems to suggest that eventually the government will employ all the people and tax away all their earnings in order to pay all their wages. In its final stage of development, government thus becomes the ultimate self-eating watermelon.

The Phoenix Gazette

Naval Aviation News

"*It had been a crash project.*"

EPILOGUE

"If this is the best of possible worlds, what then
are the others?"   —Voltaire

Perhaps more than anything else other than its freedom
and its democracy, the thing that has made America so
enormously successful is the free enterprise system. With
about one-twentieth of the world's population, America
generates one-quarter of all the goods and services produced here on Earth. Its gross national product ap-
proximates that of the entire European economic
community and Japan, combined. Nonetheless, today,
some two centuries after the nation's founding, the free
enterprise system still seems to be widely misunder-
stood in America. A poll conducted each year for the
past forty years by the Opinion Research Corporation,
has consistently revealed that the average citizen believes industry profits—after-tax—are of the order of
30 percent of sales (revealing a lack of understanding
of the tax laws which is only rivaled by the lack of
recognition of the fact that average profits generally
approximate 5 percent or less). In another survey recently conducted by the same organization, 54 percent
of the high school students questioned, when asked
whether or not government should take over U.S. industry, expressed "no opinion." This is perhaps the
most alarming observation in this entire volume.

Truly, businessmen, aided and abetted greatly by some of the practices they and others have perpetuated over the years, do many things that when examined under a microscope can only be described as strange and mystical. Yet, the accomplishments of American business are enormous indeed and are held in high esteem by most everyone the author has met in traveling in some forty countries throughout the world, including several Communist countries. This respect, at least until recently, was particularly true of the aerospace industry, which has most assuredly been subjected to an undue share of bruises in these pages for having committed no greater crime than having afforded the author a lifetime of excitement, opportunity, and friendships among a group of extraordinarily decent people. The author understands what Charles Lindbergh had in mind when he said, "Science, freedom, beauty, adventure. What more could you ask of life? Aviation combined all the elements I loved."

Perhaps only a field with such abundant accomplishments to its credit can withstand, perhaps even welcome, intense, critical self-scrutiny. In spite of all the pratfalls and foibles spotlighted in these pages, there are few endeavors in the entire history of mankind that can point to greater achievements than those associated with the aerospace industry and in particular that subset which has been stimulated by the need to help provide for the security of the free world, build a worldwide transportation and communications system, and assault the frontiers of space.

In 1903, well within the lifetime of people living today, Wilbur Wright made that first faltering flight which was eventually to lead not only to modern supersonic aircraft, aircraft which cross the Atlantic in a little over three hours, but also to wide-body commercial jets which have changed the entire concept of transportation and transportation safety. In an average year, more Americans die of bee stings than in commercial aircraft accidents.

Less than eight decades elapsed from the time the Wright brothers took to the air until the Space Shuttle took to space, the latter propelled by fuel carried in a tank so large that the trajectory of Wright's famous flight could fit inside it.

Similarly, only five decades elapsed from the time Robert Goddard wrote a paper in 1919 describing how a rocket might be constructed which could reach the moon until Neil Armstrong set foot there, having been propelled by a rocket reaching twice as high while still attached to the launch pad as the *altitude* achieved by Goddard's famous missile.

The first rocket to propel a man into space some two decades ago was about the same size as the lightning rod attached to the Space Shuttle launch pad. Man has now gone on to explore at close range most of the planets using "robots," including conducting detailed analyses of our neighbor, Mars, and has performed important missions in space while flying untethered as a human satellite circling the earth at over 20,000 miles per hour.

In the field of electronics, the Army's Ballistic Research Laboratory was, in 1947, to become the home of the world's first large digital computer, the ENIAC. Weighing 30 tons, employing 18,000 vacuum tubes, filling a large room, and consuming the same power that is needed to illuminate some 1700 light bulbs, the ENIAC less than four decades later has been supplanted by computers which can be bought for a hundred dollars, carried in one's pocket, operate sixty times as fast with over ten times the capacity, and use sunlight for energy.

Indeed, much has been accomplished for an industry which traces its beginnings to two people laboring in a bicycle shop and another flying rockets in a cabbage patch.

Yet, each of the "laws" presented herein results from real-world experience with real-world projects with real-world problems. In spite of past accomplishments, there obviously remains much to be done. Further, these laws and the problems from which they stem seem to show no predilection for any single industry or field of endeavor.

Most of the lessons to be learned herein are self-evident; a few are summarized in the paragraphs which follow:

- ***People*** *are the key to success in most any undertaking, including business. The foremost distinguishing feature of effective managers seems to be their ability to recognize talent and to surround themselves with able colleagues. Once such colleagues are found, it is the ultimate in sound management to reward them generously to assure that they are not lost.*
- ***Teamwork*** *is the fabric of effective business organizations. Soloists are inspiring in opera and perhaps even in small entrepreneurial ventures, but there is no place for them in large corporations. This is most assuredly not to say there is no place for the individualist, only that it is necessary for members of the team to be willing to suppress individual desires for the overall good of the team.*

- *Self-image* is as important in business as in sports. A corporate team must think of itself as a winner—customers, like patients selecting doctors, will seldom entrust themselves to organizations or people who do not exude legitimate, quiet pride and confidence in their own accomplishments and ability to produce.

- *Motivation* makes the difference. In sports this is sometimes equated with "mental toughness"—how else can one explain the numerous occasions each season when a team soundly beats another only to find itself thrashed by the loser a few weeks later? Motivation will almost always beat mere talent.

- *Recognition* of accomplishment (and the lack thereof) is an essential form of feedback. To reward poor performance or neglect outstanding performance is like placing the controls for each separate half of an electric blanket on the wrong side of the bed. Think about it.

- *Listening* to employees and customers pays dividends—they know their jobs and needs better than anyone else. One often hears the remark "He talks too much," but when did anyone last hear the criticism "He listens too much"?

- *Delegation,* whenever practicable, is the best course. Centralize goal setting, policy formulation, and resource allocation and decentralize execution. Managers at all levels need the latitude to do their jobs. As Plato suggested, justice is everyone doing his own job.

- *Openness* with employees and customers alike is essential to building trust. Both must be treated like the decent, important people they almost al-

ways are—and if treated as such they are likely to behave as such. Intentionally concealed problems seldom improve with age. Tell it like it is.

- **Customers** *deserve the very best. It would be helpful if everyone in business could, to paraphrase the American Indian expression, walk a mile in their customer's moccasins. The author once asked a man pumping gas at a filling station why his station was always so busy while the one across the street selling comparable gas at an identical price was almost always empty. This sage businessman replied, "They're in a different business than us. They're a fillin' station—we're a service station." Ironically, at the other end of the spectrum, one wonders why patients visiting their doctors must struggle on their crutches through snow drifts from the back of the parking lot because all the spaces near the building are "reserved for doctors," not for the paying customers.*

- **Quality** *is the key to customer satisfaction. It means giving the customer what was agreed upon— every time. To achieve quality one must have a goal of perfection, measure one's progress toward achieving that goal, and take corrective actions whenever they are needed.*

- **Stability** *of funding, schedules, goals, and people is critical to any smooth business operation. Conversely, turbulence produces work disruption, increases cost, generates delays, deters investment, diverts management attention, undermines accountability, and demotivates employees.*

- **Demanding** *that last little bit of effort from one-*

self is essential—it can make the difference against competitors who don't have the will to put out the extra effort. Business is fun, but it is also hard work.

- **Provision** for the unexpected is a businessperson's best insurance policy. It has been said that the ultimate form of management is managing under uncertainty. One must identify sources of risks and unknowns and make provision to overcome them—in the form of financial reserves, schedule reserves, and performance reserves. Promise only that which can be produced and produce that which has been promised.

- **"Touch-Labor"**—people who actually come into contact with the product—are the only certain contributors in any organization. Others may contribute—managers, lawyers, accountants, consultants, auditors—but they may not. The addition of members of these latter sets should be approached with particular skepticism.

- **Rules,** regulations, policies, reports, and organization charts are not a substitute for sound management judgment. One cannot legislate problems out of existence. It has been tried.

- **Logic** in presenting decision options, consequences, benefits, and risks is imperative. Whenever parameters can be quantified, it is usually desirable to do so.

- **Conservatism,** prudent conservatism, is generally the best path in financial matters. Calculated risks are sometimes in order, but only when bounded in consequence. One can make the high roll only so many times before the law of averages

> *will exert itself. On the other hand, in evaluating new ideas, one should be prepared to reach to the outer limits.*
> - ***Integrity** is the* sine qua non *of all human endeavors including business. It has even been said that if rascals knew the value of honesty they would be honest simply because of their rascality.*

Much of the above simply boils down to DISCI-PLINE—and in particular that finest form of the art, SELF-discipline. Discipline not to take the easy way out, discipline to forego "nice-to-have" features, discipline to minimize changes, discipline to demand a quality product, discipline to treat a customer fairly even when it costs, and discipline to "tough out" and solve the problems which will occur in even the best-managed undertakings. As Robert Townsend, chairman of Avis, put it in his book *Up the Organization,* managers must have the discipline not to keep pulling up the flowers to see if their roots are healthy.

Most of our problems, it seems, are, as could be their solutions, self-imposed.

> So in the Libyan fable it is told
> That once an eagle, stricken with a dart,
> Said, when he saw the fashion of the shaft,
> "With our own feathers, not by others' hands,
>   Are we now smitten."
> —Aeschylus

> Law is like sausage. If you like it, you shouldn't watch it being made.
> —Bismarck

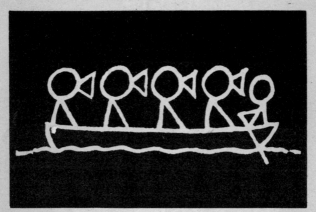

Courtesy of Columbia Business School